FUNDAMENTAL FREEDOMS

Eleanor Roosevelt and the Universal Declaration of Human Rights

With a Foreword by Allida M. Black & Mary Jo Blinker, the Eleanor Roosevelt Papers Project

FACING
HISTORY
AND
OURSELVES

A Facing History and Ourselves Publication

Facing History and Ourselves is an international educational and professional development organization whose mission is to engage students of diverse backgrounds in an examination of racism, prejudice, and antisemitism in order to promote the development of a more humane and informed citizenry. By studying the historical development of the Holocaust and other examples of genocide, students make the essential connection between history and the moral choices they confront in their own lives. For more information about Facing History and Ourselves, please visit our website at www.facinghistory.org.

Cover art photos: *Eleanor with the UDHR Poster*, UN Photo. The following photos are © Bettmann/Corbis: *Roosevelt, Cook and Dickerman; Visiting Infantile Paralysis Victims; Eleanor at the UN General Assembly; Eleanor with Marian Anderson; Eleanor in the Coal Mine;* and *Eleanor and Franklin.*

To order classroom copies, please fax a purchase order to 617-232-0281 or call 617-232-1595 to place a phone order.

To download a PDF of this publication, please visit www.facinghistory.org/fundamentalfreedoms.

ISBN-13: 978-0-9819543-2-5

Headquarters
16 Hurd Road
Brookline, MA 02445
(617) 232-1595
www.facinghistory.org

ABOUT FACING HISTORY AND OURSELVES

Facing History and Ourselves is a nonprofit educational organization whose mission is to engage students of diverse backgrounds in an examination of racism, prejudice, and antisemitism in order to promote a more humane and informed citizenry. As the name Facing History and Ourselves implies, the organization helps teachers and their students make the essential connections between history and the moral choices they confront in their own lives, and offers a framework and a vocabulary for analyzing the meaning and responsibility of citizenship, and the tools to recognize bigotry and indifference in their own worlds. Through a rigorous examination of the failure of democracy in Germany during the 1920s and 1930s, and the steps leading to the Holocaust, along with other examples of hatred, collective violence, and genocide in the past century, Facing History and Ourselves provides educators with tools for teaching history and ethics, and for helping their students learn to combat prejudice with compassion, indifference with participation, myth and misinformation with knowledge.

Believing that no classroom exists in isolation, Facing History and Ourselves offers programs and materials to a broad audience of students, parents, teachers, civic leaders, and all those who play a role in the education of young people. Through significant higher education partnerships, Facing History and Ourselves also reaches and impacts teachers before they enter their classrooms.

By studying the choices that led to critical episodes in history, students learn how issues of identity and membership, ethics and judgment, have meaning today and in the future. Facing History and Ourselves' resource books provide a meticulously researched, yet flexible, structure for examining complex events and ideas. Educators can select appropriate readings and draw on additional resources available online, or from our comprehensive lending library.

Our foundational resource book, *Facing History and Ourselves: Holocaust and Human Behavior*, embodies a sequence of study that begins with identity—first, individual identity, and then group and national identities, with their definitions of membership. From there, the program examines the failure of democracy in Germany, and the steps leading to the Holocaust—the most documented case of twentieth-century indifference, dehumanization, hatred, racism, antisemitism, and mass murder. It goes on to explore difficult questions of judgment, memory, and legacy, and the necessity for responsible participation to prevent injustice. Facing History and Ourselves then returns to the theme of civic participation to examine stories of individuals, groups, and nations who have worked to build just and inclusive communities, and whose stories illuminate the courage, compassion, and political will that are needed to protect democracy today, and in generations to come. Other examples in which civic dilemmas test democracy, such as the Armenian Genocide and the U.S. civil rights movement, are presented to expand and deepen the connection between history and the choices we face today—and in the future.

Facing History and Ourselves has offices or resource centers in the United States, Canada, and the United Kingdom, as well as in-depth partnerships in Rwanda, South Africa, and Northern Ireland. Facing History and Ourselves' outreach is global, with educators trained in more than 80 countries, and delivery of our resources through a website accessed worldwide with online content delivery, a program for international fellows, and a set of NGO partnerships. By convening conferences of scholars, theologians, educators, and journalists, Facing History and Ourselves' materials are kept timely, relevant, and responsive to salient issues of global citizenship in the twenty-first century.

For more than 30 years, Facing History and Ourselves has challenged students and educators to connect the complexities of the past to the moral and ethical issues of today. They explore democratic values and consider what it means to exercise one's rights and responsibilities in the service of a more humane and compassionate world. They become aware that "little things are big"—that seemingly minor decisions can have a major impact, and change the course of history.

For more about Facing History and Ourselves, visit our website at *www.facinghistory.org*.

ACKNOWLEDGMENTS

Primary Writer: Dan Eshet

From its inception, *Fundamental Freedoms: Eleanor Roosevelt and the Universal Declaration of Human Rights* has been a collaborative effort. Facing History and Ourselves extends gratitude to all who contributed to the development of this publication.

We would like to thank Jill Garling and Thomas Wilson for their generous support of the *Making History Series*. It is a great pleasure to thank Allida M. Black, project director at the Eleanor Roosevelt Papers Project and professor of history and international affairs at George Washington University, as well as her staff. Allida's affectionate writings about Eleanor shaped our views of "ER" as an independent political activist and as one of the most progressive and influential thinkers of her generation. Sam Gilbert, our long-time editor, spent many hours improving the style of this text. We thank him for his passionate work on this project. We would also like to thank Daniel Cohen, a dear friend and professor of history at Rice University, who read the text several times and whose advice and thoughtful discussions, shaped not only the text of this book, but also the way we thought about and approached the Universal Declaration of Human Rights. Carol Hillman, chair of the Honoring Eleanor Roosevelt Project at Val-Kill, also made valuable contributions to the discussions of Eleanor's role in the creation of the Universal Declaration of Human Rights. Special thanks to Mary Ann Glendon, who advised at critical stages during development, especially around issues of cultural differences as they played out in the UDHR drafting process. We thank the staff of the Franklin D. Roosevelt Presidential Library for their patience, advice, and cooperation throughout the research process. We also want to thank Sharon Lindenburger who reviewed the manuscript in its later drafts and enhanced its style. We also want to thank the design and editorial teams at Brown Publishing Network for their solid judgment and devotion in producing this resource.

While writing this book, Facing History and Ourselves has been fortunate to benefit from the perspective, insight, and passion of many of its staff members. We owe credit for the inspiration to read about Eleanor Roosevelt to Margot Stern Strom. This book bears the marks of her passionate interest in Eleanor's life, actions, and ideas. We owe many kinds of thanks to Adam Strom for his broad perspective and deep understanding of human rights, and for his careful reading of every word written. His knowledge of civil rights history kept our research honest and our writing balanced and fair. We also deeply thank Dan Eshet, primary writer of the text, for his dedication to this project. He collected ideas from a wide range of scholars and many fields and then crafted them into a comprehensive narrative of which we are proud. We are indebted also to Marty Sleeper, a veteran educator, for his insights and deep understanding of the challenges America faced during the 1930s and 1940s. Marc Skvirsky dutifully read all the drafts of this book; thanks to his suggestions, the book is deeper and broader in its scope than it would have been otherwise.

Many thanks to Elisabeth Fieldstone Kanner, whose experience as a teacher and curriculum writer helped make this publication more accessible and easy to use in classroom settings. Nicole Breaux supervised the first half of the project's life, while Eva Radding managed its final stages. Jen Gray brought the text to life through her photo research and permissions work. Ilana Klarman edited parts of the text. We would like to thank Catherine O'Keefe and Maria Hill, our publishing colleagues, who managed the design and printing of this book. Dimitry Anselme, Mary Johnson, Adrianne Billingham Bock, Milton Reynolds, Steve Becton, and Phredd MatthewsWall contributed constructive criticism and commentary during the writing of this book, and their suggestions influenced many aspects of the development of the text. A special acknowledgment is due to our grant writer, Jan Stanwood, for her dedicated work to fund this project.

Lastly, we also want to give warm thanks to the interns who helped us write this publication: Gillian Grossman, who worked days and nights to complete an impressive first draft of the sections dealing with the deliberation of the Declaration in the United Nations; Megan Henry, who sought out our organization and worked here selflessly during most of the summer of 2009; and Gillian Hawley, who donated so much of her precious time to see that this book was ready for publication. We'd also like to acknowledge the hard work of Alicia Tuzour and Chelsea Prosser, whose efforts on this project's behalf are very much appreciated.

When will our consciences grow
so tender that we will act to
prevent human misery rather
than avenge it?

  —Eleanor Roosevelt, 1946

Surely a world that can achieve
the atomic bomb, but fail in the
creation of the United Nations, is
morally bankrupt. And this moral
bankruptcy is the reason for our
failure to organize peace.[1]

  —John Humphrey, 1949

TABLE OF CONTENTS

PREFACE

By Adam Strom, Director of Research and Development, Facing History and Ourselves

Eleanor Roosevelt's story is one of possibility, although not in the way one might think. Hers is no rags-to-riches story. In fact, Eleanor Roosevelt grew up in an environment of privilege. Her uncle, Theodore Roosevelt, was an American president; she went to finishing school in Europe; and she danced in debutante balls. Yet it was not among the wealthy that Eleanor found her voice. It was on the streets of immigrant New York, among the poor, working with women and African Americans, and speaking out against injustice that she developed as a political force. Eleanor Roosevelt was not without flaws, but what is so compelling about her story is that we can read for ourselves the evolution of her public voice and concern. Her papers reveal both her desires and frustrations, enabling us to trace her thinking through the multiple perspectives revealed in her public and private writings.

In many ways, this book follows the scope and sequence of what we think of as the Facing History and Ourselves "journey." That journey is built around a developmental model with the fundamental assumption that all of us are lifelong learners. The name *Facing History and Ourselves* reflects the belief that we learn history in dialogue with ourselves, our history, and the world. Eleanor's story begins that way as well.

Part I focuses on the development of Eleanor's identity as a person, and as a political thinker and activist. You will read about how she formed her own universe of responsibility, with particular attention to her understanding of the people many saw as the "other."

In Part II, we learn how those values were tested as the United States entered World War II, causing Eleanor to face the limits of her own power, and we see her response to the Nazi Holocaust and the growing refugee crisis in Europe. At the same time, this section traces Eleanor's broadening understanding of democracy and her vision for the post–war world.

Part III, and the major focus of this book, is Eleanor Roosevelt's role in creating the Universal Declaration of Human Rights. After confronting the horrors of the Nazi Holocaust, and after her husband's death, Eleanor's role at the

United Nations and on the human rights committee gave her a new means of expressing her desire to participate and the opportunity to have a lasting impact on the lives of others.

Part IV of the guide examines the legacy of the Universal Declaration of Human Rights. The UDHR is an unusual international document. It is neither law nor a treaty. It is an aspirational statement. It was not written by one person; it went through several drafts with many different authors. Yet, it was Eleanor who, directing the project with subtle force, ensured that the result would be a moral yardstick by which people all over the world could measure their own communities and conditions. The process was far from easy. Try to imagine gathering a group of people who do not know each other, who represent different political interests, and who come from different countries, cultures, and religions, and asking them to agree on a statement about basic human values and to describe what everyone in the world needs to do to ensure that those values are upheld. Eleanor guided the team drafting the document through committee, and then through the process of ratification in the United Nations.

Eleanor and the other drafters of the Universal Declaration of Human Rights well knew that the Declaration was only a beginning. International cooperation on human rights issues stalled during the Cold War and the post–Cold War era has brought new alliances that make the human rights project a difficult one.

Too often, the story of human rights is removed from history. It is important to reposition this history in the wake of World War II and the Holocaust. The images of the concentration camps of Europe were never far from Eleanor's mind as she undertook this work, nor were the conditions of African Americans in her own country. As a diplomat, Eleanor balanced her personal interests and her public role. Some have criticized her for not speaking out loudly enough on some issues, and speaking too loudly on others. This story is about negotiation, and compromise. It is also about the challenges of trying to make a difference.

Eleanor Roosevelt did not write laws or build buildings. Instead, she believed firmly in giving people the tools they needed to advocate to improve their own lives. By studying the particular story of the Universal Declaration of Human Rights, students will begin to make connections to their own communities. Adults have failed to stop war, violence, and terrorism. Hopefully, in this story, students will find insights and inspiration to do a better job than previous generations have done in the sixty-plus years since the Declaration was passed.

Eleanor holds the completed Declaration of Human Rights.

FOREWORD

By Allida M. Black, Director and Editor, the Eleanor Roosevelt
Papers Project; and Mary Jo Blinker, Associate Editor,
the Eleanor Roosevelt Papers Project

Early in 1946, with the horrors of two world wars uppermost in their minds, a group of dedicated men and women, representing 18 nations, gathered under the auspices of the United Nations Commission on Human Rights to craft a vision so powerful that it could combat the nightmare of fifty million deaths inflicted on the world. Their chairman was Eleanor Roosevelt (ER), former First Lady, social justice activist, nationally syndicated journalist, and one of the twentieth century's most renowned human rights leaders. As they set to work, none of the drafters, ER included, imagined that the document they would produce would become the centerpiece of the modern human rights movement and affect the lives of millions of people around the world. However, they knew from the outset that they had no alternative. If they failed to create a shared vision, or if they failed to secure international support for the document they produced, the world might quickly be on the path to World War III. "You can measure the extent of physical damage done to cities, you can restore water supplies, gas and electricity, and you can rebuild the buildings needed to establish a military government," Eleanor argued. But the real challenge was "how to gauge what has happened to human beings—that is incalculable."

This educational resource tells the story of the growth and development of both the Universal Declaration of Human Rights (UDHR) and Eleanor Roosevelt. ER's determination to conceal her influence, others' determination to overstate their influence, and historians' narrow focus kept many details of both stories obscure. This educational resource provides students with a fuller picture of the UDHR and of the woman who played such a pivotal role in its creation.

Eleanor Roosevelt, who as a young child survived the enduring sadness of both her parents' deaths, the loss of a younger brother, and the absence of the courage and confidence that love provides, knew how fear could cripple one's soul. In fact, her greatest fear was that she would succumb to fear when called upon to combat an egregious crisis. As a ten-year-old orphan shipped off to live with a stern, strict grandmother, ER recognized that she had to find strength she did not know she had in order to make her own way in the world. With the support of a remarkable teacher, a devoted aunt, and her own immense reservoir of courage, ER grew from a fearful child to a bold social activist to a precedent-shattering First Lady to political pundit to diplomat to the world's most prominent voice for human rights. Her journey was neither easy nor safe. Her actions generated as much fierce ridicule as they did praise and respect. Yet she persevered, determined to develop effective working relationships with the various constituencies essential to making the UDHR "real." "Staying aloof," she wrote," is not a solution. It is a cowardly evasion."

Part I of this resource, and the documents that accompany it, detail ER's growth and development as a person and as an activist. During the 1920s and 1930s, ER worked on issues related to women, labor, housing, education, and race. She honed her political skills and built networks among like-minded individuals. She also became adept at mediating political disputes between her husband and his top aides, a skill that would stand her in good stead once she reached the United Nations. After the American voters elected FDR president in 1932, ER worried that her husband's victory would force her to curtail her work on the issues she thought were critical to surviving the Great Depression and expanding democracy. Together, with the wise counsel of Louis Howe, the Roosevelts developed a partnership unique in American political history. Within eight months of FDR's inauguration, ER would travel 40,000 miles promoting the New Deal and collecting political and policy advice for the New Deal's architects. She also resurrected her journalism career with her monthly magazine column *Mrs. Roosevelt's Page*. After her fourth column, she had received and answered 350,000 letters. Her conversation with the American people had begun. It continued throughout her extensive travels, with her regular White House press conferences, and beginning in January 1936, in a nationally syndicated daily column *My Day*.

She also redefined her position as First Lady to advocate consistently for unpopular causes, such as racial equality and humane treatment of refugees. The most famous example of her White House civil rights activism occurred in 1939, when she used *My Day* to announce her resignation from the Daughters of the American Revolution after that group denied African American contralto Marian Anderson the use of its hall. ER then not only helped organize Anderson's concert at the Lincoln Memorial but also, in championing her performance, equated the discrimination Anderson encountered to the Aryan policies Hitler imposed on Fascist Germany.

Eleanor Roosevelt brought the same passion and commitment to the cause of refugees. As the clouds of war gathered over Europe, and the plight of those fleeing from the Nazis grew more desperate, she worked closely with such groups as the Emergency Rescue Committee and the United States Committee for the Care of European Children. She also spoke out against the United States' restrictive immigration policies and worked to increase the number of visas available to refugees. "When will our consciences grow so tender," she asked, "that we will act to prevent human misery rather than avenge it?"

Part II focuses on Eleanor Roosevelt's activities during World War II and the early postwar period. After addressing the nation on the evening of the December 7, 1941, Pearl Harbor attack (hers was the first official voice Americans heard), she traveled the nation opposing the "politics of fear," arguing that victory did not require "hate," and insisting that racial divisions weakened the war effort. She lent her public support and private counsel to those who opposed the internment of Japanese Americans. She also championed the creation of the Fair Employment Practices Commission and urged the racial integration of the armed forces.

A 1943 visit to Allied troops in the Pacific convinced her that the only way to redeem the courage and sacrifice she saw there was to create a better world. To that end, she followed the development of the United Nations closely. Indeed, as FDR lay dying in Warm Springs in 1945, ER was meeting with a State Department official in preparation for the San Francisco conference that would ratify the UN Charter.

FDR's death opened a new chapter in ER's life. Though uncertain about what she could achieve through her "own momentum," she by then possessed all the skills and attributes of a seasoned political operative. She also had an impressive international reputation as an advocate for the discounted, disparaged, and ignored.

Things changed when President Harry S. Truman suddenly appointed ER to the first American delegation to the United Nations. Although ER initially had doubts about her qualifications, and concerns about the Senate confirmation process, she embraced the nomination. Her fellow United States delegates, all male and all senior political leaders and cabinet secretaries, did not. They resented her appointment and, in retaliation, assigned her to the Social,

Humanitarian and Cultural Committee, an appointment they considered "safe" and inconsequential. Ironically, that committee ended up being the most contentious, since it dealt with the repatriation of European refugees. The sight of these people, many of them Holocaust survivors whom she saw during a 1946 visit to displaced persons camps, filled ER with horror and anger. "There is a feeling of desperation and sorrow . . . which seems beyond expression," she wrote in *My Day*. When Andrei Vyshinsky, the chief Soviet delegate to the United Nations, argued that all such persons were "quislings" and "traitors" and should be returned to their countries of origin, Eleanor Roosevelt rose to rebut him. Calmly and deliberately, she told him that it would be "foreign" to the United States' concept of democracy "to force repatriation on any human being." ER prevailed. The UN rejected Vyshinsky's proposal.

Eleanor Roosevelt brought the same blend of courage, political savvy, and common sense to the creation of the Universal Declaration of Human Rights. As chairman first of the nuclear committee to set up the commission, and then as the commission's first chairman, she faced a daunting assignment— the drafting of an international **bill or declaration of human rights**. Proposals, models, and ideas had poured in from all over the world. Her colleagues were an equally varied group who brought their own ideas and cultural norms to the debate. Keeping everyone at the table and focused on the work required more than just tact and diplomacy. It required a firm hand and a willingness to listen to and moderate between competing points of view.

As she listened, ER deepened her understanding of what constituted human rights. She had long insisted that education, housing, and access to employment were basic human rights that society had both a moral and political obligation to provide. Now she recognized anew the importance of food and physical safety as fundamental to human dignity and well-being. As her own awareness grew, she persuaded the State Department to move toward a more international understanding of human rights (i.e., to accept that social and economic rights were as important to many parts of the world as political and civil rights were to the United States) even as she continued to advance her country's position on the topic.

Part III illuminates the debates and struggles over the development of the UDHR and details ER's role in the process. Besides serving as chairman of the commission, she also chaired the subcommittee charged with drafting the document. There she insisted that the Declaration be a document "which will be readily understood by all people." Once the drafting process was completed, she took a leading role in "selling" it—first to the United Nations itself and then to the world. Her 1948 Sorbonne speech, given at a time of heightened international tensions, underscored the United Nations' commitment to human freedom and helped create a climate in which the General Assembly could approve the Declaration.

It is my belief, and I am sure it is also yours, that the struggle for democracy and freedom is a critical struggle, for their preservation is essential to the great objective of the United Nations to maintain international peace and security.

Among free men the end cannot justify the means. We know the patterns of totalitarianism—the single political party, the control of schools, press, radio, the arts, the sciences, and the church, to support autocratic authority; these are the age-old patterns against which men have struggled for three thousand years. These are the signs of reaction, retreat, and retrogression.

The United Nations must hold fast to the heritage of freedom won by the struggle of its peoples; it must help us to pass it on to generations to come.

The development of the ideal of freedom and its translation into the everyday life of the people in great areas of the earth, is the product of the efforts of many peoples. It is the fruit of a long tradition of vigorous thinking and courageous action. No one race and no one people can claim to have done all the work to achieve greater dignity for human beings, and greater freedom to develop human personality. In each generation and in each country there must be a continuation of the struggle, and new steps forward must be taken since this is preeminently a field in which to stand still is to retreat. "[2]

Part IV, and the documents that it contains, looks at the legacy of the Universal Declaration of Human Rights and provides more information about other members of the Human Rights Commission. The contributions of Charles Malik of Lebanon, René Cassin of France, and Hansa Mehta of India, to name three, underscore the international character of the Universal Declaration.

Eleanor in talks with Soviet Communist Party head Nikita Khrushchev on September 28, 1957, in Yalta, Ukraine. Eleanor strove to build productive relationships with Soviet leaders, even during the Cold War era.

This section also asks students to connect the Declaration to contemporary human rights problems.

Although Eleanor Roosevelt considered the adoption of the UDHR her finest achievement, she continued to risk her income, reputation, and health to implement its principles.

At home, she opposed Senator Joe McCarthy's attack on American civil liberties. She thought race was "the litmus test for democracy" and supported legal challenges to segregation and extralegal protests, boycotts, and demonstrations. When management and many political leaders remained determined to curtail the labor movement, she adamantly defended a worker's right to join a union (she joined the Newspaper Guild) and held union leaders accountable for the policies and tactics they adopted. As the nation's most visible post-war Democrat, she challenged her party to be true to its principles, and not to succumb to what she called the "politics of fear." She so insisted that women be part of the presidential leadership team that John Kennedy responded to her pressure by creating the first Presidential Commission on the Status of Women and asking her to chair it.

ER carried these same values with her as she traveled the world. Refusing to succumb to easy political characterization of world leaders, she strove to build productive relationships with Josif Broz (Yugoslavia's "Tito"), Jawaharlal Nehru (India), and Nikita Khrushchev (Russia). As an unpaid ambassador for the American Association for the United Nations, she visited dozens of nations, urging their support for the UN and their incorporation of the UDHR's basic principles. And she used her *My Day* column to give credence to those nations emerging from colonial dominance, and to lobby for an American diplomacy, as grounded in development and aid as it was in military deterrence.

In short, ER devoted the rest of her life to the creation of a culture of human dignity at home and abroad. She believed that no one's rights were safe unless everyone's rights were respected. She argued repeatedly that "human rights began in small places close to home," that these rights were political and civil rights as well as economic, social, and cultural rights, and that their implementation required "concerted citizen action." She insisted that the world, the United States in particular, was "on trial" to show what human rights mean.

She, like her fellow commissioners, knew that this would not be easy. But she refused to succumb to cynicism. As she told anyone within earshot, she knew the pitfalls and obstacles lethargic leaders around the world used to rationalize their timid commitment to the Declaration. Declaring that "we make our own history," she argued that we have a choice. "If we want a free and peaceful world, if we want" to create a world where everyone can "grow to greater dignity as a human being, WE CAN DO IT."

---

[1] Clinton Timothy Curle, *Humanité: John Humphrey's Alternative Account of Human Rights* (Toronto: University of Toronto Press, 2007), 40.

[2] Eleanor Roosevelt, "The Struggle for Human Rights Speech at the Sorbonne, Paris (September 28, 1948)," in Allida M. Black, *The Eleanor Roosevelt Papers, Volume 1: The Human Rights Years, 1945–1948* (New York: Thomson Gales, 2007).

*It is essential, above all, that
in making history we don't
forget to learn by history,
to see our mistakes as well as
our successes, our weaknesses
as well as our strengths.*

– Eleanor Roosevelt, 1962

INTRODUCTION

Eleanor Roosevelt had not planned to work for the United Nations, nor had she planned to devote her days to the challenges of writing legal documents and international treaties. By the time she left the White House, she was recognized as a powerful political actor in her own right, and as a leading advocate of the rights and well-being of ordinary people. As First Lady, she had labored ceaselessly to extend civil rights to all and traveled on diplomatic and humanitarian missions around the globe. But she had not expected to be involved in the daily work of the peace organization that she and her husband, Franklin Delano Roosevelt, had envisioned during World War II.

As the clouds of war began to disperse over Europe, and the German slaughter of millions of Jews, Roma (Gypsies), political dissenters, homosexuals, and other innocent civilians came to light, Eleanor understood for the first time how much power modern states had over the lives of vast numbers of people. Then, in August 1945, when the United States detonated atomic bombs over two Japanese cities, the picture became even grimmer, as hundreds of thousands of human beings were killed in an instant. At that time, putting a permanent end to war became Eleanor's mission: the people of the world should set up mechanisms to resolve international conflicts peacefully, she said, or they would have to face the possibility that one day they would not wake up.

The opportunity to do something about this came before the war had ended. Just weeks before representatives from around the world first met to draft the United Nations (UN) charter, Harry Truman (who had succeeded Roosevelt to the presidency) asked Eleanor to join the United Nations delegation from the United States. Eleanor proved to be the perfect champion for this document, which many thought the United Nations could never approve.

This occurred in 1945. At the time, several prominent statesmen objected to Truman's choice because of Eleanor's well-known liberal positions, her popularity among African Americans and union members, and the fact that women were rarely considered for high-profile positions in the State Department. Nevertheless, three years later, on December 10, 1948, Eleanor presided over the adoption of the Universal Declaration of Human Rights. This document reflects the UN's determination to stem international conflicts by overcoming differences between cultures and nations. It also reflects Eleanor's worldview and lifelong interest in the needs and rights of ordinary people. Indeed, in many ways, the document reflects her journey as an advocate of individual freedoms and rights.

She did not write the Declaration on her own—no one could have. Canadian scholar and jurist John Humphrey wrote the first draft of the Universal Declaration of Human Rights; French legal expert René Cassin wrote the second draft and later won the Nobel Prize for his contribution; Lebanese philosopher and diplomat Charles Malik served as secretary for the Human Rights Commission; and several Russian diplomats, including Alexei P. Pavlov, also helped shape the Declaration. The prominence of these men and other delegates has tended to overshadow the role of the woman who ran the commission's meetings. And yet it is Eleanor, who skillfully directed their writing and kept their drafts simple and practical, to whom we owe the successful completion of the Declaration.

Eleanor possessed a combination of qualities, skills, and experiences that made her a better leader than the more formally educated members of the commission. It was her perseverance and fair-mindedness, coupled with charisma and authority, that kept things going when delegates stopped making sense or exchanges became heated. Secured by Eleanor's influence, the backing of the United States ensured that the writing was completed, adopted by the UN, and later ratified by the Senate. Such an achievement cannot be underestimated, especially against the backdrop of the Cold War and the retreat from international cooperation that came with it in the late 1940s. For example, an equally important document, the Convention on the Prevention and Punishment of the Crime of Genocide (1948), was buried in United States congressional committees for years; other international agreements never saw daylight, or, if they did, they lacked the international support needed to make them useful.

However, it is wrong to view Eleanor as a mouthpiece of the State Department. She fought hard for the principles and rights she valued, and she even threatened to resign from the United States delegation when the State Department resisted. How did she come to possess such qualities? What shaped her moral outlook? Who was Eleanor Roosevelt?

In this book, we will explore these questions as we investigate Eleanor Roosevelt's role in the creation of the Universal Declaration of Human Rights. Elizabeth Borgwardt, a historian, has written that from its inception, the United

Nations was designed to expand to the whole world certain aspects of the New Deal—the ambitious combination of legislation and executive action initiated by the American government to combat the economic and social problems faced by millions of Americans during the Great Depression of the 1930s.

The direct link between the Universal Declaration of Human Rights and the New Deal can be traced to the Anglo-American Atlantic Conference of 1941. There, the United States and the United Kingdom, facing the threat of Nazi Germany, "called for self-determination of peoples, freer trade, and several New Deal–style social welfare provisions." But the conference, Borgwardt wrote, was "best known for a resonant phrase about establishing a particular kind of post-war order—a peace 'which will afford assurance that *all the men in all the lands* may live out their lives in freedom from fear and want.'"[1] Note the wording: the leaders of two of the world's most powerful nations had spoken of *individual* rights, rather than *states'* rights. A revolution was under way. It would take several decades to spell out what that revolution meant. For some, like Winston Churchill, it had little or no political implications and therefore would not serve to undermine the empire he fought hard to maintain under British rule. For others, including Eleanor, it had far-reaching implications, with the potential to empower oppressed groups around the world.

Indeed, the phrase "all the men in all the lands" established the principle of universality, which would inspire Eleanor Roosevelt and the other members of the Human Rights Commission to set aside considerations of nationality, sex, ethnicity, age, and religion, speaking instead of the rights of every human being on earth. The discussion of human rights that began during the 1920s and 1930s blossomed and bore fruit as a reaction to the horrifying events of World War II.

SELF-ANNIHILATION

Just two decades after World War I, a conflict that killed 18 million soldiers and civilians, Germany forced Europe into a new war. This war pitted Germany, Japan, and Italy—the main Axis powers—against the United Kingdom, the United States, and the Soviet Union, the main Allies. Though World War II began when Germany invaded Poland, the conflict expanded into North Africa, China, the Soviet Union, and many of the other nations of Europe and Asia, bringing a whirlwind of death and destruction that far exceeded the unprecedented previous bloodbath of 1914–1918. This new war was nearly global in scope, and it was fought as a total war—each side committed all of its human and material resources to combat. After early Axis victories, the resolute defense mounted by the Soviet Union and the long-awaited entry of the United States on the side of the Allies changed everything.

Allied victory, however, would come only at the highest price: millions of human corpses and entire cities in ruins. Germany's barbarism did not diminish with the Allied advances. Quite the opposite occurred: the more defeats and losses the Nazis suffered, the faster they gassed and shot innocent men, women, and children. Only when the war in Europe ended in May 1945 did the world begin to confront the largest genocide in human history—the systematic murder of close to six million Jews, over 220,000 Gypsies (Roma and Sinti), and thousands of homosexuals and other minorities, many of whom perished in the last year of the war.[2] All told, the war had claimed the lives of 58 or 59 million civilians and combatants.[3] Over 30 million people were displaced by the Germans and the Soviets alone, and many millions more began the uncertain life of homelessness, displacement, and exile (for example, an estimated 25 million people in the Soviet Union, and 20 million in Germany, became homeless by the end of the war).[4]

In Asia, the Allied war against Japan raged. On August 6, 1945, two months after the end of the fighting in Europe, the Allied powers' systematic bombing of Japanese cities culminated in President Truman's decision to drop an atomic bomb on the city of Hiroshima. The bomb incinerated the entire city of 300,000 people. In a matter of seconds, it obliterated one quarter of the population, and many more deaths followed from exposure to deadly levels of radioactive fallout. Three days later, the United States dropped a second atomic bomb on the city of Nagasaki. Shortly thereafter, Japan surrendered unconditionally.

Clearly, in the course of one generation, the destructive forces in the world had grown at an unprecedented rate, leaving little doubt in the minds of many that if a third world war were to erupt, human civilization was in serious peril. In a *My Day* essay published two days after the first bomb, Eleanor struggled to come to terms with the bomb's awesome power:

> *If wisely used, it may serve the purposes of peace. But for the moment, we are chiefly concerned with its destructive power. That power can be multiplied indefinitely, so that not only whole cities but large areas may be destroyed at one fell swoop. If you face this possibility and realize that, having once discovered a principle, it is very easy to take further steps to magnify its power, you soon face the unpleasant fact that in the next war whole peoples may be destroyed.[5]*

In this essay, Eleanor took a position that very few in Washington were able or willing to take. Her renewed focus was on prevention: "We can no longer indulge in the slaughter of our young men," she declared. "The price will be too high, and will be paid not just by young men, but by whole populations."[6] In the weeks after Japan's surrender, she did not publicly object to the use of atomic bombs; she assumed it had ended the war more quickly than any other course of action could have.[7] But several months later, Eleanor somberly reminded a group of reporters that humankind now possessed the capacity to eradicate itself:

> *I think that if the atomic bomb did nothing more, it scared people to the point where they realized that either they must do something about preventing war, or there is a chance that there might be a morning when we would not wake up.[8]*

Faced with the possibility of self-annihilation, many groups, politicians, lawyers, and intellectuals began to call for measures to ensure the safety of the human race. Eleanor was among them. Her response to the enormous challenges that arose in the wake of World War II grew out of her lifelong commitment to social and political justice and her work to advance international peace. Indeed, by the time she joined the United States delegation to the UN, she had already completed a long personal and political journey that put her at the forefront of the struggle for civil rights in America. By then she had already acquired plenty of experience in deliberating policies and was perhaps one of the most under-recognized advocates for peace and international cooperation in America (for example, she chaired the Edward Bok Peace Prize Committee, which reviewed plans for reintroducing the United States into peacekeeping efforts around the world after the country refused to join the League of Nations).[9] Her new work would soon make her the face of the human rights campaign around the globe.

NO ORDINARY LIFE

"My mother," Eleanor wrote in the first line of her autobiography, "was one of the most beautiful women I have ever seen."[10] Later passages revealed how Eleanor saw herself: as a plain, serious, awkward girl.[11] "I must have been a more wrinkled and less attractive baby than the average…. I was a shy, solemn child even at the age of two, and I am sure that even when I danced, I never smiled."[12] Such impressions, Eleanor suggested, were driven into her by her mother, Anna Roosevelt, who often picked on her, mocking Eleanor's clothing and shyness—one of Anna's favorite nicknames for her daughter was "Granny." Eleanor later recalled that at such moments, she "wanted to sink through the floor in shame."[13] Anna set the moral standards in the family

Eleanor (far right) at the age of six with her father and brothers in New York, New York, circa 1890. Eleanor saw herself as a "plain, serious, awkward girl" and a "shy, solemn child."

so high that Eleanor felt it was "utterly impossible" for her to live up to her mother.[14] In the world inhabited by the Roosevelts—New York's elite Protestant society—where the ability to dress, speak, and dance elegantly meant a great deal, the mother's critical assessments only added to the daughter's feelings of inadequacy.

Fifth cousins once removed, Eleanor and Franklin Delano Roosevelt were descendants of Nicholas Roosevelt, a New York City alderman whose Dutch father had immigrated to America in the 1640s. Other family members arrived even earlier, some aboard the *Mayflower*; among the Delano family were descendents of the Protestant Huguenots who escaped religious persecution in France and arrived in America in 1621 (their original French name was de Lannoy). Later generations, especially on Franklin's side, prospered in commerce and industry and amassed great fortunes. If ever there was an American aristocracy, Franklin and Eleanor belonged to it.[15] But in spite of its material advantages, her family endured a series of blows. First to fall ill was Anna Roosevelt, who died of diphtheria in 1892; she was not yet 30 years old. Her husband, Elliott Roosevelt, an alcoholic who had formerly spent long periods away from home, tried to rally and care for his three children, but before long he was on the road again.[16] Eleanor and her two younger brothers, Elliott, Jr., and Gracie, were left in the care of their maternal grandmother, Mary Livingston Ludlow Hall. Despite Elliott's shortcomings, he played a tremendously important role in Eleanor's life: "He provided me," she said, "with some badly needed reassurance, for in my earliest days I knew that I could never hope to achieve my mother's beauty, and I fell short in so many ways of what was expected of me. I needed my father's warmth and devotion more perhaps than the average child."[17]

Her brother Elliott, Jr., then contracted scarlet fever, followed by diphtheria, and died six months after his mother, when he was not yet four years old. A little more than a year later, shortly before her tenth birthday, Eleanor learned that her father had died as a result of his alcohol and drug addictions.[18] In two years' time, Eleanor had lost a brother and both parents.

In 1899, Eleanor was sent to a boarding school in England named Allenswood, where she was to expand her education before taking her place in a society defined by great hereditary wealth. Under the sympathetic eyes of the headmistress, Marie Souvestre, Eleanor blossomed. Studying among the sons and daughters of the European elite inspired her, and she was able to cast off the memory of her mother's disapproval and emerge from the darkness

Eleanor at her school, Allenswood, in England in 1900. Eleanor was sent to boarding school to acquire a first-rate education. The school stressed intellectual courage, taught its students openness, and had them practice arguing their opponents' views.

of her family tragedy.[19] An early feminist, Souvestre took great interest in her American pupil, and in time they developed a warm mutual affection that lasted until Souvestre's death in 1905. Academic discipline and the guidance of a devoted mentor gave Eleanor the skills and confidence that she later displayed. Souvestre, who stressed intellectual courage, taught her students openness and had them practice arguing their opponents' views. She also made Eleanor her personal companion for her European summer travels. During these travels, Eleanor was exposed to new cultures, learned many new skills, and, at Souvestre's insistence, visited the poor and underprivileged— along with the usual mix of tourist destinations. Later in life, Eleanor concluded that Souvestre had the biggest influence on her childhood. She noted her teacher's legacy:

> As I look back, I realize that Mlle. Souvestre was rather an
> extraordinary character. She often fought seemingly lost causes, but
> they were often won in the long run. . . . I think I came to feel that
> the underdog was always the one to be championed![20]

After three years in England, Eleanor returned to the United States, where she spent the remainder of her adolescence among the "Knickerbockers." These members of New York's high society had abundant leisure time; they spent it visiting one another's mansions, riding horses, playing polo and golf, and hunting—the traditional pursuits of the British aristocracy. Though they did not need to work, many of the men pursued higher education and careers in law, business, politics, or the military. The young women were trained in the skills needed for the life of upper-class wives; they were encouraged to socialize, read, paint, improve their writing skills, and help the poor.

The 17-year-old Eleanor could not manage to summon any excitement for the standard Knickerbocker existence. She was particularly unhappy about the formal balls she was obliged to attend: at 18, young women of the approved sort were formally presented to elite society at spectacular debutante balls that marked their readiness for marriage. Like other eligible young ladies, Eleanor was expected to make her debut in adult society (this is why they were called "debutantes").

Instead of balls and tea parties, Eleanor developed a keen interest in politics and good works. She was especially drawn to the challenges faced by New York City's newest arrivals—Italian, Jewish, and German immigrants who labored in the city's most exploitative sweatshops and factories. Clearly, her interest in decent housing and living wages—two fundamental rights Eleanor would fight for all her life—predates the New Deal. In fact, she was the one who introduced her young lover, Franklin Roosevelt (then a law student at Columbia University), to the hardships of the poor on the Lower East Side. Franklin, who sometimes met Eleanor at Rivington Street Settlement House after class (see below), got firsthand experience of life in the poor neighborhood.[21] Later in life, Eleanor argued that it was her father who steered her interests toward the suffering of the disadvantaged:

> *Very early, I became conscious of the fact that there were people around me who suffered in one way or another. I was five or six when my father took me to help serve Thanksgiving dinner in one of the newsboys' clubhouses which my grandfather, Theodore Roosevelt, had started. . . . My father explained that many of these ragged little boys had no homes, and lived in little wooden shanties in empty lots, or slept in vestibules of houses or public buildings, or any place where they could be moderately warm. . . .[22]*

In 1903, she joined the staff of the College Settlement on New York City's Rivington Street, where young men and women just out of college lived among the poor, taught them calisthenics and dance, and attempted to facilitate their assimilation into American society. She also worked with the New York Consumers' League to improve women's deplorable working conditions, particularly in the textile industry. The more she saw of the living conditions in New York City's tenements, the stronger her commitment grew to helping those in a part of society quite different from her own. Although rich Americans had long assisted the poor, the Knickerbockers preferred to help the poor from behind the physical and social barrier that set them apart. Eleanor refused to give charity from arm's length; she preferred to give it firsthand. Indeed, Eleanor now began to challenge the old methods of dispensing charity, and she got to know the needy in person—a very different approach from the one favored by her parents' generation.

During the nineteenth century, the rich were obligated by religion, honor, and tradition to serve their community, and they contributed both time and money. But this charity was given from above, in keeping with the values of a patriarchal social structure in which the father exercised all authority. Within the family, he was expected to protect and provide for his children, who were obligated to respect his authority and to obey his directions. Similarly, the rich and powerful dispensed charity in return for deference from the poor. Though this type of aid provided a rudimentary social safety net, it cast the poor as "children" of the rich and reinforced America's class system.

Eleanor on December 1, 1932, serving food to unemployed women and their children. Eleanor challenged traditional upper-class forms of charity and sought firsthand knowledge of social problems.

Over the course of her lifelong social activism, Eleanor sought to break free from tradition. To the dismay of her family, she refused to simply sit on the boards of charitable organizations; she sought firsthand knowledge of social problems. Instead of charity—which she viewed as demeaning—she believed in reform, in institutions that promoted equal opportunities for everyone and that preserved the dignity of those who had nothing.

Reporting on this decisive period, Eleanor wrote in her autobiography,

> *I had a great curiosity about life, and a desire to participate in every experience that might be the lot of a woman. There seemed to me to be a necessity for hurry; without rhyme or reason, I felt the urge to be a part of the stream of life.*[23]

Though Eleanor often felt uneasy about Knickerbocker rituals, she seems never to have doubted that, for her, "the lot of a woman" involved marrying someone who moved in elite circles. This was why, "in the autumn of 1903, when Franklin Roosevelt, my fifth cousin once removed, asked me to marry him, though I was only nineteen, it seemed entirely natural."[24]

ELEANOR AND FRANKLIN

Franklin Delano Roosevelt was born on January 30, 1882, in Hyde Park, New York, to James Roosevelt and Sara Delano Roosevelt. As a boy, Franklin pursued outdoor activities with zeal, always under the adoring watch of his mother. He was tutored privately in academic subjects, and, as a result, he had a very secluded early childhood. At the age of 14, Franklin was sent to board at Groton, a prestigious preparatory school in Massachusetts. Sharp and articulate, Franklin graduated from Groton and went on to obtain a bachelor's degree in history from Harvard. Franklin, who studied history, government, and economics, also devoted many hours of his time to the *Harvard Crimson* newspaper, of which he was an editor and president. Never an "honors student," Franklin nevertheless entered Columbia Law School. He departed that institution without a degree, but he passed the New York bar exam anyway! With Franklin came his overbearing mother, Sara. A widow since 1900, Sara had long dominated her only son's life, and she did not hesitate to make decisions for her new daughter-in-law.

Eleanor and Franklin were married on St. Patrick's Day in 1905, and their marriage united the two branches of this prominent New York family. President Theodore Roosevelt, Eleanor's uncle, walked Eleanor down the aisle. Shortly after their marriage, Eleanor and Franklin set to building their family. Between 1906 and 1916, Eleanor gave birth to six children, but she often felt that it was Sara, and not she, who raised them. The relationship became even more strained when Sara announced that she was building a pair of houses in Manhattan, one for her son's family and one for herself. They would be next-door neighbors. Since Eleanor loathed confrontations, she simply resigned herself to the arrangement:

My early dislike of any kind of scolding had developed now into a dislike for any kind of discussion, and so, instead of taking an interest in these houses . . . I left everything to my mother-in-law and my husband. I was growing dependent on my mother-in-law, requiring her help on almost every subject, and never thought of asking for anything that I thought would not meet with her approval.[25]

But when the houses were finished, Eleanor finally broke down:

I sat in front of my dressing table and wept, and when my bewildered young husband asked me what on earth was the matter with me, I said I did not like to live in a house which was not in any way mine, one that I had done nothing about, and which did not represent the way I wanted to live.[26]

Nothing came of this outburst; it would take Eleanor several years to stand up to Sara.

In 1913, Franklin was selected to serve as assistant secretary of the navy, and the family moved to Washington, DC. When World War I broke out, Eleanor revived her interest in public service and went to work for the Red Cross. There was hardly a soldier who left Union Station in Washington, DC, without witnessing Eleanor give out coffee, sandwiches, and handmade wool socks.[27] Franklin's career as an assistant secretary thrived as he prepared the American navy for war. Eleanor assumed many social obligations: there were the usual cocktail parties, dinner parties, and charitable events, and her schedule began to fill up. To help with the demands of being the wife of a public official, she decided to hire a social secretary, a woman named

Lucy Mercer. A charming, easygoing woman, Mercer caught Franklin's eye. Later, in 1918, Franklin traveled to visit American naval outfits in Europe and saw the war firsthand. On his return that year, he contracted influenza (in 1918, Europe and other areas around the world were hit hard by the "Spanish flu" in what became one of the worst influenza epidemics). Bedridden, Franklin arrived in the United States and was greeted by his wife. Eleanor, who received his luggage, discovered a stack of letters revealing what she had previously suspected—Franklin and Lucy Mercer had become lovers. Eleanor acted resolutely. She gave her husband an ultimatum: he would either give her a divorce or never see Mercer again. Informed by his mother that a divorce would mean losing his rights to the family, Franklin agreed to break off the affair.[28]

Eleanor and FDR at the family house on Campobello Island. Though Eleanor often defied elite rituals, she nevertheless married within the upper social class.

Credit: © Bettmann/Corbis

INDEPENDENCE

Despite the affair, wife and husband would move on and forge a new partnership based on shared political values and ambitions—a partnership that would reach almost every corner of American life.

Biographer Allida Black wrote that World War I "radicalized" Eleanor's outlook. After the armistice, Eleanor traveled to France with Franklin to see the devastated cities and shell-shocked soldiers. Was there a way to protect future generations from such a fate? Upon her return, she joined a campaign for the League of Nations, an international organization many hoped would do just that.[29] In retrospect, Eleanor's work to bring about the United States' entry into the League of Nations was especially important for her role in the United Nations two decades later. So was her fervent advocacy, during the 1920s, on behalf of the International Court of Justice (also known as the World Court), which was established by the Covenant of the League of Nations with the goal of settling international conflicts.[30] It educated her about the challenges of organizing for global peace and earned her a reputation as an avid advocate of international cooperation. But when President Woodrow Wilson asked Congress to approve American membership, the legislative body declined. In Eleanor's eyes, this was a costly choice. A decade later, when it looked as though another conflict would engulf much of Europe, the League of Nations proved too weak to stem German aggression. But the principles laid out by the League's founders shaped both Eleanor's and Franklin's responses to World War II.

In the 1920s, Eleanor "poured all her pent-up energies into a variety of reformist organizations dedicated to the abolition of child labor, the establishment of a minimum wage, and the passage of protective legislation for women workers."[31] She traveled nonstop, gave innumerable speeches, delivered radio addresses, and became involved in slum clearance, electrification of rural regions, civil rights, and education reform. Her husband continued his official duties, which included managing the demobilization of America's vast wartime navy. After an unsuccessful campaign for the New York state senate, Franklin was selected in 1920—the first year women could vote—to run as the vice-presidential candidate on the Democratic ticket. Eleanor served as the only woman on the campaign trail.

The campaign introduced Eleanor to Louis Howe, Franklin's close political advisor. At first, Eleanor disliked Howe. But during the campaign, Howe showed a growing interest in Eleanor's opinions, as well as in her own political career. He soon began to coach her on how to read a crowd, how to handle the press, and how to move beyond the role of a community organizer and become a political actor on a national scale. A brilliant speechwriter and a talented artist, Howe attracted her attention and quickly became a dear friend and confidant. As she learned to trust Howe, Eleanor also began to depend on his advice, and he, in turn, devoted himself to furthering her career and "to bridging the emotional distance" between her and Franklin.[32] "By the end of the campaign," wrote Allida Black, "while other journalists aboard the Roosevelt campaign train played cards, Louis Howe and Eleanor could frequently

Eleanor at a 1924 Democratic meeting in New York, New York, with Louis Howe, Mrs. Henry Morgenthau, Sr., Herbert Pell, Caroline O'Day, Henry Morgenthau, Sr., and Nancy Cook. Louis Howe, FDR's close political advisor, eventually coached Eleanor to play a national political role.

be found huddled over paperwork, reviewing FDR's speeches and discussing campaign protocol."[33]

During the summer of 1921, the Roosevelts were vacationing on a small island off the Maine coast when Franklin began to feel ill. Eleanor recounted the events in a letter written on August 14:

> *We have had a very anxious few days as on Wed. evening Franklin was taken ill. It seemed a chill, but Thursday he had so much pain in his back and legs that I sent for the doctor; by Friday evening he lost his ability to walk or move his legs, but though they felt numb, he can still feel in [sic] them.*[34]

Within a few days, he was paralyzed from the waist down. Franklin had contracted polio. Tremendous determination and Eleanor's unwavering assistance permitted him to recover much of his energy, but he remained in a wheelchair for the rest of his life.

When recovery was in sight, in defiance of her mother-in-law's wishes, Eleanor urged Franklin to push on with his political career, and she helped him keep his name in the press. She resumed her work for social justice, took up the cause of women's equality, and developed a wide network of colleagues and friends who became increasingly influential in the Democratic Party. Indeed, during the 1920s, the Roosevelts emerged as a powerful political force.

WOMEN IN POWER

At Sara Roosevelt's estate in Hyde Park, a town 60 miles from New York City, the big family house filled up on weekends with children, their friends, and Franklin's political cronies. In 1926, to find a measure of peace, Eleanor had a cottage built two miles from the house, giving it the name early Dutch settlers had used for nearby Fallkill Creek: Val-Kill. Franklin, who supported the idea fully, provided the land and oversaw the design and construction. When the cottage was completed, Eleanor had a place of her own. She shared it with two of her closest friends: Marion Dickerman and her partner, Nancy Cook.[35] Val-Kill was more than a retreat or home. In the first place, the cottage afforded Eleanor a place to develop her social and political ties. In Hyde Park—in the so-called "Big House" she and Franklin shared—Sara continued to be a foreboding presence. She constantly intervened in Eleanor's relationship with her children, and she did not hesitate to pass judgment on her visitors. Indeed, Sara's views of people who sympathized with the working poor—she often called them "socialists"—were notoriously negative, as were her prejudices against Jews and immigrants.[36] Away from Sara, Eleanor was able to see whomever she wanted.

Courtesy of the FDR Library

Eleanor with Nancy Cook, Caroline O'Day, and Marion Dickerman in New York in 1929. The friendship these women began in 1922 developed into a strong political partnership in the next decade.

Many friends came and went through the doors of the cottage, but for a few years Val-Kill united in particular Eleanor, Cook, and Dickerman in a vigorous campaign. Cook was a strong advocate of world peace, of women's voting rights, of women's right to fair wages and safe jobs, and of the abolition of child labor. Eleanor believed in these causes, and a close friendship grew on the basis of a shared social and political vision. The friendship began in 1922, when Cook became executive secretary of the Women's Division of the New York State Democratic Committee and asked Eleanor to campaign with her for progressive causes and Democratic candidates. Overcoming her shyness and awkwardness, Eleanor began to be recognized as a charismatic public speaker (an art she perfected over the decade) and as a visionary among an emerging new liberal constituency.

As the partnership expanded, the women established a furniture factory on the premises. It was presided over by Cook, whose woodworking skills were outstanding. The idea was to introduce some form of industry into rural areas so that young men would be able to learn new skills and supplement their income during agricultural downtimes (Eleanor would continue to pursue this idea during the 1930s). They also bought an elite private school for girls in New York called Todhunter, where Eleanor taught literature, drama, and history. Dickerman became the principal, and Eleanor shaped the school's curriculum. In its focus on female intellectual achievement and leadership, the school was similar to Allenswood, the boarding school Eleanor had attended in England.[37]

Val-Kill quickly developed as the center of gravity for a dynamic group of political activists who spearheaded campaigns for better housing, improved sanitation and wages, public parks and recreation, job-safety legislation, and many social reforms that the New Deal would later feature: unemployment insurance, workers' compensation, child labor protections, and equal rights and pay for women in the workplace, among other causes. Building on the experience they gained during the struggle for women's right to vote (suffrage), the group members further developed their political skills and sharpened their understanding of the challenges a professional political career presented.

"Nan" Cook, Marion Dickerman, and Eleanor added a fourth key player to their team: wealthy activist and future congresswoman Caroline O'Day, who was elected chairperson of the Women's Division of the New York Democratic Party in 1923. Eleanor, too, was elected to an official post: she became the vice president and finance chairperson of the Women's Division of the New York State Democratic Committee. In addition, Eleanor worked closely with the Women's Trade Union League, which promoted the rights and well-being of women in the workplace, the League of Women Voters, and the Women's City Club, an umbrella group that united activists from many New York organizations.

Working together with Cook and O'Day, Eleanor led statewide grassroots campaigns in support of Democratic candidates and causes. The women activists adopted new techniques to mobilize supporters, which included the use of radio broadcasts, newsletters, and magazines, in addition to such well-tested methods as public debates, speeches, fundraisers, and community events. Indeed, Eleanor came to believe that "fundamental change requires active and committed women who are willing to go door to door, block by block, and educate people on an individual basis about the real needs and conditions of society."[38] Soon she emerged as the most powerful leader among New York activists, and by the end of the 1920s, she was one of the most well-known figures in the Democratic Party. Together with Eleanor's close friend Elinor Morgenthau—a Hyde Park resident and wife of Henry Morgenthau, Jr.—Eleanor, O'Day, Cook, and Dickerman "dominated the Women's Division of the New York State Democratic Committee" in the late 1920s.[39] The five women also started their own political journal, *Women's Democratic News,* with Eleanor serving as editor, author, and treasurer.[40] With Eleanor as the emerging leader, she and her partners rallied the Democratic Party behind Al Smith's and Franklin Roosevelt's gubernatorial and presidential campaigns in 1928 and 1932.

Readers of Eleanor's autobiographical writings are led to believe that her social activism and the political roles she took on were not terribly significant. Moreover, Eleanor frequently presented herself as a dutiful wife in the service of her husband's aspirations, and she made few personal claims to this period's legacy. Regardless of how Eleanor chose to present herself, her contribution to the development of an American progressive agenda in the 1930s and 1940s cannot be underestimated—nor can the roles she played in promoting this new movement. From the early 1920s, she was clearly working toward her own independence—financial, social, and political—as well as that of women and others.

While the impact of women was clearly noticeable at the grassroots level, political leadership by women was repeatedly denied. Indeed, women secured the right to vote in 1920, but their political voices remained largely unheard. "Old boys"-style networking, tradition, and prejudices left women on the margins of the political process. In an essay written in 1928, Eleanor captures both the growing strengths she and her female friends found in the 1920s and the set of prejudices—often held by men and women alike—that kept them on the sidelines:

Women have been voting for ten years. But have they achieved actual political equality with men? No. They go through the gesture of going to the polls; their votes are solicited by politicians; and they possess the external aspect of equal rights. But it is mostly a gesture without real power. With some outstanding exceptions, women who have gone into politics are refused serious consideration by the men leaders.[41]

In part, Eleanor argued, the problem was with the political establishment. Women were kept out of the loop when important decisions were made, and the old-boys' alliances made sure they had neither the information nor the tools to make an impact:

In those circles which decide the affairs of national politics, women have no voice or power whatever. . . . Politically, as a sex, women are generally "frozen out" from any intrinsic share of influence in their parties. . . . When it comes to giving the offices or dealing out favors, men are always given precedence . . . Beneath the veneer of courtesy and outward show of consideration universally accorded women, there is a widespread male hostility—age-old, perhaps— against sharing with them any actual control.[42]

However, Eleanor placed equal blame on women for their political marginalization. Many of the talented and courageous women who fought for the right to vote "dropped out of politics" and returned to domestic duties, squandered their energies, and were not willing to put in the hard work required to build an effective political career. The fact remains, "attaining the vote was only part of a program for equal rights—an external gesture toward economic independence, and social and spiritual equality with men." How, then, Eleanor asked, "can we bring the men leaders to concede participation in party affairs, adequate representation, and real political equality?"[43] Her answer was simple, direct, and radical:

Our means is to elect, accept, and back women political bosses. . . . Perhaps the word "boss" may shock sensitive ears. To many it will conjure all that is unhealthy and corrupt in our political machinery.

Yet when I speak of women bosses, I mean bosses actually in the sense that men are bosses. . . . As things are today, the boss is a leader, often an enlightened, high-minded leader. . . .

"Voters who are only voters, whether men or women, are only the followers of leaders," Eleanor concluded. "The important thing is the choosing of leaders."[44] Eleanor's essay reflected frustrations, but it also showed that she and other women of her circle were learning how to wield political power. Like Eleanor, whose income at that time equaled that of her husband, these women were financially independent, and they played leading roles in grassroots and party organizations.[45]

FIRST LADY

It took Franklin several years to recover from his loss in the vice–presidential campaign of 1920, and from his affliction with polio, which forced him to wear heavy steel braces for the rest of his life. Eleanor did not just encourage him to keep his political hope alive; with support, coaching, and advice from Howe, she "became his stand-in with the Democrats. She kept his name in front of the public. She brought people to see him—key party officials, and public personalities."[46]

Franklin learned how to cope with (and hide) his paralysis, and he was preparing to resume his political career. While Eleanor delved into the political machinery of the Democratic Party as a grassroots organizer, Franklin decided to enter the race for the post of New York governor. He campaigned and won in 1928. During the same year, Eleanor joined former New York governor Al Smith's presidential campaign against Republican Herbert C. Hoover. With Belle Moskowitz, Smith's campaign manager, Eleanor "put together one of the most efficient campaign organizations in political history." Leading a group of women activists, Eleanor headed the National Women's Committee of the Democratic Party, oversaw press releases, gave radio talks and interviews, and delivered speeches to voters on the campaign trail.[47]

Hoover won the presidential election, and Eleanor felt it was not just Smith who was defeated, but also the entire progressive agenda she had been promoting. Moreover, between the 1928 and 1932 presidential elections, the American economy had collapsed. After the stock market crashed in October 1929, the many individual investors who had driven up the value of stocks saw their investments vanish. Around the world, many feared that currency was losing its value and redeemed paper money for gold, depleting national treasuries. As every institution that had issued loans demanded repayment, banks failed, and individuals lost everything. As the financial system buckled, the United States economy ground to a halt, and millions of Americans lost their jobs. As the situation went from bad to worse, Franklin capitalized on public dissatisfaction and offered a set of new and old solutions to combat the national crisis.

By the time 57 percent of the electorate voted for Roosevelt in 1932, America was in its deepest economic crisis ever: a crisis now known as the Great Depression. Blanche Wiesen Cooke, one of Eleanor's biographers, described the country in 1933, on the eve of the inauguration:

> *America was at a standstill. Men, women, and children begged on street corners, sold pencils, apples, old clothes. People spoke about gloom, despair, suicide, revolution. When farm prices fell to pennies, farm owners burned their crops, killed their livestock. Banks foreclosed mortgages and reclaimed farms and homes. There were riots at garbage dumps as people fought each other for scraps of food and kindling. Over two million people . . .wandered the country looking for work. . . . Giant "Hoovervilles" made of tin cans and frayed tires, scraps of wood and debris, appeared along river shores and railroad sidings, in parks and woodlands. People were living in caves and culverts all over America.[48]*

In his first inaugural address, President Franklin Delano Roosevelt declared that "the only thing we have to fear is fear itself," and he set about the monumental task of rebuilding the national economy. For her part, Eleanor turned her attention to the people who had lost everything in the crash.

A UTOPIA SOFTLY SKETCHED

Despite what many believed at the time, Eleanor dreaded the life she was about to enter. She was a campaigner for the Democratic Party, a teacher, an editor, a writer, a radio commentator, and an activist for various causes. But Eleanor knew that as First Lady, she would have to give up at least some of her positions. Indeed, once "FDR won the election, he asked her to resign her positions with the Democratic National Committee, the Todhunter School, the League of Women Voters, the Non-Partisan Legislative Committee and the Women's Trade Union League."[49] Public criticism of her activism, independence, and direct contact with ordinary Americans also grew and forced her to reconsider what activities were appropriate for the First Lady. In addition, there was the gossip, love affairs, power grabbing, and political selfishness she despised so much about Washington. Eleanor entered the White House, therefore, only reluctantly.

After the inauguration, Eleanor was determined to continue her work on social and economic issues. Without a defined role, she felt that her years of experience could benefit the new administration as it faced an enormous economic crisis; the problems of the unemployed and impoverished offered endless possibilities for activism. A group of 20,000 veterans who marched peacefully on Washington provided her first opportunity. These veterans of World War I

> had been promised a government bonus, to be paid at some future time. They wanted it now, while their need was so desperate. During the summer [of 1932] they had staged a march on Washington, had managed to erect rows of little shanties on the Mall, in front of the Lincoln Memorial, and were bringing all the pressure they could on Congress to grant them their bonus immediately.[50]

"Their bitterness mounted to fury" when, under orders from President Hoover, "General Douglas MacArthur, as the army's chief-of-staff, had his soldiers drive them out of Washington, and burn their shanties."[51] But a few remained in Washington when Franklin took office. On Louis Howe's suggestion, Eleanor went to the veterans' encampment and sat down to listen to their concerns. Soon she was seen delivering sandwiches and coffee and singing by the campfire. The veterans cheered when she left, and one of them remarked, "Hoover sent the army, Roosevelt sent his wife." In a short time, this statement came to describe the public perception of Eleanor's new role.

Franklin was not unaware of Eleanor's actions. In fact, he quickly discovered that if he could harness her energy, his administration could gain a smart and widely popular ambassador. In the next few months, while Franklin remained essentially rooted in the White House (he was bound by his political commitments and by his infirmity), Eleanor made her way to the most remote corners of the country to hear firsthand the stories of those who had lost their jobs.

Refusing secret-service protection, she drove her own car, caught taxis on the street corners of New York, and rode the subway. She ran into ordinary people on the streets, at the grocery stores, and on trips she took to study America's social crisis. In one year, she traveled 40,000 miles—more than any president ever had!

As more than the president's eyes and ears, Eleanor drew information she needed from many sources. For example, several months after entering the White House, she started a monthly column called *Mrs. Roosevelt's Page* in the widely read *Woman's Home Companion*. The page was designed to give advice but also to receive it, opening a direct line of communication between millions of readers and the First Lady. The title of her first essay, "I Want You to Write to Me," declared,

> *The invitation which forms the title of this page comes from my heart, in the hope that we can establish here a clearing house, a discussion room, for the millions of men, women, and young people who read the Companion every month. . . . Please do not imagine that I am planning to give you advice that will eventually solve all your problems. We all know that no human being is infallible, and on this page I am not setting myself up as an oracle. But it may be that in the varied life I have had, there have been certain experiences which other people will find useful, and it may be that out of the letters which come to me, I shall learn of experiences which will prove helpful to others. And so I close my first page to and for you, as I opened it, with a cordial invitation—I want you to write to me.[52]*

As a result of this invitation, Eleanor received 300,000 letters in the first months of Franklin's presidency alone.

Her proactive approach shocked the public. A widely circulated 1933 *New Yorker* cartoon showed one amazed coal miner who, upon hearing that Eleanor decided to go down the mine shaft, said to another, "For gosh sakes, here comes Mrs. Roosevelt." Sure enough, two years later, Eleanor insisted on descending into a mine shaft in Ohio to see the men at work. Breaking a longstanding taboo that prohibited women from going down into the mine, Eleanor's actions caused a public row. In an essay titled "In Defense of Curiosity," Eleanor challenged these norms and the scope of interests women were allowed to entertain. "Somehow or other," she protested, critics "seemed to feel that it was unbecoming in a woman to have a variety of interests." This criticism "arose from the old inherent theory that [a] woman's interests must lie only in her home" and that women ought to leave public affairs to men.[53] Such views, Eleanor argued, were too narrow. Indeed, the ideas that defined "home" and the things that were needed to protect it required revision:

> *Few seem capable of realizing that the real reason that home is important is that it is so closely tied, by a million strings, to the rest of the world. That is what makes it an important factor in the life of every nation. . . . The women of the country are discovering their deep concern as to the policies of government and of commercial agencies, largely because these policies are reflected in many ways in their daily lives. . . .*

> *This correlation of interests is something that every woman would understand if she had the curiosity to find out the reason for certain conditions, instead of merely accepting them. . . .*

> *So many of us resent what we consider the waste of war, but if in each home there is no curiosity to follow the trend of affairs in various nations, and our own conduct toward them, how can we expect to understand where our interests clash, or to know whether our Government's policies are fair and just, or generally selfish?*

> *Out of the homes of our nation comes the public opinion which has to be back of every Government action. How can this public opinion be anything but a reaction to propaganda unless there is curiosity enough in each home to keep constant watch over local, state, national, and international affairs?*

> *Therefore, anyone who fully appreciates the value of home life must, of necessity, reach out in many directions in an effort to protect the home, which we know is our most valuable asset.[54]*

"Perhaps," Eleanor concluded, "the day will come when our curiosity will not only carry us out of our homes and out of ourselves to a better understanding of material things, but will make us able to understand one another."[55] She clearly called for women's participation in politics, without directly challenging the conventional roles of men and women. She did so by connecting the home to national—and even international—affairs, and she was thus able to provide a justification for the ever-expanding interests of a new generation of women activists.

In his acceptance speech for the Democratic nomination of 1932, Franklin pledged to Americans a "new deal" in the struggle to avert the economic crisis. Yet it was not until several months into his presidency, after initial New Deal legislation and actions failed to bring about drastic changes, that he realized how deep this crisis was. In 1934, he therefore initiated what has become known as the Second New Deal. At the center of this new effort was a daring plan: it set out to guarantee work and health care for most Americans, to limit working hours, to ensure reasonable wages, to eliminate child labor, to improve housing, and to improve and broaden education across the nation. The government fed cash into the economy to keep businesses afloat, created jobs, and imposed stricter regulations on banks, stock brokerages, and other financial institutions. The Social Security Act of 1935 ensured that the retirees, the disabled, and the unemployed would receive regular payments, much like the paychecks of working people. Other acts strengthened labor unions, so that workers could unite to bargain with the owners of private enterprises for adequate wages and job security.

Eleanor's fingerprints could be found on many of these innovative policies. In fact, living wages, proper housing, social security, and broader education programs had been on her agenda for many years. Indeed, since Eleanor's early work at the College Settlement on Rivington Street and the Consumers' League, Eleanor had recognized the duty of society to protect the well-being of the individual—but now she was learning how negotiations between government and the people worked. Eleanor took credit only for starting the National Advisory Committee of the New National Youth Administration—one of the elements of the New Deal—which provided "work projects, vocational guidance, apprenticeship training, educational and nutritional guidance camps for unemployed women, and student financial aid."[56] But many other New Deal programs began literally in the living room of her apartment in New York. Often playing down her role, Eleanor was well versed in wielding political power in non-traditional ways. In short, *she introduced programs for groups not originally included in New Deal plans; supported others which were in danger of elimination, or having their funds cut; pushed the hiring of women, blacks, and liberals within federal agencies; and acted as the administration's most outspoken champion of liberal reform.*[57]

This education was to serve her well later.

During her first years at the White House, Eleanor published hundreds of articles and gave innumerable interviews and lectures. "Her speeches and writings," wrote Joseph Lash, "called for the building of a new world, and though her language was that of the [Christian scriptures] and the Declaration of Independence, rather than the *Communist Manifesto,* her underlying message was revolutionary."[58] Eleanor, who had known tragedy and struggle, had great sympathy for those "in want, in need, in trouble"—and the people she met, along with others who read her words, sensed this.[59] But she was not a martyr: the mission gave her purpose and meaning, and it introduced her to people from all walks of life. Rich or poor, black or white, these people often became her close friends.

Eleanor descending into a coal mine in Neffs, Ohio, on May 21, 1935. As more than the president's eyes and ears, Eleanor sought firsthand experience with the American people.

"She had her own concept of utopia," Lash argues. "She sketched it softly, in phrases disarmingly modest and simple."[60] At a time when the world had been shaken, when governments had to reacquaint their citizens with the essential value of work, Eleanor wrote an essay entitled "What I Hope to Leave Behind" (published in April 1933), in which a man dreamed of living

in a community where no individual had an income that could not provide his family with the ordinary comforts and pleasures of life, and where no individual had an income so large that he did not have to think about his expenditures, and where the spread between is not so great, but that the essentials of life may lie within the possession of all concerned.[61]

Such an arrangement did not seem impossible to her.

In studying the effects of economic crisis, Eleanor relied heavily on her connections with the press, and particularly on reports provided by Lorena Alice Hickok. Hickok, a brilliant reporter, covered the conditions of ordinary Americans for the White House at Eleanor's request. "Hick," as she was known to her friends, became Eleanor's loyal advisor, and it was her advice that led to the "no men allowed" policy at some of the First Lady's press conferences.[62] Hickok also suggested that Eleanor use her love of writing for the benefit of the public: "You know," Hick said in 1935, "you send me these long 10-, 12-, 15-page letters, filled with your daily doings. The entire nation would like to know what you are doing every day, and what you think about it all."[63] Taking this suggestion, Eleanor wrote a weekly column, called *My Day*, almost uninterruptedly from 1936 until her death in 1962; it was carried in 200 newspapers.[64]

In one of Hickok's many letters to Eleanor, she described a West Virginia mining community:

Morgantown was the worst place I'd ever seen. In a gutter, along the main street through the town, there was stagnant, filthy water, which the inhabitants used for drinking, cooking, washing, and everything else imaginable. On either side of the street were

Children playing at the Arthurdale Subsistence Homestead project in Reedsville, West Virginia, in October 1934. Eleanor drove this project in the hope that that it would fulfill her vision of agriculture balanced by industry.

ramshackle houses, black with coal dust, which most Americans would not have considered fit for pigs. And in those houses, every night children went to sleep hungry, on piles of bug-infested rags, spread out on the floor.[65]

After she had made her own visit to the part of Morgantown called Scott's Run, Eleanor wrote about a visit to a house where six children were living. Their diet consisted of scraps: "the kind you or I might give to a dog." After several minutes, two of the bolder children approached their visitors, one holding a white rabbit tightly to his chest. "It was evident," Eleanor wrote, that

it was a most cherished pet. The little girl was thin and scrawny, and had a gleam in her eyes as she looked at her brother. Turning to me she said: "He thinks we are not going to eat it, but we are," and at that the small boy fled down the road clutching the rabbit closer than ever.[66]

For Eleanor, the Great Depression was the result of greed, materialism, specu-lation, and selfishness. She believed that the time had come for America to discard wealth as the only measure of success, and she argued that the crisis would end only after a basic change of priorities: a renewed focus on the interdependence of American citizens and on their ability to overcome hard-ships by working together to achieve common goals.[67]

Some believed that the plight of West Virginia's miners could be alleviated by creating new independent farming communities. In an essay from 1934, Eleanor outlined her social vision. At its core was the idea

> *that families engaged in subsistence farming consume their own garden products locally. . . . They are not expected to support themselves entirely by raising food. The plan is that they shall be situated near enough to an industry for one member of the family to be employed in a factory a sufficient number of days in the year to bring in the amount of money needed to pay for the things which the family must have, and cannot produce for themselves. In this way farming will be helped by industry, and industry will be helped by farming.*[68]

The experiment served as a model for other communities in the United States (including a small town named after Eleanor in West Virginia that survived the test of time). It was carried out in 1934, 10 miles southeast of Morgantown at Arthurdale, where 1,200 acres purchased by the federal government were settled by 165 families. Many of them were miners from Scott's Run. Along with Clarence Pickett, an official from the Department of the Interior, Eleanor drove the project forward, hopeful that it would match her vision of agriculture balanced by industry.[69] By the 1940s, however, the experiment had failed. Many in the public thought that the government had gotten in over its head and that Arthurdale was not able to survive on its own.[70]

Arthurdale may have failed, but the public debate continued. It was a debate between those who championed the free market and those who believed in vigorous government intervention—a reflection of a basic disagreement about individual responsibility and the role of government. To those who believed that the individual had sole responsibility for his or her financial well-being, Eleanor replied that while that might have been true in the past, when those who wished to work soon found jobs, "[w]e are up against a different problem now."[71] The truth of the matter was that "[m]ost of the people who are out of work are ready and willing to work." The time had come, she continued, to

> *recognize the fact that no civilization can possibly survive which does not furnish every individual who wishes to work a job at wages on which he can live decently.*[72]

Eleanor and many other female activists, campaigners, and indeed politicians were at the heart of the gentle revolution in values embodied in the New Deal policies of the 1930s. These women stressed the point that if people were to be invested in the future of their society, they needed not only to get by, but also to thrive. This position called for a sea change in the government's responsibilities. Rather than placing the responsibility for one's life entirely in the hands of the individual, these proponents of the New Deal shifted responsibility, at least in part, to the government. Franklin Roosevelt echoed many of these principles in his second inaugural speech of 1937. In this speech, he summarized the ideas of the New Deal. Since 1933, he explained,

> *[w]e recognized the need to find through government the instrument of our united purpose to solve for the individual the ever-rising problems of a complex civilization. Repeated attempts at their solution without the aid of government had left us baffled and bewildered. For, without that aid, we had been unable to create those moral controls over the services of science which are necessary to make science a useful servant, instead of a ruthless master of mankind. To do this, we knew that we must [also] find practical controls over blind economic forces and blindly selfish men.[73]*

"We refused," Franklin said, summarizing the revolutionary message of the New Deal, "to leave the problems of our common welfare to be solved by the winds of chance and the hurricanes of disaster."[74]

Like Franklin, progressive women (as they were called in sympathetic circles) argued that the government could not afford to sit back and watch while harsh economic conditions left millions unemployed, hungry, uneducated, unhealthy, and poorly housed. Furthermore, it was the government's responsibility to ensure that all American families enjoyed a measure of comfort and security, fair employment and education, and something to fall back on in times of sickness and old age. Help with those issues was not a matter of charity; rather, it was a social duty, something the government owed to every citizen.

These were also the views of Frances Perkins, an unsung hero of this social transformation, who served as secretary of labor throughout Roosevelt's entire presidency. The first woman to be selected for a cabinet post, she worked tirelessly from within the administration to protect the rights and well-being of workers. In a dinner honoring the new secretary of labor in 1933, Eleanor toasted the appointment and noted that Perkins didn't accept it to

> *gain anything material for herself or her friends, but because she sees an opportunity for government to render a permanent service to the general happiness of the working man and woman and their families. That is what we mean, as I see it, by the "new deal."*[75]

In fighting for their ideals, Eleanor and her colleagues also shaped new roles and goals for a new generation of women in the public sector. Perhaps the first person to recognize—and support—this new development was Louis Howe, who, over the years of their friendship, encouraged Eleanor to consider running for an elected post. One day many years later, Howe came into Eleanor's sitting room, sat down across from her, and, in a business-as-usual manner, said, "Eleanor, if you want to be president in 1940, tell me now, so I can start getting things ready."[76] While Eleanor dismissed such suggestions, she was forever grateful for Howe's thoughtful advice, and when he died in 1936, she felt she had lost one of her closest allies. Howe was perhaps a better judge of Eleanor's political clout than she was. Entry into the White House in 1933 had marked the beginning of a new journey for Eleanor.

RACIAL AWKWARDNESS

As Eleanor immersed herself in projects meant to end poverty, she saw that racial prejudice had been intensified by the economic crisis. She would have liked the subsistence farmsteads she championed to buck the trend, but "the residents of Scott's Run, who had worked together and unionized together, picketed and demonstrated to keep Arthurdale white." From that moment, combating racism became an unofficial tenet of Eleanor's New Deal.[77]

Long after Abraham Lincoln's Emancipation Proclamation of 1883, the legacy of slavery continued through segregation and through the Jim Crow laws that codified discrimination against blacks and other minorities. The Jim Crow laws were created to limit contact between blacks and whites and to ensure

Eleanor with Thurgood Marshall, Dr. James McClendon, Walter White, and Roy Wilkins in 1947. Eleanor's close ties with such African American leaders formed as a result of her efforts to combat racism in America.

white dominance. These laws were designed to separate services for blacks: they ordered separate entrances to public buildings, separate schools, separate seats on public transportation—even separate drinking fountains. Marriage between a black person and a white person was illegal in most states.

Jim Crow laws were upheld by the state police and the courts, especially in the South. But there was another, much more brutal practice that ensured that color lines were not crossed: lynching. The most brutal symbol of American racism, lynching typically targeted African Americans. The whites who carried out this form of ritualized murder terrorized blacks and forced them to accept white supremacy. A conservative estimate is that 5,000 people, mostly black, were lynched between 1882 and President Roosevelt's first term.[78] Indeed, since the end of the nineteenth century, lynching had become a form of public execution—a gruesome spectacle of torture, burning, and murder. It was carried out by vigilantes who held no respect for the legal process of arrest, trial, and verdict, and its practice was attended by large crowds that often included elected officials, sheriffs, and schoolchildren. In some cases, newspapers boasted of lynchings attended by thousands; postcards were available as instant souvenirs for those who wished to send news of the recent "entertainment" to others.

The economic hardships of the 1930s exacerbated racial tensions in America. As the struggle over every available job intensified, some whites took out their frustrations on their black neighbors. Occasionally, violence, riots, and even lynching ensued both in the South and the North. Indeed, during Franklin Roosevelt's first five years in office, 83 blacks—roughly 17 a year—were lynched.[79]

In the 1930s, daring civil rights activists forced the treatment of blacks in America out into the open. Eleanor was among these very few. Though at times the language of the day makes her sound condescending, very few other whites condemned racism as forcefully and frequently as she did.

Shortly after the beginning of her husband's first term, Eleanor began to invite black leaders to the White House. Her frankness about racial inequality earned her the wrath of many who were determined to protect Jim Crow laws.

Among the first black leaders Eleanor invited to the White House was Walter White, the lifelong leader and executive secretary of the National Association for the Advancement of Colored People (NAACP). After a series of racially inspired murders in the early 1930s—particularly the barbaric lynching of Claude Neal, who was tortured for hours and then murdered by a white mob in Florida in 1934—White convinced Eleanor to impress upon her husband the need to take action. The goal of the legislation that emerged, called the Costigan-Wagner Anti-Lynching Bill (1934–35), was to assign a special federal authority to prosecute local authorities when they failed to exercise their duties in the event of a lynching, and to provide compensation to the victims' families.[80] When Walter White met with Franklin to discuss the bill, the president found a number of other things to talk about:

"As was his custom, when he wished to avoid discussing a subject," White remembered, "he told many gay and amusing anecdotes to postpone an anticipated ordeal." After some time, White finally was able to broach the subject of the meeting.

"But Joe Robinson [Senate majority leader] tells me the bill is unconstitutional," Roosevelt said.

When White carefully refuted this claim, as well as many other
objections to the bill that FDR raised, the president snapped, only
half [jokingly], "Somebody's been priming you. Was it my wife?"[81]

While the president was supportive of the bill—and was the first president to call lynching murder—Franklin refused to put his weight behind it. Pressed to explain his position, he answered that southerners occupied a strategic position in Congress—one that gave them great leverage: "If I come out with an anti-lynching bill now, they will block every bill I ask Congress to pass to keep America from collapsing. I just can't take that risk."[82] Indeed, Franklin was convinced that southern Democrats, who controlled most of the congressional committees, would shut down all funding for his New Deal policies.

Friendships with blacks did not always come easily for Eleanor, despite her activism. At a dinner party in 1927, she had been seated next to Mary McLeod Bethune, the founder of a school that bore her name. Eleanor found herself immediately drawn to Bethune's integrity and frankness. But she had to work to overcome lingering biases.

[Eleanor] liked to kiss people whom she knew well when greeting
them and when saying good-bye, but it took some time and a

Eleanor with National Youth Administration leaders Aubrey Williams and Mary McLeod Bethune at the National Conference of the Negro and Negro Youth in Washington, DC, on January 7, 1937. Eleanor collaborated with Bethune on such issues as education and civil rights.

*conscious effort for Eleanor to give Mrs. Bethune a peck on the
cheek, and it was not until she kissed Mrs. Bethune without thinking
of it, that she felt she had at last overcome the racial prejudice
within herself.*[83]

Later in her life, Eleanor credited that friendship with helping her overcome
her racial awkwardness; she liked to say that Mary Bethune was the closest
friend she had among those her own age.[84]

Upon moving to the White House, Eleanor invited Bethune to serve on the
National Advisory Committee of the new National Youth Administration,
and Bethune eventually became the director of its Division of Negro Affairs.
Dubbed the "First Lady of the Struggle," Bethune became the most powerful
black woman in the country.[85] As her reputation grew, Bethune was able to
use her influence to form a "black cabinet"—an interdepartmental, informal
group of African American leaders who advised the president.[86] Bethune and
Eleanor developed a lifelong and fruitful relationship, collaborating on issues
such as education, civil rights, and the protection of poor black farmers in the
South. Eleanor's determination to fight prejudice and segregation were put to
the test at the end of 1938, when she traveled with Mary Bethune to Birmingham, Alabama, to promote the abolition of the poll tax—a tax required of
voters in the South that was widely used to disenfranchise black voters. She
also planned to attend the inaugural meeting of the Southern Conference for
Human Welfare. As part of the Roosevelt administration's progressive social
policies, the organization had been created to fight for social justice and civil
rights in the South. Since "[t]he South cannot be saved by middle class liberals alone," the organizers invited black leaders from the region to join the
discussions.[87] Defying segregation laws, blacks and whites sat side by side at
the meetings held ahead of the conference, and they expected to do the same
in Birmingham. But on the second day of the conference, the city police commissioner, Eugene "Bull" Conner, announced that the Jim Crow laws would
be strictly enforced. The result:

*Under threats of arrest, and with limited options available,
participants decided to comply with the ordinance so that the
meeting might continue. Whites sat on one side of the auditorium,
blacks on the other. Further attention was drawn to the matter when
Eleanor Roosevelt, arriving late for the afternoon session, sat among
the black participants. A policeman immediately informed her that*

she would have to move. Roosevelt did not move to the white side. She took her chair and put it on top of the line set down to divide the two sides. . . . The Afro-American [Magazine] *observed, "If the people of the South do not grasp this gesture, we must. Sometimes actions speak louder than words."*[88]

A few weeks later, Eleanor again sided against condoning intolerance. The famous black opera singer Marian Anderson had been invited by faculty members of the historically black Howard University to sing in Washington, DC. By then, Anderson was recognized in Europe as one of the greatest opera singers of her time (she trained and performed with great success in Europe in the 1920s and early 1930s, after suffering discrimination in her home country). But even in Washington, she was a familiar face by that time—this was to be her fourth performance there. When the concert's organizers approached the owners of the only auditorium in the area that was large enough to host the anticipated crowd, Constitution Hall, they were turned away. The Daughters of the American Revolution (DAR), a women's organization whose members could trace their ancestors back to the American Revolution, first denied that race was the issue in their prevention of the hall's use, but soon the truth was revealed: the DAR declared "that no Negro artist would be permitted to appear there."[89] A member of the organization at the time, Eleanor discussed with black leaders (including Walter White) the right response to the DAR's position. Eleanor had suspected for a long time that the organization disliked her views and that the DAR would not care if she chose to resign. Without a better option, Eleanor decided that she could no longer be a member of the group and that the best way to

© Bettmann/Corbis

Eleanor with Marian Anderson on July 3, 1939. When the DAR refused to allow Marian Anderson to perform at Constitution Hall in Washington, DC, because she was African American, Eleanor publicly resigned from the organization and helped arrange for Anderson to sing at the Lincoln Memorial.

draw attention to its anti-black policy was to resign. In her letter of resignation, written on February 26, 1939, she wrote,

I am in complete disagreement with the attitude taken in refusing Constitution Hall to a great artist. You have set an example which seems to me unfortunate. And I feel obliged to send in to you my resignation. You had an opportunity to lead in an enlightened way, and it seems to me that your organization has failed.[90]

The next day, without directly attacking the DAR (or even mentioning it by name), Eleanor explained in her daily newspaper column that she usually believed in working within an organization for change, even if bringing about change was a painfully slow process. But, in this case, she felt that she had no choice: "They have taken an action that was widely talked of in the press. To remain as a member implies approval of that action, and therefore I am resigning."[91] The same day, singer Marian Anderson herself spoke out:

I am not surprised at Mrs. Roosevelt's actions . . . because she seems to me to be one who really comprehends the true meaning of democracy. I am shocked beyond words to be barred from the capital of my own country after having appeared almost in every other capital in the world.[92]

Published in hundreds of newspapers across the nation, the denunciations from the First Lady politicized the conflict with the DAR and transformed it from a local byline into a national sensation. The federal government responded, and Secretary of the Interior Harold L. Ickes, who had been working with White and Anderson's manager Sol Hurok, invited Anderson to perform on the steps of the Lincoln Memorial. On Easter Sunday, April 9, 1939, 75,000 people attended the concert, which drew wide support from whites and blacks alike and inspired many new civil rights leaders and supporters. By choosing this national forum, Eleanor, Ickes, and Anderson set a precedent for a new generation of activists. Twenty-four years later, Martin Luther King, Jr., gave his famous "I have a dream" speech from the same spot, concluding his sermon with the first verse of "America"—the song with which Anderson had opened her recital.[93]

The events surrounding Anderson's performance helped Eleanor realize how influential she had become. Though she never held an office in the Roosevelt White House, Eleanor nevertheless amassed considerable power, some of it at odds with official policy. "As time went by," she wrote humbly, "I found that people no longer considered me a mouthpiece for my husband, but realized that I had a point of view of my own with which he might not at all agree."[94] Always cautious not to draw too much attention away from Franklin, Eleanor pushed him to address controversial issues himself. The president occasionally distanced himself from her statements, she noted: "If some idea I expressed strongly . . . caused a violent reaction, he could honestly say that he had no responsibility in the matter, and that the thoughts were my own."[95]

By the end of the 1930s, Eleanor was among the most famous advocates of civil rights in America. And by the early 1940s, she had begun to see civil rights as "the litmus test for American democracy" and argued that until white supremacy was eradicated root and branch, American democracy would be incomplete.[96] In her wartime analysis "The Moral Basis of Democracy" (1940), Eleanor listed the countries Hitler conquered, and she declared,

> [o]ur Democracies must realize that from the point of view of the individual and his liberty, there is no hope in the future if the totalitarian philosophy becomes dominant in the world.[97]

Eleanor focused on racial inequity, but she viewed a lack of political and social liberties as only part of the problem. For her, fighting for economic opportunity was equally essential to the survival of democracy. In confronting totalitarianism, she argued,

> [e]ither we must make our economic system work to the satisfaction of all our people, or we are going to find it extremely difficult to compete against the one which will be set upon on the European continent.[98]

Eleanor's outspokenness about racial and economic inequality in America now put her at great risk, especially because she continued to refuse secret-service protection. The danger to her life became apparent later, when members of the Ku Klux Klan threatened and actively attempted to kill her. (As the civil rights movement mobilized in the mid-1950s, Eleanor went to speak against segregation in Guilford, North Carolina. Her opponents detonated a bomb that shattered a 100-year-old oak less than 300 yards from the church where Eleanor spoke.[99] Undeterred, she continued to speak against Jim Crow and to support the civil rights movement, even when the Klan placed a bounty of $25,000 on her head.)

During the first half of the twentieth century, a significant shift was taking place in America. While in the 1920s the majority of Americans still lived on farmland, by the 1940s, the majority of the population had either migrated to or already lived in urban centers, where new and expanding industries were creating the nation's increasingly spectacular wealth. Rapidly growing cities, built around industries, mines, ports, and transportation hubs, presented a set of new challenges: population density and housing shortages, questions of education and welfare, unemployment and the need for job training, and regulation of workers' wages and the concerns of unions. These new social issues generated tension, strikes, demonstrations, and even riots. The economic crisis that the Roosevelt administration faced—the Great Depression—ensured that none of these problems would be easily resolved.

The New Deal was designed to respond to these new challenges. Under its innovative programs, America for the first time afforded the poor and the marginalized federally mandated rights and protections. Eleanor Roosevelt played a crucial part in advancing the changes. World War II would expand her thinking about rights, adding moral urgency to the impulse she felt to protect the rights of every individual.

"A...MOTHER HEN FOR ALL RESCUE AGENCIES"

After 1933, the Roosevelt administration initiated a set of reforms aimed not only at economic recovery but also at expansion of the scope of American democracy. While progress on racial issues was slow, President Roosevelt's social reforms sought to reintroduce into society those whom the Great Depression had pushed to the sidelines. The president's message, while populist, was one of hope, openness, and greater opportunities for all.

At the same time as the Roosevelts were attempting to extend opportunities to everyone in the United States, Germany began a fast-paced transformation from democracy to dictatorship. In 1933, torchlights in Berlin celebrated Adolf Hitler's appointment as Germany's new chancellor. What followed was a series of unprecedented changes that transformed Germany into the most notorious dictatorship in history. Book burning, censorship, political repression, and, above all, the ruthless persecution of Jews and other minorities marked the destruction of German democracy. Step by step, Germany became a militarized society whose members were mobilized to serve the outlandish goals of a ruthless dictator. Those who dissented were brutally silenced. Those who opposed were fired, arrested, and summarily killed. And the weak, the sick, and the "racially inferior" faced statelessness, exile, and cruel death.

Finally, after six years of militarization and expansion without war, Hitler sent his troops to the battlefield. On September 1, 1939, German bombers destroyed the Polish city of Wielun, signaling the beginning of World War II. The attack transformed America's national agenda, presenting the Roosevelts with new challenges. Declaring war on Germany was out of the question; in spite of close ties to the United Kingdom, most Americans opposed getting involved in what they saw as European affairs. Still, President Roosevelt worked both publicly and behind the scenes to provide as much assistance to Britain as the public would tolerate. The mobilization of American military and industrial might to serve the Allies ended the Depression, but when the time came to consider the victims of Germany's new policies, the administration faltered at first.

After claiming victory in a series of important elections in 1932 and 1933, Hitler's National Socialist Party, the Nazis, organized a coalition government to run the country and immediately enacted a series of anti-Jewish policies that culminated in the Nuremberg laws of 1935. These racial laws defined who was Jewish and who was not. Effectively, they deprived Germany's 600,000 Jews of all legal rights, took away their citizenship, and essentially turned them into refugees in their own country. Segregated and legally barred from owning property, the Jews were violently persecuted, starved, and murdered. Many emigrated, a choice at first encouraged by the government and applauded by the Christian majority.

Outside Germany, widespread xenophobia and antisemitism worsened the plight of refugees, and only a small number of countries moved to increase their immigration quotas. The situation deteriorated further when Germany annexed Austria and occupied Czechoslovakia, rendering stateless hundreds of thousands more persecuted Jews. Many considered moving to Palestine, the focus of Jewish national aspirations at the time, but the British authorities announced that the refugees were not welcome, leaving them stranded on a hostile continent.

Three years after the Nuremberg laws had been announced, President Roosevelt finally hosted an international conference to discuss the growing humanitarian crisis in Europe. Évian-les-Bains on the shores of Lake Geneva, in France, was the site of the conference. One after another, the participants professed the importance of sheltering those who fled from Nazi violence, then contritely explained that they could not help.[100] The Dominican Republic was the only one to accept larger numbers of Jewish refugees; the nation's leader, Rafael Trujillo, hoped that Jews would marry local inhabitants and "lighten" the race of the population. The country offered several thousand visas, though less than 1,000 were in fact used. When he heard the news, Hitler concluded, "Nobody wants these criminals."[101]

Indeed, few Americans wished to open the country to all comers, and only a trickle of refugees found a place. Surveys at the time reveal that this nation of immigrants feared and resented foreigners—and Jews were particularly suspect. Charles E. Coughlin, a priest who used his popular regular radio program to attack President Roosevelt's programs, portrayed Jews as greedy loan sharks, cunning capitalists, trade unionists, and communist agents.[102] Among Roosevelt's foes, some called the New Deal the "Jew Deal" and called Roosevelt "Rosenfeld"; some even suggested that the Roosevelts were of Jewish descent (which, incidentally, Eleanor refused to refute). According to public opinion surveys, antisemitism remained virulent and widespread, and most Americans viewed Jews as uncivilized, noisy, and stingy.[103]

Sara Delano Roosevelt, Franklin's mother, held strong prejudices against Jews. Fearing Sara's sharp tongue, Eleanor often avoided having her close Jewish friends in her company. For many of the rich Protestants among whom Eleanor had grown up, prejudice against Jews was commonplace. Both in the North and the South, many hotels, country clubs, and even universities prohibited Jews outright or placed strict quotas to constrain "Jewish influence." Eleanor too entertained some of these prejudices in her youth. In an often-quoted letter to Sara Delano Roosevelt written in 1918 after a party with the financier (and, much later, Franklin's trusted financial advisor) Bernard Baruch, she wrote: "The Jew party [was] appalling." She added, "I never wish to hear money, jewels, or sables mentioned again"—repeating centuries-old stereotypes about greedy Jews.[104] However, years of political and civic engagement broadened her mind. Although the greatest transformation in her personal attitude toward Jews would come during World War II, already in the 1920s Eleanor had many Jewish friends and colleagues, among them Belle Moskowitz, with whom she worked on Alfred E. Smith's presidential campaign, and the Roosevelts' neighbors, Elinor Morgenthau and her husband, Henry Morgenthau, Jr. (who later served as secretary of the treasury during the Roosevelt administration). Elinor Morgenthau was more than a friend or horseback-riding companion: "Elinor Morgenthau was . . . part of a political alliance with Eleanor Roosevelt." As mentioned earlier, with Nancy Cook, Marion Dickerman, and Caroline O'Day, the "five women . . . 'dominated' the Women's Division of the New York State Democratic Committee."[105] Indeed, many Jews played leading roles in social causes and shared Eleanor's political outlook. For example, despite her earlier misgivings, Eleanor collaborated with Baruch, who went out of his way to support Arthurdale with his own money.[106]

Eleanor's sympathies were with the victims of Nazi terror, but what could she do? She was not an elected official, and the president was fighting to extend New Deal policies while preparing for reelection, so she used the tools at her disposal. In November 1938, during Kristallnacht (known as the Night of the Broken Glass), when Nazi thugs attacked Jewish synagogues, arrested thousands, and destroyed homes and businesses throughout Germany and Austria, Eleanor began to speak out frequently against antisemitism in America. She did so primarily because Franklin and his advisors repeatedly cautioned her that she could not criticize the administration's immigration policies. Wrapped in secrecy, denial, and unrealistic fears of communist infiltrators and Nazi spies, these policies were closely monitored by the State Department. Still, for Eleanor and a small group of rescue organizations, the news about Kristallnacht was a call to action.[107]

Several weeks after Kristallnacht, in an essay titled "Keepers of Democracy," Eleanor protested against growing fears of minorities in America, connecting these to xenophobia, antisemitism, and racism: "There is a growing wave in this country of fear, and of intolerance which springs from fear. Sometimes it is a religious intolerance, sometimes it is a racial intolerance, but all intolerance grows from the same roots."[108] She felt that America was in need of a "rude awakening." Democracy itself was at great risk if, for the sake of feeling secure, America would embrace dictatorial policies toward its minorities (as was the case in Germany, where hatred of Jews was used to promote Hitler's racist policies).[109]

A week later, on January 23, 1939, Eleanor scolded the public directly for its attitudes toward efforts to save German Jews:

What a curious thing it is when a great musician like Mischa Elman[110] offers the proceeds from a concert trip throughout the country to the fund for refugees, that he has to be guarded on the way to and from his first concert. What has happened to us in this country? If we study our own history, we find that we have always been ready to receive the unfortunates from other countries, and though this may seem a generous gesture on our part, we have profited a thousand fold by what they have brought us.[111]

Later, in July 1939, Eleanor received official numbers regarding immigrants who came to the United States. She reported that despite the urgency of the situation in Germany, refugees arrived in the United States in very small numbers, much smaller than what the official quotas had allowed.[112] Barred from criticizing the administration's policies in public for this discrepancy, Eleanor turned to unofficial channels in her attempts to help families of Jewish refugees. Behind the scenes, Eleanor met with Justine Polier, a judge who was also the daughter of the influential New York rabbi Stephen Wise. Polier, hoping to enlist Eleanor's support, presented a plan that would allow German Jewish children, who were fleeing Nazi persecution, the right to enter the United States. Eleanor promptly agreed to help, and she advised Polier on legislative strategy:

My husband says that you had better go to work at once and get two people of opposite parties in [Congress] and have them jointly get agreement on the legislation which you want for bringing in children. The State Department is only afraid of what Congress will say to them, and therefore if you remove that fear the State Department will make no objection. He advises you [to] get all the Catholic support you can.[113]

Following this advice, the bill was introduced in February 1939 with two sponsors: Senator Robert F. Wagner, a Democrat from New York, and congresswoman Edith Nourse Rogers, a Republican from Massachusetts. But opposition was shrill, and over thirty prominent associations lined up against the Wagner-Rogers bill, including the American Legion, the Daughters of the

American Revolution, and the Veterans of Foreign Wars. Their position was that "charity begins at home"—that as the nation recovered from the Depression, the focus had to be on protecting American children from hunger and want. Others espoused explicitly antisemitic views.

As the fight over immigration intensified, Eleanor cabled Franklin, who was traveling in the Caribbean. He did not respond, and when Eleanor sought help from White House staff, she was told that if the president spoke out, his opponents might present legislation to cut the already stringent immigration quotas. Eleanor wrote Polier, sharing the bad news: "I cabled [my husband] and he said . . . he would be pleased to have the bill go through, but he did not want to say anything publicly at the present time."[114] Without presidential support, the bill stalled and was withdrawn. Roosevelt and Polier continued to lobby the Department of State but made little headway.

Then, in 1940, a more general concern about child refugees inspired the formation of the Committee for the Care of European Children. At Franklin's instigation, Eleanor served as the group's honorary chairwoman. Meanwhile, she also lent her support to a number of other organizations and initiatives, including the Emergency Rescue Committee and the Crusade for Children. She tirelessly worked the Washington bureaucracy and routinely thwarted efforts of the Department of State to seal the borders. Through her wartime role she became, in the words of one historian, "a . . . mother hen for all rescue agencies."[115]

While Eleanor spoke more and more critically about antisemitism—often noting the parallel between it and the racist attitudes toward blacks in America—her efforts to save European refugees faced tough opposition in the State Department. On May 15, 1939, a large ocean liner, the *St. Louis*, left Germany for Cuba with over 930 Jewish refugees on board. When the ship arrived at its original destination, the port of Havana, the Cuban government refused to allow anyone to disembark. Blocked, the *St. Louis* then sailed for Miami, Florida, anchoring offshore during the weeks of negotiations that followed. The curious who wandered down to the docks took photographs of desperate refugees waving from porthole windows, so close was the vessel to safety. In the end, the *St. Louis* was turned away, leaving the captain no choice but to sail back to Europe, where many of his passengers later died in Nazi concentration camps.

"PAPER WALLS"

Eleanor and other critics blamed the Department of State, which was entrusted with the country's foreign affairs. "The seven hundred members of the foreign service," wrote Franklin Delano Roosevelt biographer Jean Smith,

> *primarily prep school [graduates] with Ivy League pedigrees, were predisposed to political conservatism. Prone to the prejudices of their . . . backgrounds, they were anti-immigrant, anti-Semitic, antiblack, and anti–New Deal.*[116]

Matters of immigration visas were handled by Breckinridge Long, who served as the assistant secretary of state starting in 1940. A longtime friend of Franklin's, Long did much to shore up the institutional objections to immigration and built, in the words of historian David Wyman, bureaucratic "paper walls" to stop refugees from coming into America.[117] Soon after he assumed office, he reversed a Roosevelt policy designed to ease the very restrictive immigration policies intact since 1924. When Eleanor told Franklin she thought Long was a fascist, he replied harshly, "I've told you, Eleanor, you must not say that." But she insisted, "Well, maybe I shouldn't say it, but he is!"[118] Long "had a visceral dislike of Jews and foreigners that bordered on the xenophobic." He viewed Jews as "lawless, scheming, defiant, in many ways unassimilable."[119] In a memorandum dated June 26, 1940, Long outlined how American consulates in Europe could

> *delay and effectively stop for a temporary period of indefinite length, the number of immigrants into the United States. We could do this by simply advising our consuls to put every obstacle in the way, and to require additional evidence, and to resort to various administrative devices which would postpone and postpone and postpone the granting of the visas.*[120]

It took months for supporters of the Jewish cause to uncover and expose such secret policies. The consequences were dire, and while thousands made it to safety in the United States, millions more were abandoned and died on European soil.

The fate of Jewish refugees in France illustrates the obstacles activists faced. From as early as 1933, many German Jewish artists, politicians, and intellectuals sought refuge in this traditionally liberal and democratic country. But in May 1940, Nazi forces overwhelmed the French army, occupied the northern part of the country, and established a crony government called "Vichy" in the south. Terrified, many of the Jewish refugees fled to the south. When the Vichy collaborationist government began to round up Jews and turn them over to the Nazis, the refugees were trapped.

In response, concerned citizens in the United States formed the Emergency Rescue Committee (ERC) to rescue European refugees—especially the German refugees in France. Sent by the ERC, Varian Fry, an idealistic American journalist, arrived in France and set up, with little money or help, a secret operation designed to save some of the brightest minds of the century. In a little over a year, Fry was able to get 1,500 refugees out. But many others—famous painters, intellectuals, and authors who often criticized the Nazi Party—remained trapped and were eventually caught and murdered. Eleanor's intervention on behalf of Fry's mission was met with a wall of prejudice, suspicion, and antisemitism. In the end, Franklin was dissuaded by Long from opening the immigration quotas.

Fry was assisted by American Unitarian minister Waitstill Sharp and his wife Martha, who also attempted to rescue refugees in France. Setting their base in neutral Portugal, they helped smuggle individuals for whom they secured visas to the United States. Among the refugees the Sharps directly helped escape was the German Jewish author Lion Feuchtwanger, whose sharp criticism of Nazism placed him at the top of the German blacklist. When Feuchtwanger was identified in one of the concentration camps in southern France, activists knew that it was a matter of time before the Germans would discover his location and kill him. It is said that word of his situation reached Eleanor, and that she whispered in Franklin's ear, "We need to do something about people like this." Shortly thereafter, Lion Feuchtwanger was secretly taken out of the camp and put into a diplomatic car. He and his wife Marta were led to the home of American Vice-Consul Hiram Bingham. From there, accompanied by the Sharps, the Feuchtwangers were smuggled at great risk across Spain into Portugal. The two later sailed from Lisbon to America, where they made their home for the rest of their lives. In another dramatic rescue, the Sharps secured visas for another 29 children and 10 adults.[121]

Sadly, of the 567 names of intellectuals, scholars, and artists seeking asylum that the ERC and other Jewish organizations submitted to the Department of State, only 40 were allowed into the United States.[122]

On another memorable occasion, in the summer of 1940, 83 refugees did manage to slip past the unofficial barriers against incoming Jews. "Filled to capacity with 317 passengers," wrote scholar Doris Kearns Goodwin,

the Quanza had steamed into New York Harbor in late August. All those in possession of American visas were allowed to debark. The remaining passengers, refugees who had escaped from occupied France, pleaded with authorities to let them come ashore, too. "Impossible," said the officials, "no one can step onto American soil without the proper papers." The Quanza sailed on to Veracruz, hoping to find a more receptive port, but the Mexican authorities ordered the ship to return to Europe. "Complete despair overwhelmed the passengers," one young woman traveling with her parents recalled. Europe to them was "a German concentration camp." Preparing for the return trip, the Quanza docked at Norfolk, Virginia, to load up with coal. While the ship remained in the harbor, Jewish organizations appealed to Mrs. Roosevelt for help.

Courtesy of the USHMM Photo Archives

American Unitarian minister Waitstill Sharp and his wife Martha prior to departing for a relief mission in Europe. The Sharps helped smuggle German refugees from France to the United States.

Eleanor was at Hyde Park when she received word of the situation.
Convinced that something should be done, she appealed to her
husband directly. He agreed to send Patrick Malin [one of his
advisers on refugee issues] . . . to Norfolk to see what he could do
to secure visas for children, for aliens holding visas from other
countries, and for bona fide political refugees. Working quickly,
Malin certified all the documents that were presented to him, and
construed everybody else to be a political refugee, so that the entire
ship could disembark.[123]

Goodwin argues that Long responded to what he viewed as betrayal by tightening immigration procedures even further. By July 1943, refugees hoping to reach the United States needed to find two American citizens willing to sponsor them, as well as furnishing character references. They had to fill out a lengthy application form typed almost illegibly. And they were expected to submit a clean police record from their former place of residence. For European Jews, such a record of good conduct could only have been obtained by appealing to a Nazi official. Under the best circumstances, obtaining an American visa took nine months. For German Jews, who were categorized as "enemy aliens," the wait was even longer, and approval was less likely.

While Eleanor continued her activism on behalf of refugees, more and more Jews were being slaughtered in Nazi death camps. Deep into the war, in 1943, Henry Morgenthau, the secretary of the treasury, uncovered the State Department's secret scheme to keep refugees at bay. When he informed the president, Franklin set up the War Refugee Board. Under Morgenthau's supervision, it saved about 200,000 Jews through a combination of diplomacy, bribery, and extraordinary commitment. John Pehle, who headed the board, later remarked, "What we did was little enough. It was late. . . . Late and little, I would say."[124] Eleanor said much the same, on many occasions. According to her son, Jimmy, her failure to convince Franklin to admit more refugees was "her deepest regret at the end of her life."[125]

By 1943, when news about the killing of millions of Jews in Europe reached the United States, Eleanor made one of her strongest appeals to the public to treat the Jews as individuals. In an August 1943 column, she argued that

[t]he Jews are like all the other people of the world. There are able
people among them, there are courageous people among them, there
are people of extraordinary intellectual ability along many lines.

There are people of extraordinary integrity, and people of great
beauty and great charm. . . . In other words, they are a cross-section
of the human race, just as is every other nationality, and every other
religious group.[126]

Sensing perhaps that the fate of the European Jews was sealed, Eleanor somberly reflected at the end of her column, "I do not know what we can do to save the Jews in Europe and to find them homes."[127]

JAPANESE INTERNMENT CAMPS

On December 7, 1941, the war came home. A surprise attack by the Japanese navy destroyed the American fleet at Pearl Harbor, on the Hawaiian island of Oahu. The stunning vulnerability of a nation so distant from the European and East Asian battlefields ignited panic and paranoia. Many, including some government officials, cast suspicious eyes on Americans of Japanese descent, whom they saw as a potential "fifth column"—traitors spying for the enemy. Could Japanese citizens living in the United States be trusted? While the public debate raged on, Eleanor traveled to the West Coast, where most Japanese immigrants lived, and then devoted her newspaper column to the subject. She implored her readers to rise above hysteria, not to give in to fear and prejudice. Three excerpts convey the sober, reasonable tone of her plea:

This is, perhaps, the greatest test this country has ever met. Perhaps
it is the test which is going to show whether the United States can
furnish a pattern for the rest of the world for the future. Our citizens
come from all the nations of the world. Some of us have said from
time to time, that we were the only proof that different nationalities
could live together in peace and understanding, each bringing
his own contribution, different though it may be, to the final unity
which is the United States.

If, out of the present chaos, there is ever to come a world where free
people live together peacefully, in Europe, Asia or in the Americas,
we shall have to furnish the pattern. . . .

Perhaps, on us today, lies the obligation to prove that such a vision
may be a practical possibility. If we cannot meet the challenge of
fairness to our citizens of every nationality, of really believing in

*the Bill of Rights, and making it a reality for all loyal American
citizens, regardless of race, creed, or color; if we cannot keep in
check anti-semitism, anti-racial feelings, as well as anti-religious
feelings, that we shall have removed from the world, the one real
hope for the future on which all humanity must now rely.[128]*

By this time, Eleanor fully appreciated the essential connections among all of
the struggles for respect and legal protection waged in America and around
the world. Writing in 1943, she described the situation of Japanese Americans
as war broke out between the United States and Japan.

*We have in all 127,000 Japanese or Japanese-Americans in
the United States. Of these, 112,000 lived on the West Coast.
Originally, they were much needed on ranches and on large truck
and fruit farms, but, as they came in greater numbers, people began
to discover that they were competitors in the labor field.*

*The people of California began to be afraid of Japanese
importation, so the Exclusion Act was passed in 1924 [in fact, it
was passed in 1917]. No people of the Oriental race could become
citizens of the United States by naturalization, and no quota was
given to the Oriental nations in the Pacific.*

*This happened because, in one part of our country, they were feared
as competitors, and the rest of our country knew them so little, and
cared so little about them that they did not even think about the
principle that we in this country believe in: that of equal rights for
all human beings.*

*We granted no citizenship to Orientals; so now we have a group
of people (some of whom have been here as long as fifty years)
who have not been able to become citizens under our laws. Long
before the war, an old Japanese man told me that he had great-
grandchildren born in this country and that he had never been back
to Japan; all that he cared about was here on the soil of the United
States, and yet he could not become a citizen. . . .*

*Now we come to Pearl Harbor, December 7, 1941. There was no
time to investigate families or to adhere strictly to the American rule*

that a man is innocent until he is proved guilty. These people were not convicted of any crime, but emotions ran too high. Too many people wanted to wreak vengeance on Oriental-looking people. Even the Chinese, our allies, were not always safe from insult on the streets. The Japanese had long been watched by the FBI, as were other aliens, and several hundred were apprehended at once on the outbreak of war and sent to detention camps.[129]

When talk turned to a massive relocation of Japanese Americans, Eleanor tried to rally opposition, even recruiting Attorney General Francis Biddle. Still, on February 19, 1942, President Roosevelt issued Executive Order 9066, handing Secretary of War Henry Stimson the power to create domestic military zones "from which any or all persons may be excluded."[130] In effect, Roosevelt's decree forced all people of Japanese descent to register with the government and to prepare to leave their homes for unknown destinations. By May, virtually all Japanese American residents of the West Coast were moved into internment camps (also called relocation centers), located from Idaho to Texas, until the last year of the war.

For critics, the injustice could not have been better illustrated when, almost simultaneously, the government began to recruit Japanese Americans for the military. The majority of these loyal citizens were sent to serve together when the 442nd Infantry Regimental Combat Team was formed in 1943. The 442nd, one of the most decorated units in American history, fought alongside white units for the liberation of Europe from the Nazis.

As internment became a national policy, Eleanor was forced to temper her criticism. In a radio broadcast, she told her audience, "It is obvious that many people who are friendly aliens have to suffer temporarily in order to insure the safety of the vital interests of this country while at war."[131]

A barber shows his anti-Japanese sign shortly following FDR's Executive Order 9066, which forced all people of Japanese descent to prepare to leave their homes for internment camps.

Privately, Eleanor expressed different views altogether. She wrote to a friend that the internment of American citizens "is just one more reason for hating war—innocent people suffer for a few guilty ones."[132] But even publicly, she managed to use her celebrity to try to combat prejudice. After a visit to the Gila River Relocation Center near Phoenix in 1943, she wrote an article for *Collier's Weekly* about the lives of Japanese internees, inviting her readers to "try to regard them as individuals, and not to condemn them before they are given a fair chance to prove themselves in the community." Though by this date few Japanese Americans lived among the whites who accounted for most of Eleanor's readership, the focus of Executive Order 9066 was the West Coast; those living elsewhere had not been forced to leave their homes. She continued:

> *We have no common race in this country, but we have an ideal to which all of us are loyal: we cannot progress if we look down upon any group of people amongst us because of race or religion. Every citizen in this country has a right to our basic freedoms, to justice and to equality of opportunity. We retain the right to lead our individual lives as we please, but we can only do so if we grant to others the freedoms that we wish for ourselves.[133]*

In the end, not a single Japanese American was charged with spying for Japan. In 1988, President George H. Bush apologized to Japanese Americans for the injustices and losses associated with the relocation, uprooting, and internment during the war. Their families received $20,000 from the government as compensation.

BECOMING ELEANOR

How do you become the person you are? What factors shape the way you see yourself and the world around you? In 1951, Eleanor explored these questions in an essay called "The Seven People Who Shaped My Life," which was published in a popular mainstream magazine, *Look*. In it, she listed the people who affected her most and discussed their contributions to her growth as a person:

What you are in life results in great part from the influence exerted on you over the years by just a few people.

There have been seven people in my life whose influence on me did much to change my inner development as a person.

The first were my mother and father. . . .

My mother always remained somewhat awe inspiring. She was the most dignified and beautiful person. But she had such high standards of morals that it encouraged me to wrongdoing; I felt it was utterly impossible for me ever to live up to her!

My father, on the other hand, was always a very close and warm personality. I think I knew that his standards were nowhere nearly as difficult to achieve, and that he would look upon my shortcomings with a much more forgiving eye. He provided me with some badly needed reassurance, for in my earliest days I knew that I could never hope to achieve my mother's beauty, and I fell short in so many ways of what was expected of me. I needed my father's warmth and devotion more perhaps than the average child, who would have taken love for granted and not worried about it.

My mother died when I was six. After my father's death when I was eight years old, I did not have that sense of adequacy and of being cherished which he gave me until I met Mlle. Marie Souvestre when I was 15.

The headmistress of the school I went to in England, she exerted perhaps the greatest influence on my girlhood. . . . She liked Americans and attributed to them qualities of character and intelligence, which shortly began to give me back some of the confidence that I had not felt since my father's death.

I had lived in a family with some very beautiful aunts and two attractive uncles who looked upon me as a child to whom they were always kind, but about whom there was certainly nothing to admire. I was conscious of their pity because my looks fell so far below the family standards, and I had no special gifts of any kind to redeem my looks.

Mlle. Souvestre, on the other hand, laid a great deal of stress on intellectual achievements, and there I felt I could hold my own. She took me traveling with her. . . . For three years, I basked in her generous presence, and I think those three years did much to form my character and give me the confidence to go through some of the trials that awaited me when I returned to the United States. . . . As I look back, I realize that Mlle. Souvestre was rather an extraordinary character. She often fought seemingly lost causes, but they were often won in the long run. . . . I think I came to feel that the underdog was always the one to be championed! . . .

The next important and stimulating person in my life was Mrs. W. Forbes (Hall) Morgan, the young aunt with whom I lived when I first came home from Europe. . . . It happened that my family was distinctly a part of what was then called society, not by virtue of having money, but because it had held a place in what might be called the Four Hundred for several generations. . . .[134]

I admired her inordinately, but I knew that I must not be a nuisance. After a none too happy childhood, I was lonely, friendless, shy, and awkward, and not a society success. For a [member of the] Hall [family], that was not easy to understand, but it hardened me in much the way that steel is tempered. The fires through which I passed were none too gentle, but I gained from them nevertheless and each new ordeal was a step forward in the lessons of living.

The personalities of my husband and my mother-in-law, I am sure, exerted the greatest influence in my development.

My mother-in-law was a lady of great character. She always knew what was right and what was wrong. She was kind and generous and loyal to the family through thick and thin. But it was hard to differ with her. She never gave up an idea she had, whether it was for herself or for you. And her methods of achieving her own ends at times seemed a bit ruthless if you were not in accord. She dominated me for years.

But I finally developed within myself the power to resist. Perhaps it was my husband's teaching me that there was great strength in passive resistance. Perhaps it was that, having two such personalities as my husband and his mother, I had to develop willy-nilly into an individual myself. . . .

Both wanted to dominate their spheres of life, though they were enough alike to love each other dearly. My husband was just as determined as his mother, but hated to hurt people, and never did so unless they really angered him. She won even with him sometimes, but usually he simply ignored any differences in their point of view.

His illness finally made me stand on my own feet in regard to my husband's life, my own life and my children's training. The alternative would have been to become a completely colorless echo of my husband and mother-in-law and be torn between them. I might have stayed a weak character forever, if I had not found that out.

In some ways, my husband was a remarkable teacher . . . [he] opened the windows of the world for me. As I think it over, he was perhaps the greatest teacher of the many who contributed to my education.

The last person, probably, to have influenced me much as an individual was Louis Howe, my husband's adviser. He pushed me, not for my own sake but for my husband's, into taking an interest in public affairs.

This was a field I had carefully shunned, feeling that one member of the family with a knowledge of politics was all that one family could stand. But, little by little, I found myself beginning to understand why certain things were done, and how they came about. Before I realized it, I was at least interested in the fields of domestic and of foreign affairs.[135]

CONNECTIONS

1. What are the most important qualities you have learned about Eleanor, based on the people and elements she lists as having shaped her life? What does she wish to reveal to her audience? What does she value?

2. How did Eleanor differ from other female members of "high society"? How did this shape her life's work?

3. Eleanor states that she "came to feel that the underdog was always the one to be championed." What is an underdog? What attracted Eleanor about sympathizing with the underdog?

4. Eleanor writes that her husband was "a remarkable teacher" and that Louis Howe pushed her into "taking an interest in public affairs" for her husband's sake. However, biographer Joseph Lash notes that Howe, at one point, suggested she run for president.[136] Why does she deny herself such independence in this essay? What does this say about her audience and about women's roles in society and politics during this time period?

REFUSING TO BE "FROZEN OUT"

During the 1920s, Eleanor became more and more involved in the work of the Democratic Party. She also forged strong connections with grassroots activists and community organizers, such as Marion Dickerman and Nancy Cook. Together with other activists, many of whom were former members of the suffragist movement, the three women launched many campaigns to improve housing conditions in New York, to shorten the working hours of laborers, to prevent child labor, and to secure decent working conditions and compensation for working women. During these years, Eleanor honed her political skills and, while working to support Democratic candidates, emerged as a leading voice in the Democratic Party. Yet she and her female colleagues were met with strong resistance and prejudices. Many men and women of the time were skeptical about women's capacity to serve in critical leadership positions. Thus, eight years after the fight for suffrage was won, women were still playing secondary roles in politics. In the 1928 essay below entitled, "Women Must Learn to Play the Game as Men Do," Eleanor explains some of the challenges women faced and her definition of success for women in politics.

> *Women have been voting for ten years. But have they achieved actual political equality with men? No. They go through the gesture of going to the polls; their votes are solicited by politicians; and they possess the external aspect of equal rights. But it is mostly a gesture without real power. With some outstanding exceptions, women who have gone into politics are refused serious consideration by the men leaders.*
>
> . . .
>
> *From all over the United States, women of both camps have come to me, and their experiences are practically the same. When meetings are to be held at which momentous matters are to be decided, the women members often are not asked. . . . Politically, as a sex, women are generally "frozen out" from any intrinsic share of influence in their parties. . . . Beneath the veneer of courtesy and outward show of consideration universally accorded women, there is a widespread male hostility—age-old, perhaps—against sharing with them any actual control.*

. . .

To many women who fought so long and so valiantly for suffrage, what has happened has been most discouraging. For one reason or another, most of the leaders who carried the early fight to success have dropped out of politics. This has been in many ways unfortunate. Among them were women with gifts of real leadership. They were exceptional and high types of women, idealists concerned in carrying a cause to victory, with no idea of personal advancement or gain. In fact, attaining the vote was only part of a program for equal rights—an external gesture toward economic independence, and social and spiritual equality with men.

How, then, can we bring the men leaders to concede participation in party affairs, adequate representation, and real political equality?

Our means is to elect, accept, and back women political bosses. . . . Perhaps the word "boss" may shock sensitive ears. To many it will conjure all that is unhealthy and corrupt in our political machinery. Yet when I speak of women bosses, I mean bosses actually in the sense that men are bosses. . . . As things are today, the boss is a leader, often an enlightened, high-minded leader. . . . I therefore use the word, as it is the word men understand.

If women believe they have a right and duty in political life today, they must learn to talk the language of men. They must not only master the phraseology, but also understand the machinery which men have built through years of practical experience. Against the men bosses, there must be women bosses who can talk as equals, with the backing of a coherent organization of women voters behind them.

Voters who are only voters, whether men or women, are only the followers of leaders. The important thing is the choosing of leaders.

. . .

Certain women profess to be horrified at the thought of women bosses bartering and dickering in the hard game of politics with men. But many more women realize that we are living in a material world, and that politics cannot be played from the clouds. To sum up, women must learn to play the game as men do. If they go into politics, they must stick to their jobs, respect the time and work of others, master a knowledge of history and human nature, learn diplomacy, subordinate their likes and dislikes of the moment, and choose leaders to act for them, and to whom they will be loyal. They can keep their ideals; but they must face facts, and deal with them practically.[137]

CONNECTIONS

1. Even after women achieved the right to vote, Eleanor believed that men continued to deny women real political power. What does voting achieve in a struggle for equality? What can it not accomplish? Why did women lack political equality with men?

2. What is a "gesture without real power"? What does Eleanor mean when she says that women are "frozen out" from any influence in politics? Historically, who else has been "frozen out"? What have they done to overcome this?

3. What does Eleanor mean when she says that women "must learn to talk the language of men"? Is it important that women do this? How can language change the way people think about a situation?

4. What does it mean for women to "play the game as men do"? What are Eleanor's goals? Have you felt it necessary to play someone else's game? How do the rules of the "game" get written, and why is it so difficult to change them?

5. In the 1920s, it was considered a great achievement that women had been granted the right to vote. What does Eleanor recognize as the limitations of simply having the right to vote? How has the American definition of "democracy" changed since the 1920s? What is political equality, and why is it important for democracy?

"THE BASIC THING WE MUST DO IS TO STOP GENERALIZING ABOUT PEOPLE"

Like many of us, Eleanor's attitudes about race and civil rights evolved over time. By the time she came to Washington as First Lady, she had spent time working with the poor, as well as new immigrants on New York's Lower East Side. However, she had less experience working with African Americans. Several years later, when Eleanor left Washington, she was known as one of the most outspoken white supporters of civil rights for black Americans. This reading uses excerpts from two of Eleanor Roosevelt's many speeches, essays, and newspaper columns addressing these issues to allow us insight into changes in the way that she approached civil rights.

In 1934, the year after she came to Washington, DC, Eleanor addressed a conference on the education of African Americans. Discussions of education often expose our most basic feelings about human potential. For example, if you do not believe that all students can achieve at the same level, your expectations and assumptions for them are not the same. In the 1930s, very few schools outside of colleges and universities were integrated. In many cases, black schools received far less financial support and far fewer resources. Education for blacks was considered inferior to the education offered to the majority of white students, and this served to block opportunities later in life.

Addressing the question of education for African Americans in her speech entitled, "The National Conference on the Education of Negroes," Eleanor told her audience that education was bound to vary from one community to another, and while every race possessed certain gifts, we "cannot all become geniuses [and] we cannot all reach the same level."

> We have got to think it through and realize that, in the end, all
> of us, the country over, will gain if we have a uniformly educated
> people; that is to say, if everywhere every child has the opportunity
> to gain as much knowledge as his ability will allow him to gain.
> We know that there are in every race certain gifts, and therefore the
> people of the different races will naturally want to develop those
> gifts. If they are denied the opportunity to do so, they will always
> feel a frustration in their lives and a certain resentment against the
> people who have denied them this opportunity for self-expression.

I believe that the Negro race has tremendous gifts to bring to this country in the way of artistic development. I think things come by nature to many of them that we have to acquire, such as an appreciation of art and of music and of rhythm, which we really have to gain very often through education. I think that those things should be utilized for the good of the whole nation, that you should be allowed and helped to make your greatest contribution along the lines that you want and that give you joy.[138]

Such views reflected the stereotypes of the period. Over time, Eleanor became more involved in civil rights issues, developing personal friendships and political alliances with prominent African American leaders, such as Mary McLeod Bethune, founder of the National Council of Negro Women and later President Roosevelt's national advisor on minority affairs, and NAACP executive secretary Walter White. By the 1940s, Eleanor's public statements and advocacy for civil rights issues were well known. Lauded by some for her support of equal rights, she also received regular hate mail and death threats from white supremacists. Eleanor came to believe that civil rights were the true test of democracy.

At the same time, Eleanor understood that her positions on race were often seen as radical. So she worked to help ordinary Americans understand why she took the positions she did. In "The Minorities Question" (1945) Eleanor states:

The Second Commandment, "Love Thy Neighbor as Thyself," has often been before me when I have heard people generalize about groups of their neighbors who, like them, are citizens of the United States.

There is no use in shutting our eyes to the fact that racial and religious tensions in this country are becoming more acute. They arise partly from experiences back in the past, experiences very often in other countries where wars were carried on between people of various nationalities. I think they persist in this country largely because of the insecurity of some of our people under our economic system. If times are hard, jobs scarce, and food hard to get, we always prefer that someone else be the victim of these difficult situations, and we fight to keep ourselves on top. We come to attribute certain characteristics to different races and nationalities.

We differentiate too little, and even where religions are concerned, if they are not our own, we are apt to lump people all together as doing certain things because they are Jew or Gentile, Catholic or Protestant.

I have come to think, therefore, that the basic thing we must do is to stop generalizing about people. If we no longer thought of them as groups, but as individuals, we would soon find that they varied in their different groups as much as we do in our own. It seems to me quite natural to say: "I do not like John Jones." The reasons may be many. But to say: "I do not like Catholics or Jews" is complete nonsense. . . . It is individuals we must know, not groups!

The Negroes perhaps suffer more from this lumping together of people than any other race. Because the South has created a picture, a charming one of mammys [sic], old-fashioned butlers and gardeners and day laborers, we must not believe that that is the whole picture. They have rarely shown us the picture of the intellectual or of the soldier or of the inventor. . . .

Many people will tell you they object to breaking down the barriers between the races or to allowing them to associate together without self-consciousness from the time they are children, because of their disapproval of intermarriage between races. They feel that races should stay pure blooded as far as possible. When people say that to me, I sometimes wonder if they have taken a good look at our population. If there ever was a nation where people have mixed blood, it is right here in the United States, and yet we seem to have remained a strong and virile nation. Besides, this particular objection which people advance is somewhat irrelevant since when people want to marry, they are usually past reasoning with! . . .

If we really believe in Democracy we must face the fact that equality of opportunity is basic to any kind of Democracy. Equality of opportunity means that all of our people, not just white people, not just people descended from English or Scandinavian ancestors, but all our people must have decent homes, a decent standard of health, and educational opportunities to develop their abilities as far as they are able. Thus they may be equipped with the tools for the work

*which they wish to do, and there must be equality of opportunity to
obtain that work regardless of race or religion or color. . . .*

*What is needed is really not a self-conscious virtue which makes us
treat our neighbors as we want to be treated, but an acceptance of
the fact that all human beings have dignity, and the potentiality
of development into the same kind of people we are ourselves. When
we look at each individual without thinking of him as a Jew or as
a Negro, but only as a person, then we may get to like him, or we
may dislike him, but he stands on his own feet as an individual,
and we stand with him on an equal basis. Together we are citizens
of a great country. I may have had greater opportunity and greater
happiness than he has had, and fewer obstacles to overcome, but
basically we build our lives together, and what we build today sets
the pattern for the future of the world.*[139]

CONNECTIONS

1. How do these two documents differ? Why do you think Eleanor's ideas of
   civil rights and race changed between 1934 and 1945? What happened
   to her during that time? What happened in the country and the world
   during that period? How has the way that you think about civil rights
   changed over time?

2. Who is Eleanor addressing in both of these passages? What language does
   she employ to persuade her audience? How does she frame her discussion of race?

3. How do Eleanor's 1945 ideas about the value of the individual human
   being reflect her position on civil rights? Compare her ideas about race
   between the two documents.

MARIAN ANDERSON AND THE DAUGHTERS OF THE AMERICAN REVOLUTION

In 1939, the famous black opera singer Marian Anderson was invited by faculty members of the traditionally black Howard University to sing in the nation's capital. Following a rule they had enacted that barred black performers from their stage, the Daughters of the American Revolution barred Anderson from appearing at Constitution Hall, at that time the largest venue in the District of Columbia. The president of this group, in which membership was open only to white women who could trace their ancestors back to colonial days, stated unequivocally that "no Negro artist would be permitted to appear."[140] Reacting to this blatantly racist act, Eleanor resigned from the organization, making her decision in concert with black leadership. With her resignation, the event gained wide publicity. She gave her reasons simply in a letter to the DAR:

February 26, 1939.

My dear Mrs. Henry M. Robert, Jr.:

I am afraid that I have never been a very useful member of the Daughters of the American Revolution, so I know it will make very little difference to you whether I resign, or whether I continue to be a member of your organization.

However, I am in complete disagreement with the attitude taken in refusing Constitution Hall to a great artist. You have set an example which seems to me unfortunate, and I feel obliged to send in to you my resignation. You had an opportunity to lead in an enlightened way and it seems to me that your organization has failed. I realize that many people will not agree with me, but feeling as I do this seems to me the only proper procedure to follow.

Very sincerely yours,

Eleanor Roosevelt

The next day, Eleanor explained her feelings at greater length in her *My Day* column:

I have been debating in my mind for some time, a question which I have had to debate with myself once or twice before in my life.

Usually I have decided differently from the way in which I am deciding now. The question is: if you belong to an organization and disapprove of an action which is typical of a policy, should you resign, or is it better to work for a changed point of view within the organization? In the past, when I was able to work actively in any organization to which I belonged, I have usually stayed in until I had at least made a fight and had been defeated.

Even then, I have, as a rule, accepted my defeat, and decided I was wrong or, perhaps, a little too far ahead of the thinking of the majority at that time. I have often found that the thing in which I was interested was done some years later. But, in this case, I belong to an organization in which I can do no active work. They have taken an action which has been widely talked of in the press. To remain as a member implies approval of that action, and therefore I am resigning.

[...]

E.R.[141]

Eleanor's letter and column made the DAR's actions a national sensation. Her bold stand brought even more attention to the DAR's segregationist policy, and newspapers around the country picked up the story. One *New York Times* editorial, in particular, captured the public's outrage:

Those who love music and are unable to perceive any relationship between music on the one hand, and political, economic or social issues on the other, will regret, as Mrs. Eleanor Roosevelt does, that Washington may be deprived of the pleasure of hearing this artist.

If Miss Anderson's inability to find a suitable hall in the national capital for her April concert is due to social or racial snobbery, all that can be said is that such an attitude is inconsistent with the best American traditions, including those which were born in the fires of the American Revolution. It is hard to believe that any patriotic organization in this country would approve of discrimination against so gifted an artist and so fine a person as Miss Anderson. In fact, no organization could do so, and still merit the adjective patriotic.[142]

Anderson herself explained that she read about the controversy for the first time when she passed a newsstand and "my eye caught a headline: 'Mrs. Roosevelt Takes Stand.' ...I honestly could not conceive that things had gone so far."[143] In March of that same year, the results of a national survey were published. According to this survey, 67 percent of Americans approved of Eleanor's actions, while 33 percent disapproved. "Southerners," the report read, "dissented by an average vote of 57 percent, but even some of the dissenters declared they had no objection to Marian Anderson's singing as a paid performer. It was Mrs. Roosevelt's 'making a fuss about it' that they disliked."[144]

Eleanor and others were not satisfied. Anderson, who had given concerts all over the world, still had no place to perform in the capital of her own country. NAACP's director, Walter White, along with Eleanor, Anderson's manager (Sol Hurok), and Secretary of the Interior Harold L. Ickes, came up with a bold plan that met with Franklin Roosevelt's wholehearted approval. They arranged for Anderson to perform as planned in Washington, DC, on Easter Sunday, April 9, 1939. Defying the culture of segregation, they organized an open-air concert—open to all people—on the steps of the Lincoln Memorial. A *New York Times* reporter submitted the following description of the concert:

> *An enthusiastic crowd estimated at 75,000, including many government officials, stood at the foot of Lincoln Memorial today and heard Marian Anderson, Negro contralto, give a concert and tendered her an unusual ovation. Permission to sing in Constitution Hall had been refused Miss Anderson by the Daughters of the American Revolution.*
>
> *The audience, about half composed of Negroes, was gathered in a semicircle at the foot of the great marble monument to the man who emancipated the Negroes. It stretched halfway around the long reflecting pool. Miss Anderson was applauded heartily after each of her numbers, and was forced to give an encore.[145]*

CONNECTIONS

1. What was Eleanor's dilemma? What was the best way to resolve it? When might you decide to break away from a group you disagree with?

2. What were Eleanor's arguments for leaving the DAR? What are the advantages and disadvantages of her act?

3. What is the symbolic meaning of the Lincoln Memorial? What are the links between the site's symbolic meaning and the concert? What other memorable events have taken place at the Lincoln memorial? What do they have in common?

ELEANOR AND THE JEWISH REFUGEE CRISIS (1939)

When the Nazis came to power in Germany, some Jews began to look for a way out, despite their long ties to the country. In fact, Nazi policy was focused on trying to rid Germany of Jews. The problem was finding a place for Jews to go. In the United States, strict immigration quotas severely limited the number of Jews that were allowed into the country. Moreover, a powerful lobby of isolationists and Antisemites inside and outside the State Department made sure that even those quotas were often not met. While sympathetic to the plight of refugees, Eleanor found herself caught between fighting for her views and avoiding open criticism of her husband's policies. Behind the scenes, Eleanor worked with advocates on creating legislation aimed at extending the stay of refugees and providing visas to others.

Writing in her *My Day* column in January 1939, Eleanor tried to change the way people thought about the refugee crisis:

> *What a curious thing it is when a great musician like Mischa Elman[146] offers the proceeds from a concert trip throughout the country to the fund for refugees, that he has to be guarded on the way to and from his first concert. What has happened to us in this country? If we study our own history we find that we have always been ready to receive the unfortunates from other countries, and though this may seem a generous gesture on our part, we have profited a thousand fold by what they have brought us.*
>
> *It may be that some of these very refugees may make discoveries which will bring us increased employment. Many of them represent the best brains of the countries from which they come. They are not all of one race or religion, and the wherewithal to keep them alive and get them started is being provided by such generous spirits as Mischa Elman. Must his wife and children tremble for his safety because of this gesture? He is giving concerts for the Committee for Non-Sectarian Refugee Aid. Wherever he goes, I hope he will be enthusiastically supported, not only because people enjoy his music, but because they admire the extraordinary generosity which he is showing.[147]*

After the Nazi invasion of Poland in September 1939, war broke out across Europe. Even more refugees began to seek relief in the United States. In May of 1939, the MS *St. Louis*, a ship carrying 937 refugees who had been denied permission to land in Cuba despite having visas, sailed north to the east coast of the United States. The State Department refused to make an exception for the passengers, who were sent back across the Atlantic to Europe. The story of the *St. Louis* so troubled Eleanor that during the summer of 1940, when another ship filled with refugees, the SS *Quanza*, sailed along the coast, Eleanor directly intervened, allowing the passengers to disembark. Assistant Secretary of State Breckinridge Long was furious. In a memorandum issued to State Department employees that same year, Long stated his intentions to keep immigrants out of the United States by bureaucratic means.[148]

As the war continued, mobile death squads targeted some Jewish civilians, others were transported to ghettos and starved to death, and still others were sent to a growing system of concentration and death camps in eastern Europe. In her August 13, 1943, *My Day* column, responding to reports asserting that Germany had already killed over a million Jewish women, children, and men, Eleanor urged the public to shed their prejudice.

> *Some people think of the Jewish people as a race. Others think of them purely as a religious group. But in Europe the hardships and persecution which they have had to endure for the past few years, have tended to bring them together in a group which identifies itself with every similar group, regardless [of] whether the tie is religious or racial. . . .*
>
> *[T]hey have suffered in Europe as has no other group. The percentage killed among them in the past few years far exceeds the losses among any of the United Nations [Allies] in the battles which have been fought throughout the war.*
>
> *Many of them, for generations, considered Germany, Poland, Romania, and France, their country and permanent home. This same thing might happen to any other group, if enough people ganged up against it and decided on persecution. It seems to me that it is the part of common sense for the world as a whole to protest in its own interest against wholesale persecution, because*

none of us by ourselves would be strong enough to stand against a big enough group which decided to treat us in the same way....

It means the right of survival of human beings, and their right to grow and improve. . . .

I do not know what we can do to save the Jews in Europe, and to find them homes, but I know that we will be the sufferers if we let great wrongs occur without exerting ourselves to correct them.[149]

CONNECTIONS

1. What is a refugee? How does a person become a refugee?

2. Do the United States and other countries have an obligation to take in people whose own countries persecute them?

3. Many people believe that the Jewish refugee crisis presented a dilemma for Eleanor. What is a dilemma? What was her dilemma? How did she address it?

4. Compare the way Eleanor wrote about the plight of Jews in 1939 and in 1943. What is similar? What differences seem most striking? How do you account for those differences?

5. As First Lady, what leverage did Eleanor have to use for her cause? What were some of the limitations of her power?

1 Elizabeth Borgwardt, *A New Deal for the World: America's Vision for Human Rights* (Cambridge: Harvard University Press, 2005), 4.

2 Tony Judt, *Postwar: A History of Europe since 1945* (New York: Penguin, 2005), 18.

3 Niall Ferguson, *The War of the World: Twentieth-Century Conflict and the Descent of the West* (New York: Penguin, 2006), 651–52.

4 Judt, *Postwar*, 16–17, 23.

5 Eleanor Roosevelt, *My Day* (column), August 8, 1945. The full text of Eleanor Roosevelt's *My Day* columns can be found at the Eleanor Roosevelt Papers Project website, http://www.gwu.edu/~erpapers/myday/.

6 *My Day*, August 8, 1945.

7 See, for example, the letter from Eleanor Roosevelt to Harry S. Truman, August 12, 1959, Post-Presidential Files, Harry S. Truman Papers, in the Truman Library, http://www.trumanlibrary.org/eleanor/eleanordoctemplate.php?documentid=hst19590812&pagenumber=1 (accessed December 29, 2008); Lois Scharf, *Eleanor Roosevelt: First Lady of American Liberalism* (Boston: Twayne, 1987), 145.

8 Memorandum of press conference held by Mrs. Eleanor Roosevelt (January 3, 1946); Allida M. Black, ed., *The Eleanor Roosevelt Papers* (New York: Thomson Gale, 2007), 184; Joseph P. Lash, *Eleanor: The Years Alone* (New York: Norton, 1972), 29.

9 Allida M. Black, private communication (August 11, 2009). Her work there introduced her to the language of international treaties and law, as well as to the ideas of many peace activists and scholars. The prize itself, $50,000 (one million dollars or more today), was enormous and generated wide publicity. Isolationists in the House, however, were livid and petitioned successfully for a Senate investigation into the "un-American" activities and "communistic internationalism" of Eleanor, Bok, and their allies. See Blanche Wiesen Cook, *Eleanor Roosevelt, Volume 1: 1884–1933* (New York: Penguin Books, 1992), 342–45.

10 Eleanor Roosevelt, *The Autobiography of Eleanor Roosevelt* (New York: Da Capo Press, 1992), 3.

11 Ibid., 5.

12 Ibid.

13 Ibid., 9.

14 Eleanor Roosevelt, "The Seven People Who Shaped My Life," Eleanor Roosevelt Papers Project, http://www.gwu.edu/~erpapers/teachinger/q-and-a/q13-seven-influences.cfm (accessed August 13, 2009), originally published in *Look* 15 (1951), 54–56, 48. We thank Allida M. Black for this and many other valuable references.

15 The Roosevelts were made up of two principal clans: the Oyster Bay line, primarily affiliated with the Republican Party (Eleanor's father belonged to that line), and the Hyde Park line, affiliated with the Democratic Party (Franklin Delano Roosevelt, Eleanor's future husband, was born into that line). Eleanor Roosevelt's father, Elliott, for example, was the youngest brother of Theodore Roosevelt, who served as president of the United States from 1901 to 1909. On Eleanor's mother's side, the Hall family, she was a descendent of Robert R. Livingston, who administered the oath of office to President George Washington.

16 Eleanor loved and admired her father. She imagined that his return would provide her with the steady and reassuring presence she needed to shed her awkwardness. But Anna's death destroyed what little willpower Elliott possessed.

17 Roosevelt, "The Seven People Who Shaped My Life."

18 Allida M. Black, "Eleanor Roosevelt: A Lifetime of Activism," in *Eleanor Roosevelt and the Universal Declaration of Human Rights* (United States Mission to the United Nations in Geneva, 2008), http://www.usmission.ch/graphics/2008/ERooseveltBook.pdf (accessed September 9, 2009).

19 Roosevelt, *Autobiography*, 24.

20 Roosevelt, "The Seven People Who Shaped My Life."

21 Jean Edward Smith, *FDR* (New York: Random House, 2008), 47. We strongly disagree with Smith's assessment that Eleanor was a political liability to President Roosevelt and was a secondary figure among the women in his life.

22 Roosevelt, *Autobiography*, 12. Theodore Roosevelt was the father of Theodore Roosevelt the president.

23 Roosevelt, *Autobiography*, 41.

24 Ibid.

25 Ibid., 61.

26 Ibid.

27 Smith, *FDR*, 147.

28 Doris Kearns Goodwin, *No Ordinary Time: Franklin and Eleanor Roosevelt: The Home Front in World War II* (New York: Simon and Schuster, 1994), 500.

29 Black, "Lifetime of Activism," 23. See also "The League of Nations," Eleanor Roosevelt Historic Site website, http://www.nps.gov/archive/elro/glossary/league-of-nations.htm (accessed July 13, 2009).

30 "World Court," Eleanor Roosevelt National Historic Site website, http://www.nps.gov/archive/elro/glossary/world-court.htm (accessed August 17, 2009).

31 Goodwin, *No Ordinary Time*, 98.

32 Allida M. Black, private communication (August 11, 2009); Cook, *Eleanor Roosevelt*, 283–285.

33 Allida M. Black, *Anna Eleanor Roosevelt: Biographical Essay*, Eleanor Roosevelt Papers Project, http://www.gwu.edu/~erpapers/abouteleanor/erbiography.cfm#yr1933 (accessed September 1, 2009).

34 Joseph Lash, *Eleanor and Franklin: The Story of their Relationship, Based on Eleanor Roosevelt's Private Papers* (New York: W. W. Norton & Company, 1971), 267–68.

35 Joseph Lash, *Eleanor Roosevelt: A Friend's Memoir* (New York: Doubleday & Co., 1964), 141.

36 Lash, *Eleanor and Franklin*, 304.

37 Smith, *FDR*, 219.

38 Cook, *Eleanor Roosevelt*, vol. 1, 338.

39 Michelle Mart, "Eleanor Roosevelt, Liberalism, and Israel," *Shofar: An Interdisciplinary Journal of Jewish Studies* 24 (2006): 61. We thank Daniel Cohen for this and many other references.

40 Allida M. Black, *Casting Her Own Shadow: Eleanor Roosevelt and the Shaping of Postwar Liberalism* (New York: Columbia University Press, 1996), 11.

41 *Red Book Magazine* 50 (April 1928): 78–79, 141–42.

42 Ibid.

43 Ibid.

44 Ibid.

45 Smith, *FDR*, 236. Eleanor made an average of $25,000 during this period (over $300,000 in today's terms), which roughly equals the governor's salary FDR received.

46 Lash, *Eleanor and Franklin*, 277.

47 Cook, *Eleanor Roosevelt*, 372.

48 Ibid., 25–26.

49 Black, *Anna Eleanor Roosevelt: Biographical Essay*.

[50] Lorena A. Hickok, *Reluctant First Lady: An Intimate Story of Eleanor Roosevelt's Early Public Life* (New York: Dodd-Mead, 1962), 55, available on the Internet Archive website, http://www.archive.org/stream/reluctantfirstla012830mbp/reluctantfirstla012830mbp_djvu.txt (accessed September 23, 2009).

[51] Ibid.

[52] Eleanor Roosevelt, "I Want You to Write to Me," *Woman's Home Companion*, August 1933, 4, cited in *Dear Mrs. Roosevelt: Letters to Eleanor Roosevelt through Depression and War*, ed. Cathy D. Knepper (New York: Carroll & Graf Publishers, 2004), xiv.

[53] Eleanor's spirited response appeared in *The Saturday Evening Post* on August 14, 1935. It can be found on the Eleanor Roosevelt Papers Project website, http://www.gwu.edu/~erpapers/documents/articles/indefenseofcuriosity.cfm (accessed August 19, 2009).

[54] Eleanor Roosevelt Papers Project website.

[55] Ibid.

[56] Black, *Anna Eleanor Roosevelt: Biographical Essay*.

[57] Ibid.

[58] Lash, *Eleanor and Franklin*, 382.

[59] Cook, *Eleanor Roosevelt*, 4.

[60] Lash, *Eleanor and Franklin*, 382.

[61] Allida M. Black, ed., *What I Hope to Leave Behind: The Essential Essays of Eleanor Roosevelt* (Brooklyn: Carlson Publishing, 1995), 7.

[62] Hickok, like several other friends of the Roosevelts, actually lived in the White House. When her relationship with Eleanor grew closer, Hickok resigned from her job, fearing that her reports would lose credibility.

[63] Lorena Alice Hickok, introduction to *My Day: The Best of Eleanor Roosevelt's Acclaimed Newspaper Columns, 1936–1962*, ed. David Emblidge (New York: Da Capo Press, 2001), xiv.

[64] *Eleanor Roosevelt: Close to Home*, DVD, directed and distributed by Anne Makepeace (Hyde Park, 2005).

[65] Cook, *Eleanor Roosevelt*, 130–31.

[66] Ibid. Cook's references to original documents can be found in these pages.

[67] Lash, *Eleanor and Franklin*, 382.

[68] Eleanor Roosevelt, "Subsistence Farmstead" (1934), in *What I Hope to Leave Behind*, 361–62.

[69] Cook, *Eleanor Roosevelt*, 133.

[70] Wesley Stout, "The New Homesteaders," *The Saturday Evening Post*, August 4, 1934. In 1934, Wesley Stout of *The Saturday Evening Post* described the failures of Arthurdale and called the experiment a "direct venture in planned economy." Phrases such as "planned economy" and "social engineering" were derogatory terms routinely used by conservatives to attack New Deal polices.

[71] Eleanor Roosevelt, "Helping Them to Help Themselves," in *What I Hope to Leave Behind*, 370.

[72] Roosevelt, "Helping Them to Help Themselves," 370.

[73] Second Inaugural Address of Franklin D. Roosevelt, January 20, 1937, The Avalon Project, Yale University Law School website, http://avalon.law.yale.edu/20th_century/froos2.asp (accessed November 2, 2009).

[74] Ibid.

[75] Lash, *Eleanor and Franklin*, 390.

[76] Ibid. Cf. Cook, *Eleanor Roosevelt*, vol. 2, 351.

[77] Cook, *Eleanor Roosevelt*, 152.

[78] T. H. Watkins, *The Great Depression* (New York: Little, Brown & Company, 1995), 223–24.

[79] Smith, *FDR*, 398.

[80] Watkins, *The Great Depression*, 223.

[81] Ibid., 248.

[82] Ibid.

[83] Lash, *Eleanor and Franklin*, 523.

[84] "Eleanor Roosevelt and Civil Rights," Eleanor Roosevelt National Historical Site website, http://www.nps.gov/archive/elro/teach-er-vk/lesson-plans/notes-er-and-civil-rights.htm (accessed February 4, 2009).

[85] "Bethune, Mary McLeod," in *The Eleanor Roosevelt Encyclopedia*, eds. Maurine H. Beasley et al. (Westport: Greenwood Press, 2001), 47.

[86] Cook, *Eleanor Roosevelt*, 160; "Bethune, Mary McLeod," *Roosevelt Encyclopedia*, 50.

[87] Patricia Sullivan, *Days of Hope: Race and Democracy in the New Deal Era* (Chapel Hill: University of North Carolina Press, 1996), 99.

[88] Ibid., 100.

[89] Lash, *Eleanor and Franklin*, 525.

[90] "Eleanor Roosevelt Resigns from the Daughters of the American Revolution," Eleanor Roosevelt's letter of resignation, Franklin D. Roosevelt Presidential Library and Museum website, http://www.fdrlibrary.marist.edu/tmirhfee.html (accessed September 24, 2009).

[91] Ibid.

[92] "Mrs. Roosevelt Indicates She Has Resigned From D.A.R. Over Refusal of Hall to Negro," *New York Times*, February 27, 1939.

[93] Alex Ross, "Voice of the Century: Celebrating Marian Anderson," *New Yorker*, April 13, 2009, 78, 79.

[94] Roosevelt, *Autobiography*, 193.

[95] Ibid.

[96] Allida M. Black, "Introduction," *What I Hope to Leave Behind*, xxi.

[97] Eleanor Roosevelt, "The Moral Basis of Democracy," *What I Hope to Leave Behind*, 80.

[98] Ibid.

[99] Allida M. Black, *Casting Her Own Shadow, Eleanor Roosevelt and the Shaping of Postwar Liberalism* (New York: Columbia University Press, 1996), 117.

[100] Facing History and Ourselves, *Holocaust and Human Behavior* (Brookline: Facing History and Ourselves National Foundation, 1994), 259.

[101] Facing History and Ourselves, *Holocaust and Human Behavior*, 259.

[102] Though Jews represented 3 percent of the American population, 15 percent of those who worked in the Roosevelt administration were Jewish. This remarkable number attests to the president's openness. But even as Jews like Secretary of the Treasury Henry Morgenthau, Jr., entered the highest ranks, they were not allowed into the "old lines" of government such as the Department of State. This had devastating consequences.

[103] Goodwin, *No Ordinary Time*, 102.

[104] Ibid., and Allida M. Black, personal communication, August 11, 2009.

[105] Mart, "Eleanor Roosevelt, Liberalism, and Israel."

[106] Later in life, when both were single, Baruch proposed marriage to Eleanor. See "Jews," *Eleanor Roosevelt Encyclopedia*, 282.

[107] Cook, *Eleanor Roosevelt*, 570.

[108] Eleanor Roosevelt, "Keepers of Democracy," originally published in *Virginia Quarterly Review* 15 (Jan. 1939): 1–5, available at Eleanor Roosevelt Papers Project, http://www2.gwu.edu/~erpapers/documents/articles/keepersofdemocracy.cfm (accessed September 8, 2009).

[109] Eleanor bluntly stated that

> [i]f you are in the South, someone tells you solemnly that all the members of the Committee of Industrial Organization are Communists, or that the Negroes are all Communists. This last statement derives from the fact that, being for the most part unskilled labor, Negroes are more apt to be organized by the Committee for Industrial Organization. In another part of the country someone tells you solemnly that the schools of the country are menaced because they are all under the influence of Jewish teachers and that the Jews, forsooth, are all Communists. And so it goes, until finally you realize that people have reached a point where anything which will save them from Communism is a godsend; and if Fascism or Nazism promises more security than our own democracy, we may even turn to them. (Eleanor Roosevelt, "Keepers of Democracy.")

[110] Mischa Elman was a legendary Jewish violinist who immigrated to the United States from the Ukraine, and became a citizen in 1923.

[111] Lash, *Eleanor and Franklin*, 575.

[112] *My Day*, July 19, 1939.

[113] "My Dear Justine, My Dear Eleanor," American Jewish Historical Society website, http://www.ajhs.org/publications/chapters/chapter.cfm?documentID=295 (accessed September 9, 2009).

[114] Ibid.

[115] Lash, *Eleanor and Franklin*, 636.

[116] Smith, *FDR, 417.*

[117] David S. Wyman, *Paper Walls: America and the Refugee Crisis, 1938–1941* (Amherst: University of Massachusetts Press, 1968). In this pioneering work, Wyman charted American failure to respond to the refugee crisis in Europe between 1938 and 1941. He attributed it to deep-seated anti-immigrant and antisemitic attitudes in the country in general, and in the State Department in particular.

[118] Goodwin, *No Ordinary Time*, 175–76.

[119] Ted Morgan, *FDR: A Biography* (New York: Simon & Shuster, 1985), 584.

[120] Memo from Assistant Secretary of State Breckinridge Long to State Department officials dated June 26, 1940, PBS, American Experience website, http://www.pbs.org/wgbh/amex/holocaust/filmmore/reference/primary/barmemo.html (accessed January 22, 2009).

[121] Eleanor's quote and the information in this paragraph were taken from a movie script on the Sharps, date of release yet to be determined. We thank Artemis Joukowsky, III, for sharing the script with us.

[122] Morgan, *FDR*, 585–86.

[123] Goodwin, *No Ordinary Time*, 174.

[124] "Establishment of the War Refugee Board," PBS website, http://www.pbs.org/wgbh/amex/holocaust/peopleevents/pandeAMEX102.html (accessed September 9, 2009).

[125] Goodwin, *No Ordinary Time*, 176.

[126] *My Day*, August 3, 1943.

[127] Ibid.

[128] *My Day*, December 16, 1941.

[129] Eleanor Roosevelt, "A Challenge to American Sportsmanship" (October 16, 1943), in *Courage in a Dangerous World: The Political Writings of Eleanor Roosevelt*, ed. Allida M. Black (New York: Columbia University Press, 1999), 141–42.

[130] "Japanese American Internment," *Eleanor Roosevelt Encyclopedia*, 279, originally cited in Roger Daniels, The Decision to Relocate the Japanese Americans (Philadelphia: Lippincott, 1975), 113.

[131] Ibid., 279.

[132] Ibid., 280.

[133] Eleanor Roosevelt, "To Undo a Mistake is Always Harder Than Not to Create One Originally," in J. Burton, M. Farrell, F. Lord, and R. Lord, "Confinement and Ethnicity: An Overview of World War II Japanese American Relocation Sites," *Anthropology* 74 (2000), available at the National Park Service website, http://www.nps.gov/history/history/online_books/anthropology74/index.htm (accessed September 23, 2009).

[134] The term "Four Hundred" loosely described the most powerful people in New York at the end of the nineteenth century. They belonged to a selective circle defined by aristocratic aspirations and etiquette, by wealth, and by genealogy (many of them were distantly related to the first settlers who arrived in America in the seventeenth century).

[135] Eleanor Roosevelt, "The Seven People Who Shaped My Life"; The Eleanor Roosevelt Papers Project website.

[136] Lash, *Eleanor and Franklin*, 390.

[137] Eleanor Roosevelt, "Women Must Learn to Play the Game as Men Do," *Red Book Magazine* 50 (April 1928): 78–79, 141–42, available at Eleanor Roosevelt Papers Project, http://www.gwu.edu/~erpapers/documents/articles/womenmustlearn.cfm (accessed October 8, 2009).

[138] Eleanor Roosevelt, "The National Conference on the Education of Negroes" (address delivered at the National Conference on Fundamental Problems in the Education of Negroes, Washington, DC, May 11, 1934), reprinted in *What I Hope to Leave Behind: The Essential Essays of Eleanor Roosevelt*, 142.

[139] Eleanor Roosevelt, "The Minorities Question," as quoted in *What I Hope to Leave Behind*, 167–69.

[140] Lash, *Eleanor and Franklin*, 525.

[141] "Eleanor Roosevelt Resigns from the Daughters of the American Revolution," Franklin D. Roosevelt Presidential Library and Museum website.

[142] "Marian Anderson," *New York Times*, March 1, 1939.

[143] Allan Keiler, *Marian Anderson: A Singer's Journey* (Champaign, IL: University of Illinois Press, 2002), 188–89, 202.

[144] *New York Times*, March 19, 1939.

[145] "Throng Honors Marian Anderson in Concert at Lincoln Memorial," *New York Times*, April 10, 1939.

[146] Mischa Elman was a legendary Ukraine-born Jewish violinist who immigrated to the United States and became a citizen in 1923.

[147] *My Day*, January 23, 1939.

[148] For information about the memo from Assistant Secretary of State Breckinridge Long to State Department officials, dated June 26, 1940, see PBS, American Experience website, http://www.pbs.org/wgbh/amex/holocaust/filmmore/reference/primary/barmemo.html.

[149] *My Day*, August 13, 1943.

PART II: WORLD WAR II AND THE BIRTH OF THE UNITED NATIONS

I have the feeling that we let our consciences realize too late the need of standing up against something that we knew was wrong. We have therefore had to avenge it—but we did nothing to prevent it. I hope that in the future, we are going to remember that there can be no compromise at any point with the things that we know are wrong.[1]

– Eleanor Roosevelt, 1946

"WHAT ARE YOU FIGHTING FOR?"

The war opened doors for many of those who suffered during the Depression and who had previously faced scorn and contempt. As early as 1940, the Roosevelt administration began to convert many American plants into armament factories. The government funneled millions of dollars in federal contracts to main industrial centers, and especially to Detroit's auto industry. Indeed, a year before America entered the war in 1941, President Roosevelt had issued "a call to arm and support" the Allies in Europe. He knew well that isolationists still had the upper hand and would not allow America to enter the war directly at this point. In a famous fireside talk to the nation, President Roosevelt argued that America had to use its vast industrial capacity to protect the free world. Furthermore, it had to serve as the "arsenal for democracy" and supply America's bankrupt ally, Britain, with the "material support" necessary to fight Hitler's aggression.

Soon ships, ammunition, shells, tanks, and military vehicles began to roll off American assembly lines. Millions of workers were retrained and hired to serve in factories converted to wartime production use. Among them were many women, who trained as industrial workers and took on jobs that traditionally went to men. Fueled by federal dollars, the defense industry shifted to high gear, eliminated large pockets of unemployment, and began to pull America out of the Depression of the 1930s. However, African Americans, who were called upon to participate in the war against German racism, did not share the same benefits of the economic boom as whites. Responding to industry recruiters, many blacks migrated from the South to industrial centers in the North and the West (an estimated 1.5 million blacks emigrated from the South during the 1940s).[2] Many of them, however, were turned down; racial discrimination and segregation were widespread. Those who did find jobs experienced discrimination in other areas, including in transportation, in schools, and in housing opportunities.

Responding to stories of flagrant discrimination in the media, civil rights activists, including Eleanor, began to protest: How could the same government that sent blacks to fight Nazi racism allow racial discrimination in almost every aspect of American life?[3]

Leon Bass, an African American veteran of World War II, recently recalled his conflicting feelings about the role of African Americans in the war. After volunteering to serve in the war, he was trained in the segregated South. He was then sent to Europe, where his experiences provoked deep doubts about what he was doing. "What are you fighting for?" he asked himself.

I asked that question because I remembered I could not get a drink of water at a public water fountain back home; I couldn't get a meal at a restaurant back home; they would not let me have a seat on a bus back home. So what was I doing here? What was I fighting for? I was but 19 years of age. . . . I was an angry, angry, young black soldier. I felt my country was using me, abusing me, putting me out there in harm's way to fight and maybe die, to preserve all those wonderful things that every American should enjoy, but at the same time my country was saying to me, "Leon, you are not good enough to enjoy what you are fighting for!"[4]

The war instilled a stronger sense of urgency in the hearts of many. For activists such as Eleanor, the birthplace of the New Deal could only thrive if every group participated in the American dream. This was a time of reckoning: "There is going to be almost an entire continent of vast natural resources under the direction of an opposing philosophy to ours, and an opposing economic system," she warned her readers in 1940. Americans, she argued, could no longer shun certain questions: "[H]ow much Democracy [do] we have and how much [do] we want to have"? How much democracy America had—indeed, how democratic it was—was intimately connected to the issue of racial and economic injustice. For, in America, Eleanor stated plainly, "[w]e have poverty which enslaves, and racial prejudice which does the same." Eleanor, who raised the issues of housing, education, and equal employment opportunity for all to the top of her agenda during the war, spelled out what choosing democracy should mean: at the very least, it would be "achieving an economic level below which no one is permitted to fall." One could not expect to beat Hitler at his own game, she added. He was far too efficient,

---

Description of map on next page: World War II began when Nazi Germany invaded Poland in September 1939. Germany and its allies, known as the Axis Powers, advanced north, east, and west, assuming almost complete control over Europe in the early years of the war. Japan—one of Germany's main allies—extended the war to the Pacific, and, after Japan's attack on Pearl Harbor in 1941, the U.S. actively joined Allied powers in their fight against Nazism. In 1943, facing the Allied forces' invasion of Italy and the fierce Soviet army, the Nazis' advances finally failed, marking the tipping point in favor of the Allies. The war in Europe ended in the spring of 1945 following the Allies' invasion to Normandy (D-Day); the war with Japan only ended after the U.S. dropped two atomic bombs on Hiroshima and Nagasaki in August 1945.

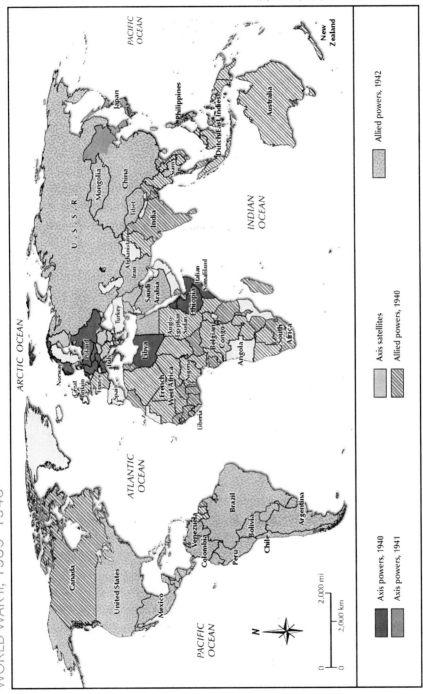

WORLD WAR II, 1939–1945

Allied powers, 1942

Axis satellites

Allied powers, 1940

Axis powers, 1940

Axis powers, 1941

organized, and brutal in enslaving the European continent to serve his expansionist aspirations. Americans therefore had a very clear choice: "Either we must make our economic system work to the satisfaction of all of our people, or we are going to find it extremely difficult to compete against the one which will be set upon on the Continent of Europe."[5]

Many Americans did not share Eleanor's moral vision of democracy, but news of flagrant discrimination in the defense industry rallied civil rights activists. The same year that Eleanor made these remarks, black activists also responded. Led by black union organizer A. Philip Randolph, they approached the administration, demanding that discrimination in the defense industry be outlawed and that the government order factories and job-retraining programs to accept people of all colors. In September of 1940, President Roosevelt denied their request.

Thus far, the struggle for civil rights had been carried out through letters, behind-the-scenes pressure, negotiation, and in the courts. Sensing the urgency of the situation, Randolph and his colleagues realized that these strategies were not likely to address the needs of hundreds of thousands of unemployed blacks. They set their eyes on a massive demonstration in Washington, DC, and began to mobilize blacks around the country. News of preparations for the demonstration reached the White House, and estimates suggested that as many as 100,000 people were planning to march on Washington in July 1940.

Eleanor, whose views about the injustice of racial inequality in America were well known by this point, had traveled and spoken to many black communities throughout the spring, gaining their trust and support. Worried about the volatile situation, Franklin asked her to pressure Randolph to cancel the march. He sent her and New York Mayor Fiorello LaGuardia to meet Walter White and Randolph in New York. Eleanor expressed her fear that anti-black sentiment was rife beneath the surface in Washington and that violence was likely to erupt if the plan was put into action. Despite the warning, the civil rights leaders did not yield. Randolph and White told Eleanor and LaGuardia that they were determined to carry out the march unless the president ordered the defense industry to integrate. On her return, Eleanor informed the president that only an antidiscrimination order would avert the crisis. A week before the march was due to take place, Roosevelt finally issued Executive Order 8802. The ordinance prohibited discrimination in the national defense industry on the basis of race and set the precedent for future legislation promoting equal opportunity in the United States. A thankful Randolph sent a telegram to Eleanor, informing her that the march would not be necessary at that time.[6]

The president's ordinance opened high-paying jobs to many African Americans, increasing their proportion of the war production force from 3 to 9 percent between 1942 and 1945. But the antidiscrimination executive order did not ease wartime racial tension and violence, which peaked in 1943 with 250 incidents in 47 cities.[7] In Detroit, the major source of tension shifted from the work situation to housing. Since the war began, over 300,000 new white workers and 50,000 blacks descended on the city to take advantage of the economic boom. Detroit became a much more crowded city in a matter of months, as the new residents strained public transportation, parks, and schools. Their arrival created a housing crisis. The administration responded by funding housing projects from which, with few exceptions, blacks were barred. Restricted to a small number of crowded neighborhoods, blacks realized that the North was often just as racist as the South. With full employment, an excessive population, and thousands of homeless or semi-homeless people, the bustling city saw an ever-growing number of street-corner fights.

Eleanor pleaded with administration officials to use public housing programs for slum clearance and for projects designed to benefit blacks as well as whites. Charles Palmer, the coordinator of this federal program, opposed her proposal. A relentless Eleanor then turned to Roosevelt's director of defense housing, Clark Foreman, who devised a plan to allocate funds to a project called the Sojourner Truth Homes. The goal was to provide homes near working-class white neighborhoods for low-income African Americans. White neighbors, many of Polish Catholic descent, were alarmed: how could the government force their neighborhoods to accept blacks? In January 1942, under pressure from white residents, officials from Washington forced Clark Foreman to resign and turned the project's intended occupants from blacks to whites. Civil rights leaders turned to Eleanor to intercede. She did, and her intervention convinced Franklin to reverse the whites-only policy.

In February 1942, escorted by a large group of supporters, two dozen black families attempted to move into their new homes. They were confronted by an armed mob. Violence and the burning of crosses followed. The black tenants turned back, and the project was temporarily suspended. Despite simmering resentment, at the end of April 1942, black families, escorted by hundreds of state and local police officers, made their way to their Sojourner Truth Project homes. But in June 1943, Detroit's racial tensions boiled over; occasional street-corner scrimmages turned into a horrific riot. During 36 hours of riots, mobs turned over cars and looted stores. In all, 1800 people were arrested, 6 policemen were shot, and 25 blacks and 9 whites died. Many more, disproportionately blacks, were injured and imprisoned. Only after President Roosevelt sent in federal troops in armed vehicles did the worst wartime race riots come to an end.

Courtesy of Detroit Public Library

The *Detroit Tribune* reports on its city's fatal June 1943 race riot. A government project aimed at providing homes near working-class white neighborhoods for low-income African Americans in Detroit, named for Sojourner Truth, spurred a 36-hour riot during which 25 blacks and 9 whites died.

Eleanor, who was involved in previous attempts to build neighborly cooperation, was distraught. Still, some held her responsible for the riots because she encouraged blacks to cross the color lines and to challenge segregation. Eleanor began receiving hate mail and threats.

In one such letter, C. B. Alexander of Knoxville, Tennessee, accused Eleanor of upsetting the existing norms that had kept race relations stable for generations. Among other things, he wrote, Eleanor encouraged "the [N]egro to think that he can sit and ride in any place he chooses. When he places himself where he doesn't belong, he causes trouble." Alexander than went on to argue that

> [w]e people of the South know the [N]egro; we know how to control him. We don't hate him, we don't persecute him, we treat him as well as he is treated anywhere so long as he stays in his place, but it must be remembered that there are inferior people just as there are

inferior animals. You know there are fine bred dogs, fine bred cattle, fine bred swine, etc. . . .

All of we Southern people teach our children that they are superior to the [N]egro. . . . Naturally our children will teach their children likewise; hence the South will always be as she is today. Treat all human beings as you would like to be treated, but remember your blood.[8]

Eleanor's position on Detroit's riots sharpened. She adamantly protested police brutality that targeted blacks and denounced the pervasive racist attitudes displayed by the police and the white mob that instigated the violence. The riots made her "sick at heart," she argued, because they "put us on a par with Nazism."[9] She went on:

We cannot settle strikes by refusing to understand their causes; we cannot prepare for a peaceful world unless we give proof of self-restraint, of open-mindedness, of courage to do right at home, even if it means changing our traditional thinking and, for some of us, a sacrifice of our material interests.[10]

She would have said a lot more, apparently, but in private she acknowledged that this was "the most F[ranklin] would be willing to have me say. He feels that he must not irritate the Southern leaders as he needs their votes for essential war bills."[11]

A LASTING PEACE

As the war in Europe spread, Eleanor and Franklin shared the concern that if the world's nations did not figure out how to negotiate and work out their differences peacefully, they would soon face an endless cycle of violence. The foundation of a lasting peace, they believed, would have to be anchored in a number of basic rights for all people. In her January 1, 1941, *My Day* column, Eleanor wrote that she was aware of how hard it was to wish anyone a happy New Year that year. And yet, she said, hope could be found by working to bring about "justice for all, security in certain living standards, a recognition of the dignity and the right of an individual human being without regard to his race, creed, or color." These fundamental rights, she added, "are the things for which vast numbers of our citizens will willingly sacrifice themselves."[12]

A wartime American antisemitic cartoon featuring FDR as a Jewish conspirator. FDR had an unprecedented number of Jews in his administration, and his perceived sympathy with Jews earned him many enemies.

Many of Eleanor's ideas influenced Franklin's thinking about human dignity, finding their way into the international conferences and agreements that took place before and after the end of the war. These efforts came to fruition when 51 nations gathered in San Francisco to form an international relief and peacekeeping organization in April 1945, shortly before Germany's final surrender. The preparations for this day had been under way throughout the war, and Franklin led the process until his death. He hoped that this new organization, which he called the United Nations after the name he had been using to describe the Allies, would defend the basic rights of all people, providing peace and security among nations.

By the end of 1940, Franklin had begun to sketch the outlines of a group that would encourage global cooperation after the war, and he unveiled his ideas at the beginning of 1941 in his "four freedoms" speech. Echoing Eleanor's *My Day* column of New Year's Day, he spoke of "a world based on 'four essential human freedoms'"—freedom of speech and expression, freedom to worship God in one's own way, freedom from want, and freedom from fear.[13] These would eventually be captured in the preamble to the Universal Declaration of Human Rights:

[T]he advent of a world in which human beings shall enjoy freedom
of speech and belief, and freedom from fear and want, has been
proclaimed as the highest aspiration of the common people.[14]

Franklin and Eleanor both sought to instill this moral vision in the core of the United Nations, as well as in the international agreements signed by the United States.[15] Eleanor summarized their goals in a speech she gave later, in 1946:

My husband often said that first the war must be won, but when
that was done, then all our efforts must be centered on building an
organization through which all men could work for peace.[16]

It was during the secret Atlantic Conference held aboard a warship near the shore of Newfoundland in the summer of 1941 that Franklin and his British counterpart, Prime Minister Winston Churchill, discussed the organization. They drafted a document that called for "self-determination of peoples, freer trade, and several New Deal–style social welfare provisions."[17] Economic concerns loomed large, as the charter emphasized

the fullest collaboration between all nations in the economic field
with the object of securing, for all, improved labor standards,
economic advancement, and social security.[18]

It sounds very much like Franklin's election campaign rhetoric, expanded to encompass the rest of the world. There was to be a "new world order," a unified system that would "afford assurance that all the men in all the lands may live out their lives in freedom from fear and want." For the first time, international standards would regulate the treatment of individuals, regardless of where they lived. To ensure human dignity, the traditional right of national governments to write and enforce every law would be balanced by international laws that protected each and every individual. This has been called the beginning of "the modern doctrine of human rights."[19]

UNITED NATIONS

After the Atlantic Conference, Roosevelt and Churchill arranged for a number of meetings with the leaders of other Allied nations. The Tehran Conference of 1943 was attended by the main Allied powers, who tentatively agreed to form a peace organization—the United Nations. These preliminary steps led to a protracted discussion held in the autumn of 1944 at a Washington, DC, mansion called Dumbarton Oaks. Representatives from China, the Soviet Union, the United Kingdom, and the United States hammered out the basic structure of the United Nations over seven weeks. They envisioned four bodies:

- The General Assembly would be the principal body of the United Nations. Composed of all United Nations members, it would enhance international cooperation and promote the welfare of the citizens of the world through peaceful means.

- The Security Council would be responsible for preventing future wars and other violence. This group would have 11 members—5 permanent and 6 selected in turn from the other member states. The permanent members would have the right to veto any resolution passed by a majority of the Security Council.

- The International Court of Justice—the judicial body of the United Nations—would adjudicate crimes that fell under international jurisdiction, such as war crimes, crimes against humanity, and what we now call genocide.

- The Secretariat would steer the organization and handle administrative matters.

In addition, there would be an Economic and Social Council to deal with economic, social, cultural, and humanitarian crises.

Much had been learned from the failures of the body that preceded the United Nations—the League of Nations. Formed after World War I, the group never had a military force at its disposal, and it never managed to attract key members. In spite of the best efforts of President Woodrow Wilson (and Eleanor), the United States never joined. The League of Nations became synonymous with powerlessness and failure. So the group that met at Dumbarton Oaks made every effort to ensure that all leading states would join and required all members to provide armed forces that would intervene in international crises.[20]

When they met at Yalta, a Soviet resort town, in February 1945, the leaders of the United States, the Soviet Union, and the United Kingdom agreed that the formation of the United Nations would be a top priority following Germany's surrender. The United Nations was established on June 26, 1945, in

Joseph Stalin, FDR, and Winston Churchill on December 1, 1943, in Tehran, Iran. The Tehran Conference was attended by the four Allied powers, who devised plans to defeat the Axis and tentatively agreed to sponsor the United Nations.

San Francisco, when 44 nations signed the charter—a treaty that defined the new organization and its organs.

However, Franklin did not live to see the fruition of his efforts. On April 12, 1945, two and a half months before his dream for a world government was realized, Franklin Delano Roosevelt died of a massive cerebral hemorrhage. Eleanor sent her sons a telegram: "Father slept away. He would expect you to carry on and finish your jobs."[21] The extraordinary compression of those words says so much.

The longest serving president in American history was succeeded by his vice president, Harry Truman. Untested and unelected, President Truman sought to tie himself to the previous administration. He asked the former First Lady to serve as a delegate to the United Nations (she refused to consider an official government post).[22] In spite of decades spent working for immigrants, female workers, blacks, and refugees, Eleanor doubted her qualification for this new role. She wrote in her autobiography, "How could I be a delegate to help organize the United Nations when I have no background or experience in international meetings?"[23]

These sentiments did not, however, reflect Eleanor's domestic and international accomplishments. A longtime activist and a widely read author, Eleanor was recognized for her leadership in improving the conditions of workers, minorities, immigrants, and women. Although she never sought an elected government post, Eleanor was a central figure in Franklin's administration and in the Democratic Party, where she was able to wield power as very few could. Her political connections with representatives in Congress, minority activists, labor leaders, and women voters expanded deeply into all facets of American society. Moreover, by the end of the war, Eleanor was no longer just a domestic icon. She had an extended network of friends among world leaders and soon advised President Truman about the best ways to win their support. She had also traveled around the world many times, visiting troops and wounded soldiers in areas of international conflict. And her work on international treaties, starting with her campaign for the League of Nations in the 1920s and 1930s, secured her reputation as a leader in the areas of peacekeeping, national rights and sovereignty, and human rights.

Three pressing issues had occupied Eleanor since the spring of 1945, and these weighed heavily on her decision regarding President Truman's offer. As World War II drew to a close, Eleanor began to focus on the need to prevent similar manmade horrors from recurring. A few days before the end of the war, Eleanor used her daily column to implore her readers to face the humanitarian crisis in Europe head-on:

> *As more and more people are liberated from prisons and concentration camps, I keep wondering if their return will not mean a great awakening among us to the realization of the full horror of war. . . . Who could make it more clear than a boy who had been in one of these camps, and in contact with the German people?*

> *I hope we are not going to be too easy with ourselves. It would be pleasant to close our eyes and ears now and say: "These things could never be. Human beings could not do such things, and therefore we will not believe them or listen to them." That would be an easy way out because we would not have to decide how we could prevent any recurrence in the future, in any part of the world, of the Fascism which brought these things about.[24]*

Yet the horrors of the war did not end when the fighting on the continent stopped. Hundreds of thousands of refugees, many of them half-starved, stateless Jews, were gathered in "displaced persons" camps awaiting the international community's decision about where they could relocate. Although this was not yet a focus of Eleanor's writings, it was becoming harder to ignore evidence of the Nazis' attempt to destroy European Jewry and to eliminate hundreds of thousands of other minorities that they viewed as "undesirable." Then, on August 6 and 9, 1945, on orders from President Truman, the United States dropped two atomic bombs on the Japanese cities of Hiroshima and Nagasaki. The bombs reduced both cities to ashes and in seconds obliterated as many men, women, and children as had been killed in weeks of fighting in Europe. Eleanor did not object to the use of the atomic bomb; she assumed it would bring a quicker end to the war in the South Pacific.[25] But several months later, she pointed to what many felt was the most important lesson of the atomic bomb—that humanity had created the possibility for its own destruction. She somberly reminded a group of reporters of this destructive force:

I think that if the atomic bomb did nothing more, it scared the people to the point where they realized that either they must do something about preventing war, or there is a chance that there might be a morning when we would not wake up.[26]

As evidence of the war's horrors mounted, many activists became increasingly convinced of the need to ensure the protection of human rights and dignity. Eleanor, with many others, shared Franklin's vision of a world order based on peace and unity, on the rule of law, and on international cooperation. Thus, after debating about Truman's offer to join the United States delegation, on December 22, 1945, Eleanor decided to accept the appointment. That same day, she wrote in her *My Day* column that every person "has a deep and solemn obligation" to create a peaceful world.[27] Our love for our country, Eleanor wrote,

must never blind us to the good of all lands and of all peoples. In the end, as Wendell Willkie said, we are "One World" and that which injures any one of us, injures all of us.[28]

These words captured the spirit of solidarity many felt in 1945. And they spoke to the shared responsibility to create a peaceful world—a responsibility that needed to transcend national boundaries. When, a year later, she

President Harry S. Truman with Eleanor on July 1, 1948, in Washington, DC. President Truman asked the former First Lady to serve as a delegate to the United Nations in 1945, an appointment she accepted.

addressed the challenges of thinking about the world as a whole, Eleanor did not pretend it would be easy:

> *It is a heavy price. It means education of a nation that has always been isolationist at heart. We love our own country. We have felt that our salvation lay in living within ourselves. Now suddenly we say to our people, "You cannot live for yourselves alone. You depend on the rest of the world and the rest of the world depends on you."*[29]

She returned to the theme of international cooperation in her newspaper column, stating, "We must become one world."[30] Only by working together could the people scattered around the globe rebuild the world and secure its peaceful future. Failing to achieve unity would mean a return to the divisive politics that had led to countless previous wars.

Two weeks after Eleanor accepted Truman's appointment to the United Nations, she boarded the *Queen Elizabeth* and sailed to London for the UN's first meeting. While aboard the ship, Eleanor held her first press conference since leaving the White House. When asked how she felt about her new job, she responded, off the record: "For the first time in my life I can say just what I want. For your information, it is wonderful to feel free."[31]

Sailing on the same ship was Republican Senator Arthur H. Vandenberg. Long an isolationist and vocal opponent of Franklin Roosevelt's policies, Vandenberg had reversed course during the war, becoming an outspoken advocate of international cooperation; he too was on his way to London to witness the opening of the first United Nations meeting. Eleanor later recalled meeting him during that voyage:

> *He stopped me.*
>
> *"Mrs. Roosevelt," he said in his deep voice, "we would like to know if you would serve on Committee Three."*
>
> *I had two immediate and rather contradictory reactions to the question. First, I wondered who "we" might be. Was a Republican senator deciding who would serve where? And why, since I was a delegate, had I not been consulted about committee assignments? But my next reaction crowded these thoughts out of my mind. I realized that I had no more idea than the man in the moon what Committee Three might be.[32]*

The Third Committee, one of six United Nations committees, dealt with "humanitarian, educational and cultural questions," issues Eleanor had worked on for many years.[33] (The General Assembly oversaw six permanent committees. The men on the delegation assigned themselves to the committees they deemed more crucial to American interests: the First Committee dealt with political issues and security, and the Second Committee dealt with economic and financial issues.) Eleanor agreed, at the age of 62, to take on the assignment, which soon became "one of the most wonderful and worthwhile experiences" of her life.[34]

"I DID NOT KNOW UNTIL I SAW"[35]

Surprisingly, the Third Committee, which took on as one of its first issues the fate of the European refugees, became the focus of the United Nations' diplomacy. Among the millions of people the war displaced, there were two million refugees who refused to be repatriated. Their fate became a significant source of conflict between the United States and the Soviet Union, because many of the refugees were Soviet subjects who refused to live under communism. Eleanor, caught in the crossfire, was quickly recognized as a formidable defender of these refugees.

Of these two million war refugees, 250,000 were Jewish survivors and former Nazi slave laborers. Some of the displaced persons were settled in hastily assembled camps, while others had set out for their distant homes, traveling by whatever means they could find. Much as Eleanor had invited poor black "sharecroppers in the White House and visited them in their tarpaper shacks in the cotton fields," so she was determined to meet the very people whom the Third Committee was supposed to assist.[36] Before returning to the United States after the first session of the United Nations, then, Eleanor made a short but fateful trip to the refugee camps in Germany to meet and speak directly with the refugees.

Nothing could adequately prepare those who were not directly affected by the war for what Eleanor was about to see in Germany. News about the horrific nature of the Holocaust began streaming in with the liberation of concentration camps in Europe in the spring of 1945. Eleanor must have been aware of these reports, such as the one filed by legendary CBS reporter Edward R. Murrow. Murrow filed this report on April 15, 1945, after visiting Buchenwald—one of the many concentration camps the Germans set up in Europe. In these camps, the Germans imprisoned, exploited, starved, and gassed to death some six million Jews. Murrow was among the first to witness the conditions in the camps immediately following liberation:

> *[This] will not be pleasant listening. If you're at lunch, or if you have no appetite to hear what Germans have done, now is a good time to switch off the radio, for I propose to tell you about Buchenwald. It is on a small hill about four miles outside Weimar, and it was one of the largest concentration camps in Germany, and*

it was built to last. . . . We drove on, reached the main gate. The
prisoners crowded up behind the wire. We entered. . . .

Men and boys reached out to touch me; they were in rags and the
remnants of uniform. Death had already marked many of them, but
they were smiling with their eyes. I looked out over that mass of men
to the green fields beyond where well fed Germans were plowing.

A German, Fritz Gersheimer, came up and said, "May I show you
round the camp? I've been here ten years." . . . It happened to
be occupied by Czechoslovakians. When I entered, men crowded
around, tried to lift me to their shoulders. They were too weak.
Many of them could not get out of bed. I was told that this building
had once stabled eighty horses. There were twelve hundred men
in it, five to a bunk. . . . I asked how many men had died in that
building during the last month. They called the doctor; we inspected
his records. There were only names in a little black book, nothing
more—nothing about who these men were, what they had done, or
hoped. Behind the names of those who had died there was a cross.
I counted them. They totaled two hundred and forty-two. Two
hundred and forty-two out of twelve hundred in one month. . . .

The doctor's name was Paul Heller. He had been there since 1938.
As we walked out into the courtyard, a man fell dead. Two others—
they must have been over sixty—were crawling toward the latrine.
I saw it, but will not describe it.

In another part of the camp they showed me the children, hundreds
of them. Some were only six. One rolled up his sleeve, showed me
his number. It was tattooed on his arm. D-6030, it was. The others
showed me their numbers. They will carry them till they die.

An elderly man standing beside me said, "The children, enemies of
the state." I could see their ribs through their thin shirts. The old
man said, "I am Professor Charles Richa of the Sorbonne." The
children clung to my hands and stared. We crossed to the courtyard.
Men kept coming up to speak to me and to touch me, professors from
Poland, doctors from Vienna, men from all Europe. Men from the
countries that made America.

We went to the hospital; it was full. The doctor told me that two hundred had died the day before. I asked the cause of death; he shrugged and said, "Tuberculosis, starvation, fatigue, and there are many who have no desire to live. It is very difficult." . . .

I asked to see the kitchen; it was clean. The German in charge had been a Communist, had been at Buchenwald for nine years, had a picture of his daughter in Hamburg. He hadn't seen her for almost twelve years, and if I got to Hamburg, would I look her up? He showed me the daily ration—one piece of brown bread about as thick as your thumb, on top of it a piece of margarine as big as three sticks of chewing gum. That, and a little stew, was what they received every twenty-four hours. He had a chart on the wall; very complicated it was. There were little red tabs scattered through it. He said that was to indicate each [group of] ten men who died. He had to account for the rations, and he added, "We're very efficient here."

We went again into the courtyard, and as we walked, we talked. The two doctors, the Frenchman and the Czech, agreed that about six thousand had died during March. Kersheimer, the German, added that back in the winter of 1939, when the Poles began to arrive without winter clothing, they died at the rate of approximately nine hundred a day. Five different men asserted that Buchenwald was the best concentration camp in Germany; they had had some experience of the others.

Dr. Heller, the Czech, asked if I would care to see the crematorium. He said it wouldn't be very interesting because the Germans had run out of coal some days ago and had taken to dumping the bodies into a great hole nearby. Professor Richer said perhaps I would care to see the small courtyard. I said yes. He turned and told the children to stay behind. As we walked across the square I noticed that the professor had a hole in his left shoe and a toe sticking out of the right one. He followed my eyes and said, "I regret that I am so little presentable, but what can one do?" . . . We proceeded to the small courtyard. The wall was about eight feet high; it adjoined what had been a stable or garage. We entered. It was floored with concrete. There were two rows of bodies stacked up like cordwood. They were thin and very white. Some of the bodies were terribly bruised, though there seemed to be little flesh to bruise. Some had been shot through the head, but they bled but little. All except two were naked. I tried to count them as best I could and arrived at the conclusion that all that was mortal of more than five hundred men and boys lay there in two neat piles.

There was a German trailer, which must have contained another fifty, but it wasn't possible to count them. The clothing was piled in a heap against the wall. It appeared that most of the men and boys had died of starvation; they had not been executed. But the manner of death seemed unimportant. Murder had been done at Buchenwald. God alone knows how many men and boys have died there during the last twelve years. Thursday I was told that there were more than twenty thousand in the camp. There had been as many as sixty thousand. Where are they now?

As I left that camp, a Frenchman who used to work for Havas in Paris came up to me and said, "You will write something about this,

The first group of displaced persons to arrive at Zeilsheim in 1945. In 1946, Eleanor visited this camp to learn firsthand about the fate of the refugees. After her visit to the camps, Eleanor wrote, "You can measure the extent of physical damage done to cities . . . [b]ut how to gauge what has happened to human beings—that is incalculable."

perhaps?" And he added, "To write about this you must have been here at least two years, and after that—you don't want to write any more."

I pray you to believe what I have said about Buchenwald. I have reported what I saw and heard, but only part of it. For most of it, I have no words. Dead men are plentiful in war, but the living dead, more than twenty thousand of them in one camp. And the country round about was pleasing to the eye. . . . If I have offended you by this rather mild account of Buchenwald, I'm not in the least sorry.[37]

Less than a year later, Eleanor was in Germany to learn firsthand about the fate of the refugees. Even before she got to her first refugee camp, she had witnessed a great deal. Mass graves, ghost towns destroyed by aerial bombing, and many more dead than alive, the survivors of German slave camps and death camps. She first went to Zeilsheim, a Jewish refugee camp near Frankfurt, Germany. Her impressions echoed Murrow's speechlessness almost a year before ("For most of it I have no words"):

There is a feeling of desperation and sorrow in this camp which seems beyond expression. An old woman knelt on the ground, grasping my knees. I lifted her up, but could not speak. What could one say at the end of a life which had brought her such complete despair?[38]

Time and again, her words failed her:

You can write and talk all you like about it. I have done my best, but to people who have never seen or heard anything similar to it, it is practically impossible to get it across. Nothing makes it live.[39]

Attempting to describe the lives whose ruin she had witnessed, Eleanor told the Women's Joint Congressional Committee, "I cannot tell you what destruction is. No one can."[40] The destruction was incomprehensible, literally beyond the grasp of language. The sheer physical destruction was not the main challenge: "You can measure the extent of physical damage done to cities," Eleanor wrote in *My Day*, "you can restore water supplies, gas and electricity, and you can rebuild the buildings. . . . But how to gauge what has happened to human beings—that is incalculable."[41]

Among the survivors, those who spoke about their experiences were often ignored. Others were too overcome by their despair to try to communicate what had happened to them. As one French woman told Eleanor, many of the survivors had suffered so much that "they either go crazy or they die or something happens to their personality so that they cannot feel any more." "Physically," the woman observed, "they may come back, but it varies how that sense of numbness goes. Sometimes it takes a long time; sometimes it never goes."[42]

At the camps, Eleanor was finally able to assess the full extent of Nazi terror: the destruction of a people's essential ties to a civic community and of things that are at the heart of our humanity.

> *It is the feeling that there has been a crumbling of the thing that gives most of us a sense of security, the feeling that we have roots, and that—as bad as the situation may be—we have a government to which we can appeal, we have people who are representing us and who can speak for us.*[43]

Where all hope had vanished, where people had been stripped of their humanity, language also ceased. The survivors shared this loss of words with those who encountered them. Eleanor linked that silence to "a kind of spiritual uprooting, a kind of being lost."[44] From another camp, Wiesbaden, she reported that she "went away . . . more hopeful, but still with a sense of depression weighing upon me. What's the ultimate answer?"[45]

HOPE AND REHABILITATION

As the sites of destruction unfolded before the world, activists, lawyers, NGOs, politicians, and intellectuals advocated for an array of responses to this manmade humanitarian and economic crisis. Some, led by Raphael Lemkin, pushed for a United Nations convention that would criminalize what he termed "genocide"—the destruction of ethnic, national, or religious groups.[46] Others demanded that the chief Nazi perpetrators be brought to justice and that their trials would create the legal foundation for persecuting future crimes of the same nature. Among those who struggled to find answers to Eleanor's question were individuals with a profound understanding of the legal and moral aspects of the German killing machine. Robert H. Jackson was the chief prosecutor of the principal Nazi war criminals during the international military tribunal at Nuremberg (1945–56). Of the people whom he referred to as "the end product of totalitarianism," he said:

> *No people are less responsible for their own misery and helplessness than they. The Nürnberg record tells the ghastly story of how they were torn from their homes, and shipped like cattle to serve as slaves in agricultural and industrial production to feed the war machine; how they were overworked and underfed; and how it was deliberately calculated to be cheaper to work these people to death and replace them with new recruits than to nourish them adequately and avoid the turnover of death. The collapse of the Nazi masters left these people in the country penniless, landless, and hopeless. They are hated aliens in the land where we now find them and they have become unwelcome aliens in the lands from which they were taken. And there they are, huddled into camps where they cannot stay permanently, with no means to go elsewhere, and no place open to them if they had means to go.*[47]

"Adequate justice to these surviving people can never be done," Jackson added, "but to keep them existing in suspense is a form of mental torture almost as harrowing as that which the Nazis inflicted."[48]

For Eleanor, the refugees could be helped by restoring their civic and political voice. In other words, she proposed a *civic* solution. "Charity," she said,

> *is a wonderful thing, but it does not give one that sense of security. What is important is rehabilitation [of the person]. . . . [T]he sooner those people can be taken where they can become citizens and feel that they are actually building a new life, the better it will be for the whole world."*[49]

European civilization lay in ruins. To rebuild it, one had to give individuals and states the power to govern themselves.

This goes a long way to explain why, when the Soviet Union lobbied in the meetings of the Third Committee for the mandatory return of war refugees to their countries of origin, Eleanor objected. Early in 1946, there were between 1.5 and 2 million refugees in Europe who refused to return to their home countries.[50] Many feared persecution on account of their religious or dissenting political views. Others simply refused to go back to places now under Soviet autocratic regime. Eleanor believed that forcing anyone who had lived through the worst of World War II to suffer any further amounted to betrayal.[51]

The head of the Soviet delegation, Andrei Vyshinsky, sharply retorted that anyone who refused to return home was a traitor—and traitors would have to be dealt with.[52] In a speech she gave on February 12, 1946, Eleanor agreed that traitors should be returned and punished. But to her, political dissenters were not traitors: many refugees had fought against their countries' enemies but were "still unwilling to go back because they do not agree with the present government in their countries."[53] Didn't the people who sacrificed so much deserve the right to choose their nationality? When Eleanor concluded her speech, she and Vyshinsky shook hands. She told the Russian delegate that while she admired his determination, she hoped that the day would come when they would see things eye to eye.[54] Whether or not Eleanor won that round of the debate—some felt certain that she had—she had established herself as a leading voice in the Third Committee.

The group most affected by the postwar humanitarian crisis was the set of Jewish survivors of the Holocaust. What rights did the world owe these people who lost their state, their property, their families? What could be done to restore their hope, their dignity, and their sense of belonging to the world?

Stateless and unwanted in Europe, a large group of these Jewish survivors wanted to emigrate to the United States, in spite of the State Department's strict immigration polices. Some who did return to their pre-war homes in Europe were attacked by the local population, who refused to give up property that had been seized during the war.[55] Another group was Zionist. They thought that the only place they could be safe was Palestine, a zone currently under British control, where they hoped to establish their own state. Even before the visit to Zeilsheim, Eleanor supported this cause. In a *My Day* column dated November 7, 1945, she wrote,

> *There is in Europe at the present time a group of 100,000 displaced persons—the miserable, tortured, terrorized Jews who have seen members of their families murdered and their homes ruined, and who are stateless people, since they hate the Germans and no longer wish to live in the countries where they have been despoiled of all that makes life worth living. Naturally they want to go to Palestine,*

the one place where they will have a status, where they will feel
again that sense of belonging to a community which gives most of
us security . . . [56]

She concluded this essay by saying, "It seems to me urgent that these people be given permission to go to the home of their choice. They are the greatest victims of this war."[57] Her personal visit to Zeilsheim, several months after the publication of this essay, left a deep and lasting impression and reinforced Eleanor's convictions about the rights of these Holocaust survivors. Years later, she recalled

an old woman whose family had been driven from home by war,
madness and brutality. I had no idea who she was and we could not
speak each other's language, but she knelt in the muddy road and
threw her arms around my knees . . . "Israel! Israel!" As I looked at
her weather-beaten face, and heard her old voice, I knew for the first
time what that small land meant to so many, many people.[58]

Eleanor believed that in Israel the Jews would be able, for the first time in centuries, to direct their own lives. While she favored a Jewish state in Palestine, Eleanor continued to think about the plight in universal terms. The right of Jewish refugees to decide their own fate, she wrote, had to be extended to all peoples around the world—be they in Europe, the European colonies in Africa, or elsewhere. This was a universal right, for

[t]he desire of every people to determine its own destiny, free from
dictation or control by others, is one of the most deep-seated of all
human feelings. Throughout history, groups of individuals having
common bonds . . . have developed a sense of solidarity as a people
and have tended to resent any effort of the outsider, the foreigner,
to interfere with them. So strong is this feeling that men of many
peoples have at various times been willing to lay down their lives to
be free from domination by others.[59]

Thus, the fate of displaced Jews inspired Eleanor to consider the needs of "humanity as a whole."[60] It sharpened her view on the questions that troubled her most during this period. How could the world prevent another war? What would spare the world from another atomic bomb? How could Europe's displaced people experience the restoration of dignity, hope, and nationality?

The opportunity to spell out those needs came as soon as the question was posed. At the conclusion of its first session, as many delegations prepared to return home, the United Nations set up a small commission to discuss the promotion and protection of human rights.[61] Eleanor, who had imagined that her stint as a diplomat was over, quickly learned that there was more to do:

> *Not long after I returned to New York I received notice that the Economic and Social Council, which had been set up by the United Nations in London, had created a ["nuclear"] committee to make recommendations on matters pertaining to the functioning of the UN Human Rights Commission.*[62]

Delegates on this committee were selected for their individual merits, not because of their nationality. The invitation to serve was a compliment, and Eleanor accepted without any misgivings or anxieties.[63] By then, the most famous member of the American delegation had won the hearts of even her staunch critics. Senator Vandenberg, who had objected when a woman he viewed as utterly lacking in diplomatic experience had been appointed to the United Nations (he nominated her to the Third Committee because the group's tasks struck him as trivial), was now singing her praises. It was reported that at a Washington, DC, dinner party, Vandenberg told the guests, "I want to say that I take back everything I ever said about her, and believe me it's been plenty."[64]

"HOW MUCH DEMOCRACY DO WE WANT?"

Eleanor's position on racial, religious, and social justice was sharpened during World War II. The injustices perpetrated by the Nazis abroad highlighted the struggle for equal rights at home. The war and its aftermath also strengthened Eleanor's belief that a true democracy must be inclusive and that it must secure the rights and freedoms of all its citizens. In her view, full democracy had not yet been achieved. There was an ongoing struggle to include different segments of the population in the political process. But freedom and equality—the moral basis of democracy—were not simply a matter of political rights. People were discriminated against and had their opportunities limited for a variety of reasons, including race, religion, or economic status. In the excerpt below from her wartime analysis "The Moral Basis of Democracy" (1940), Eleanor emphasizes the importance of equal opportunities and economic security for the strength of democracy.

We are slowly climbing out of the economic morass we fell into, but so long as we have the number of unemployed on our hands which we have today, we can be sure that our economic troubles are not over, and that we have not found the permanent solution to our problem.

Either we must make our economic system work to the satisfaction of all of our people, or we are going to find it extremely difficult to compete against the one which will be set upon the Continent of Europe.

We hear a good deal of loose talk about going to war. As a matter of fact we are already in a war—an economic war, and a war of philosophies.

Here, in this country, it seems to me that as the strongest nation in the battle today, we have to take an account of just what our condition is: how much Democracy we have, and how much we want to have.

It is often said that we are free, and then sneeringly it is added: "free to starve if we wish." In some parts of our country, that is not idle jest. Moreover, no one can honestly claim that either the Indians or the Negroes of this country are free. These are obvious examples of conditions which are not compatible with the theory of

Democracy. We have poverty which enslaves, and racial prejudice which does the same. There are other racial and religious groups among us who labor under certain discriminations, not quite so difficult as those we impose on the Negroes and the Indians, but still sufficient to show we do not completely practice the Democratic way of life.

It is quite obvious that we do not practice a Christ-like way of living in our relationship to submerged people, and here again we see that a kind of religion which gives us a sense of obligation about living with a deeper interest in the welfare of our neighbors is an essential to the success of Democracy.

. . .

We are, of course, going through a type of revolution, and we are succeeding in bringing about a greater sense of social responsibility in the people as a whole. Through the recognition by our government of a responsibility for social conditions, much has been accomplished; but there is still much to be done before we are even prepared to accept some of the fundamental facts which will make it possible to fight as a unified nation against the new philosophies arrayed in opposition to Democracy.

It would seem clear that in a Democracy a minimum standard of security must at least be possible for every child in order to achieve the equality of opportunity which is one of the basic principles set forth as a fundamental of Democracy. This means achieving an economic level below which no one is permitted to fall, and keeping a fairly stable balance between that level and the cost of living. No one as yet seems to know just how to do this without an amount of planning which will be considered too restrictive for freedom. The line between domination and voluntary acquiescence in certain controls is a very difficult one to establish. Yet it is essential in a Democracy.[65]

CONNECTIONS

1. What, according the Eleanor, is the "moral basis of democracy"? What do you think of as the moral basis of democracy?

2. What is a minimum standard of economic security? Does providing a minimum standard of economic well-being come into conflict with freedom in a capitalist society?

3. In Eleanor's opinion, what is essential for a democracy to work? Why is economic safety vital? What are the "new philosophies arrayed in opposition to Democracy," and why are they important to consider in a discussion of America's economic philosophy?

4. Who is Eleanor's audience? What values does she emphasize to make her argument more persuasive? What does she mean by a "Christ-like way of living," and what is her goal in using this imagery?

THE "FOUR FREEDOMS" SPEECH

Shortly before President Roosevelt's State of the Union address was delivered on January 6, 1941, Eleanor published her first *My Day* column of the year. The essay anticipated many of the themes the president would address in his speech. Though hope was hard to entertain, she believed that many Americans would nevertheless find a ray of hope by working together toward the attainment of "peace with honor and justice for all."[66] She then mentioned the goals (or "freedoms," in Franklin's speech) for which she thought people would be inspired to fight: "Justice for all, security in certain living standards, a recognition of the dignity and the right of the individual human being, without regard to his race, creed, or color."[67]

> *I doubt if anyone will say a thoughtless "Happy New Year." They will know that happiness is hard to achieve in a world where war and famine and poverty and injustice still hold sway. Most of us will wish each other a "Happier New Year," vowing inwardly that whatever we can do to obtain peace with honor and justice for all, we will do in the future. In our own country and in our own lives, we will try to disassociate ourselves from our personal interests sufficiently to help bring about such things as seem to be of benefit to our whole people.*
>
> *Justice for all, security in certain living standards, a recognition of the dignity and the right of the individual human being, without regard to his race, creed, or color—these are things for which vast numbers of our citizens will willingly sacrifice themselves. Progress may be slow, but as more of us keep this determination in our minds and hearts, I feel sure we will be able to say, as we look back over each year, "This has been a Happier New Year."[68]*

Several days later, when FDR addressed the nation with his "four freedoms" speech, which is excerpted below, he presented a vision of a new world order founded on a quartet of essential freedoms: freedom of speech and expression, freedom of religion, freedom from want, and freedom from fear. The first two were already enshrined in the American Constitution. But the idea that every American should enjoy freedom from want, which went beyond the traditional political and civil rights granted to most Americans, grew out of the New Deal. The last item, freedom from fear, belongs to the same impulse that drove Franklin to dream up the United Nations. All four elements found expression in the Universal Declaration of Human Rights.

Annual Message to Congress

January 6, 1941

In the future days, which we seek to make secure, we look forward to a world founded upon four essential human freedoms.

The first is freedom of speech and expression—everywhere in the world.

The second is freedom of every person to worship God in his own way—everywhere in the world.

The third is freedom from want—which, translated into world terms, means economic understandings which will secure to every nation a healthy peacetime life for its inhabitants—everywhere in the world.

The fourth is freedom from fear—which, translated into world terms, means a worldwide reduction of armaments to such a point and in such a thorough fashion that no nation will be in a position to commit an act of physical aggression against any neighbor— anywhere in the world.

That is no vision of a distant millennium. It is a definite basis for the kind of world attainable in our own time and generation. That kind of world is the very antithesis of the so-called new order of tyranny, which the dictators seek to create with the crash of a bomb.

To that new order we oppose the greater conception—the moral order. A good society is able to face schemes of world domination and foreign revolutions alike without fear.

Since the beginning of our American history, we have been engaged in change—in a perpetual peaceful revolution—a revolution which goes on steadily, quietly adjusting itself to changing conditions— without the concentration camp or the quick-lime in the ditch. The world order which we seek is the cooperation of free countries, working together in a friendly, civilized society.

This nation has placed its destiny in the hands and heads and hearts of its millions of free men and women; and its faith in freedom under the guidance of God. Freedom means the supremacy of human rights everywhere. Our support goes to those who struggle to gain those rights or keep them. Our strength is our unity of purpose. To that high concept there can be no end save victory.[69]

CONNECTIONS

1. What are the basic principles that Eleanor and Franklin discuss? How are these ideas connected to human rights?

2. The "four freedoms" speech caught the imagination of many people. What do you think it was about Franklin Roosevelt's ideas that people responded to?

3. Why does Franklin emphasize the need for a new moral order? What is a moral order? What would be the foundations of that new moral order? What would it take to put his ideas into practice?

ELEANOR AND WARTIME RACE RIOTS

American factories that were converted to war production attracted tens of thousands of new workers, including many black men and women from the South who had been impoverished by the Great Depression. The greatest industrial center was Detroit, where the automobile industry was converted for the production of tanks, military vehicles, and ammunition. In 1941, under pressure from A. Philip Randolph and the Brotherhood of Sleeping Car Porters (which threatened a massive march on Washington, DC), the president banned all racial segregation in the defense industry. But blacks were not allowed to have apartments in government-built housing projects designed to accommodate Detroit's growing population. In the summer of 1943, race riots broke out in Detroit and other urban areas as white workers continued to resist the inclusion of blacks in booming wartime industries. Eleanor spoke out, calling herself "sick at heart" because of

> *race riots which put us on a par with Nazism which we fight, and make one tremble for what human beings may do when they no longer think, but let themselves be dominated by their worst emotions . . .*
>
> *We cannot settle strikes by refusing to understand their causes; we cannot prepare for a peaceful world unless we give proof of self-restraint, of open-mindedness, of courage to do right at home, even if it means changing our traditional thinking and, for some of us, a sacrifice of our material interests.*[70]

While President Roosevelt's Executive Order 8802 succeeded in opening factories to black workers, racial conflicts often flared up in neighborhoods where blacks were denied housing alongside whites, some escalating into citywide riots. Eleanor, by this date an outspoken supporter of desegregation, was accused of inciting the violence. The letter below from C. B. Alexander (1943) is one of the many she received during this time. In some ways, it is typical of racist thinking in mid–century America:

> *Mrs. Franklin D. Roosevelt,*
>
> *Hyde Park, N.Y.*
>
> *Dear Madam:*
>
> *In my humble opinion you are doing very much harm toward race riots when you advocate no discrimination in places of amusements*

and in vehicles of transportation. No doubt you well know that we have the "Jim Crow" law in the South which prohibits [N]egroes from settling in places with the white people. Your articles cause the [N]egro to think that he can set and ride in any place he chooses. When he places himself where he doesn't belong, he causes trouble.

We people of the South know the [N]egro; we know how to control him. We don't hate him, we don't persecute him, we treat him as well as he is treated anywhere, so long as he stays in his place, but it must be remembered that there are inferior people just as there are inferior animals. You know there are fine bred dogs, fine bred cattle, fine bred swine, etc.

When God made the world he made all kinds of people, and all kinds of animals; he also made all kinds of flowers, red, white, pink, etc. It takes all colors of everything to make a world. If he had intended the white and black people to mix, he would have made them all the same color.

When God made the world, he expected people to control themselves and all other animals on the face of the earth, but he made the fowls of the air to control themselves, as he knew that man could not control them. All fowls of the air choose their mates each spring from their own species; they never mix breed; it's their God-given instinct. Then why do the different races of people want to mix breed? They were given a brain to think with, but many of them don't have even an instinct.

It is association that causes LOVE among people; this is why the white and [N]egro marry in many states. You have a law prohibiting their association in vehicles of transportation, and in places of amusement, and this will eliminate many mixed marriages. I THINK THAT ANY STATE WHICH PERMITS THE MIXED MARRIAGE IS ROTTEN...

I do not believe in persecuting a mongrel dog. I will stop my car any time to save his life, but I would not take him home to breed with my Boston Bulldog. That is the way I feel about the [N]egro; he is an inferior race to the white race. Consult your encyclopedia, and you will find the outline of his skull and other features much different from the white man's...

In one of your recent articles in our local paper, you stated that you did not believe in mixed marriages; no decent white person believes in this, but you should have stated that there should be a Federal Law prohibiting these marriages.

All of we Southern people teach our children that they are superior to the [N]egro, but we also teach them to respect them and treat them like human beings, which they do. Naturally our children will teach their children likewise; hence the South will always be as she is today. Treat all human beings as you would like to be treated, but remember your blood.

Yours truly

C. B. Alexander,

Knoxville, Tenn.[71]

CONNECTIONS

1. Eleanor suggests that to get to the root cause of the race riots, some people may have to change their traditional thinking. What does she mean?

2. According to Alexander, why is Eleanor responsible for the race-riot violence? How might Eleanor respond to that accusation?

3. Alexander's letter mentions ideas and attitudes about racial superiority and inferiority that were influenced by eugenics, or race "science" (see Facing History and Ourselves, *Race and Membership in American History: The Eugenics Movement*), which ranked some races as superior and some races as inferior. How does Alexander's letter reflect these ideas? Where do you get your ideas about race? Where do you see legacies of racist thinking today?

4. What stereotypes do you see in Alexander's letter? Where do stereotypes come from? How are they used and abused?

5. How might you respond to a letter like this?

6. The American Heritage dictionary defines the term *racism* as follows: "1. The belief that race accounts for differences in human character or ability and that a particular race is superior to others. 2. Discrimination or prejudice based on race." How do you define racism? Why is racism a danger to democracy?

7. What should teachers consider when using historical documents, like this one, that express stereotypes about people?

THE ATLANTIC CHARTER

In August 1941, President Roosevelt and Prime Minister Churchill met secretly to establish guidelines for their postwar policies. Before America had even declared war on Germany, the two leaders spoke of peace as the way to a better world: they declared that they would not seek new territories and that they would respect the rights of people worldwide to choose their own governments. The document they drew up, called the Atlantic Charter, reiterated the need for international collaboration and listed several economic and social rights to be protected by this collaboration. The two leaders pledged to work toward a peaceful world where "all the men in all the lands may live out their lives in freedom from fear and want." When they spoke of the need to ensure the basic rights of "all the men in all the lands," they moved in a new direction. Instead of reinforcing the power of government, they gave the individual a voice. This was the first step on the long road to the Universal Declaration of Human Rights. The joint statement, known as the Atlantic Charter, signed by President Roosevelt and Prime Minister Churchill, follows.

> *The President of the United States of America and the Prime Minister, Mr. Churchill, representing His Majesty's Government in the United Kingdom, being met together, deem it right to make known certain common principles in the national policies of their respective countries on which they base their hopes for a better future for the world.*
>
> *First, their countries seek no aggrandizement, territorial or other.*
>
> *Second, they desire to see no territorial changes that do not accord with the freely expressed wishes of the peoples concerned.*
>
> *Third, they respect the right of all peoples to choose the form of government under which they will live; and they wish to see sovereign rights and self government restored to those who have been forcibly deprived of them.*
>
> *Fourth, they will endeavor, with due respect for their existing obligations, to further the enjoyment by all States, great or small, victor or vanquished, of access, on equal terms, to the trade and to the raw materials of the world, which are needed for their economic prosperity.*
>
> *Fifth, they desire to bring about the fullest collaboration between*

all nations in the economic field with the object of securing, for all, improved labor standards, economic advancement and social security.

Sixth, after the final destruction of the Nazi tyranny, they hope to see established a peace which will afford to all nations the means of dwelling in safety within their own boundaries, and which will afford assurance that all the men in all the lands may live out their lives in freedom from fear and want.

Seventh, such a peace should enable all men to traverse the high seas and oceans without hindrance.

Eighth, they believe that all of the nations of the world, for realistic as well as spiritual reasons, must come to the abandonment of the use of force. Since no future peace can be maintained if land, sea, or air armaments continue to be employed by nations which threaten, or may threaten, aggression outside of their frontiers, they believe, pending the establishment of a wider and permanent system of general security, that the disarmament of such nations is essential. They will likewise aid and encourage all other practicable measures which will lighten for peace-loving peoples the crushing burden of armaments.

Signed by: Franklin D. Roosevelt & Winston S. Churchill[72]

CONNECTIONS

1. What challenges did the world face in 1941? How did the issues confronted by Franklin Roosevelt and Winston Churchill contribute to the drafting of the Atlantic Charter?

2. What was Roosevelt and Churchill's vision for the postwar world? What obstacles do you think they faced in trying to fulfill their vision?

3. At the time this document was written, America had not yet entered World War II, and the United Kingdom had colonies in the West Indies, Africa, and Asia. What obligations did the leaders take upon themselves in writing the Atlantic Charter? How might their own nations' histories have influenced their ability to fulfill their vision for the postwar world?

4. The Atlantic Charter is the first document that ensures rights for people regardless of the state to which they belong. What does this suggest about the relationship between individual rights and state rights? Why might some people consider that an infringement on the idea of sovereignty?

5. The intention of the Atlantic Charter was to guarantee individual rights and prevent future war. As you read this document, what evidence do you find that supports this?

THE UNITED NATIONS CHARTER

Following the Tehran Conference (1943), where the Allied powers tentatively agreed to form the United Nations, representatives from China, the Soviet Union, the United Kingdom, and the United States met at a mansion called Dumbarton Oaks in Washington, DC. There they decided on the structure of the United Nations. This work continued in June 1945 when delegates from 50 nations met in San Francisco to finalize and sign the United Nations Charter, which went into effect in August of that year.

The preamble to the charter below can be read as a response to the two world wars and the "untold sorrow" they inflicted on humanity. Shortly after the charter went into effect and the United Nations was formed, Eleanor was put in charge of a group dedicated to delineating and codifying the "fundamental human rights" mentioned in the preamble. The Universal Declaration of Human Rights drew its inspiration and authority from this document.

Charter of the United Nations, Preamble, 1943

We the Peoples of the United Nations Determined

to save succeeding generations from the scourge of war, which twice in our lifetime has brought untold sorrow to mankind, and

to reaffirm faith in fundamental human rights, in the dignity and worth of the human person, in the equal rights of men and women and of nations large and small, and

to establish conditions under which justice and respect for the obligations arising from treaties and other sources of international law can be maintained, and

to promote social progress and better standards of life in larger freedom,

And for these Ends

to practice tolerance and live together in peace with one another as good neighbors, and

to unite our strength to maintain international peace and security, and

to ensure by the acceptance of principles and the institution of methods, that armed force shall not be used, save in the common interest, and to employ international machinery for the promotion of the economic and social advancement of all peoples,

Have Resolved to Combine our Efforts to Accomplish these Aims

Accordingly, our respective Governments, through representatives assembled in the city of San Francisco, who have exhibited their full powers found to be in good and due form, have agreed to the present Charter of the United Nations and do hereby establish an international organization to be known as the United Nations.[73]

CONNECTIONS

1. In what ways is this document a response to the atrocities of World War II? Are the values that the drafters of this charter emphasize timeless? How does this document try to inspire people to make peace?

2. Where did the ideas in the United Nations Charter come from? What makes the UN different from its failed predecessor, the League of Nations?

3. For many, the charter of the UN expresses both hope and idealism. What is the hope that it expresses? How wide is the gap between hope and reality?

4. Though its charter presents a series of idealistic goals and values, the United Nations has not always lived up to those goals and values. What would you use to measure both the successes and the failures of the United Nations?

5. Where do you see the impact of the United Nations in the world? Is that impact positive or negative?

"NATURALLY THEY WANT TO GO TO PALESTINE"

In the fall of 1945, while helping relief organizations prepare winter supplies for the displaced persons population in liberated Europe, Eleanor began to promote the idea of a homeland in Palestine for the Jewish Holocaust survivors.[74] She thought that they were "the greatest victims" of World War II, a fact that placed a special obligation on the United States and Britain (Palestine was still under British mandate, and so Britain could control, however reluctantly, how many Jews would be admitted there). In the *My Day* excerpt below, she explains her reasons.

There is in Europe at the present time a group of 100,000 displaced persons—the miserable, tortured, terrorized Jews who have seen members of their families murdered and their homes ruined, and who are stateless people, since they hate the Germans and no longer wish to live in the countries where they have been despoiled of all that makes life worth living. Naturally they want to go to Palestine, the one place where they will have a status, where they will feel again that sense of belonging to a community which gives most of us security.

President Truman has asked Great Britain for consideration of their condition, and permission for their admittance to Palestine. Prime Minister Attlee is said to be coming over the end of this month to discuss this and other matters with the President.

It seems to me urgent that these people be given permission to go to the home of their choice. They are the greatest victims of this war. We might as well face the fact that we may be asked to assume some responsibility; and, if so, we should be prepared to do it. Our consciences can hardly be clear when we read about and see the pictures of these emaciated, miserable people who suffer while we sit comfortably, and let them die at the rate of 50 per day—which is what is happening now, I am told.[75]

CONNECTIONS

1. What arguments does Eleanor use to support her position on a Jewish state for the victims of the Holocaust?

2. What does Eleanor mean that only in their own state will the Jews have "status"? A sense of belonging? Do you agree with her assessment? Do groups need their own states to develop their own sense of belonging?

3. After massive atrocities, what is necessary for a group to heal? What conditions might foster healing? What conditions might be an obstacle to healing?

4. The United States and Britain did not cause the destruction of the European Jewry. Why do you think that Eleanor felt that the United States should be ready to assume responsibility for the creation of a homeland for the Jewish refugees in Europe? What responsibility did the war place on the victors?

5. What is the responsibility of the international community when a group or a nation falls victim to genocide, as the Jews did in the Holocaust?

ELEANOR'S VISITS TO THE DISPLACED PERSONS CAMPS

Between February 13 and 16, 1946—ten months after American forces liberated Nazi concentration camps—Eleanor met some of the thousands of displaced Jews living in camps. These were some of the survivors of the concentration camps Germany had filled during the war. First, Eleanor visited the camp at Zeilsheim. It contained some 3,200 people and was located just outside Frankfurt, in an area controlled by the United States Army. When Eleanor spoke with the refugees, many expressed a longing to emigrate to Palestine. Two days after the visit, Eleanor reported her impressions in *My Day*, the daily newspaper column she wrote from 1935 until 1962. Through her *My Day* column and a series of speeches, Eleanor struggled to comprehend the suffering and perseverance of the survivors. In the excerpts below, she speaks of the survivors who had lost not just their belongings, but so much of what made them human: their physical appearance, their families, their liberties, and their hopes.

My visit to Frankfort was packed so full of emotions, it is hard to give you an adequate idea of what I saw and how I felt. Yesterday morning, we visited the Zeilsheim Jewish displaced persons camp. It is one of the best, since the people are living in houses previously occupied by Germans.[76]

In these houses, each little family has a room to itself. Often a family must cross a room occupied by another in order to enter or leave the house, but there are doors and walls to separate them. If they like, they may bring food from the camp kitchen to their rooms and eat in what they call "home."

They made me a speech at a monument they have erected to the six million dead Jewish people. I answered from an aching heart. When will our consciences grow so tender that we will act to prevent human misery, rather than avenge it?

Someone asked a man, who looked old but couldn't have been really old, about his family. This was his answer: "They were made into soap." They had been burned to death in a concentration camp.

Outside the school, the children greeted me. They told me a little boy of ten was the camp singer. He looked six. He had wandered into camp one day with his brother, all alone, so he was the head of his family. He sang for me—a song of his people—a song of freedom. Your heart cried out that there was no freedom—and where was hope, without which human beings cannot live?

There is a feeling of desperation and sorrow in this camp which seems beyond expression. An old woman knelt on the ground, grasping my knees. I lifted her up, but could not speak. What could one say at the end of a life which had brought her such complete despair?[77]

. . .

You can measure the extent of physical damage done to cities, you can restore water supplies, gas, and electricity, and you can rebuild the buildings needed to establish a military government. But how to gauge what has happened to human beings—that is incalculable.

The men and girls in the various services have a feeling of the problem, and the misery which exists all around them. . . . And, later, another soldier said to me: "I can't think why [Europeans] had to fight each other. The language is a bar; but while our customs are different, all over, we seem to have a lot of things that are just the same." That's really a great discovery—"all over we have a lot of things that are just the same.". . . Those are the things we have to find and build on, and those, I imagine, are the only things that can give us hope.[78]

On her return to United States, Eleanor spoke about her experience in the camps to a women's group in New York:

[T]he thing that I feel is not only the physical aspect, but something that I can only describe in this way: what would happen to us if suddenly we had no real right to appeal to a government of our own? . . . Even in the worst days of the Depression, when I went down into the mining areas, at least the people came to one and said, "We want our government to know." And they had the feeling that they had a right to tell their government . . .

I have the feeling that we let our consciences realize too late the need of standing up against something that we knew was wrong. We have therefore had to avenge it—but we did nothing to prevent it. I hope that in the future, we are going to remember that there can be no compromise at any point with the things that we know are wrong. . . . We cannot live in an island of prosperity in a sea of human misery. It just can't be done. . . .

But it is not just that. It is the feeling that there has been a crumbling of the thing that gives most of us a sense of security, the feeling that we have roots, and that—as bad as the situation may be—we have a government to which we can appeal, we have people who are representing us and who can speak for us.

Charity is a wonderful thing, but it does not give one that sense of security. What is important is rehabilitation. The sooner the study is made, and the sooner those people can be taken where they can become citizens and feel that they are actually building a new life, the better it will be for the whole world. . . .

That is the thing I should like to leave with you. I think the most important thing for us to realize is the great responsibility that lies upon our shoulders and the fact that we must give something beyond what we have ever given before in the world—something that is no longer for ourselves at all, but for humanity as a whole.[79]

CONNECTIONS

1. What does it mean to be a "displaced person"? What does it mean to be a refugee? When you are a refugee or a displaced person, to whom do you appeal?

2. Why is having the ability to appeal to a government important? In what ways can Americans appeal to their government, and how is this different from Nazi Germany?

3. In Eleanor's opinion, what is hope, and why is it important? What is the role of hope in democracy? How can civil rights help restore displaced people's hopes?

4. Eleanor asks, "When will our consciences grow so tender that we will act to prevent human misery rather than avenge it?" What does she mean? What is the difference between prevention and retribution? In your opinion, what would it take to prevent human misery?

5. What is charity? What is rehabilitation? How does Eleanor see the two as different? In Eleanor's opinion, why is charity not enough?

6. What does Eleanor mean when she says that we "must give something beyond what we have ever given before in the world"? What does it mean to give something "for humanity as a whole"?

[1] Eleanor Roosevelt, "Speech Before Women's Division of the United Jewish Appeal of Greater New York," in Allida M. Black, *The Eleanor Roosevelt Papers, Volume 1: The Human Rights Years, 1945–1948* (New York: Thomson Gale, 2007), 255–58.

[2] Charles M. Lamb, *Housing Segregation in Suburban America since 1960: Presidential and Judicial Politics* (Cambridge: Cambridge University Press, 2005), 27.

[3] Doris Kearns Goodwin, *No Ordinary Time: Franklin and Eleanor Roosevelt: The Home Front in World War II* (New York: Simon & Schuster, 1994), 247.

[4] "Educator Leon Bass Speaks at the 2008 Facing History Benefit Dinner," Facing History and Ourselves website, http://www.facinghistory.org/video/educator-leon-bass-speaks-2008-facing-histor (accessed April 9, 2009). Bass was among the American soldiers who entered the Buchenwald concentration camp in Germany after its liberation in April 1945. On encountering the unspeakable crimes committed there, he realized that the struggle against racism must be carried out everywhere.

[5] Eleanor Roosevelt, "The Moral Basis of Democracy" (1940), in *What I Hope to Leave Behind: The Essential Essays of Eleanor Roosevelt*, ed. Allida M. Black (New York: Carlson Publishing, 1995), 80.

[6] Allida M. Black, ed., *What I Hope to Leave Behind: The Essential Essays of Eleanor Roosevelt* (New York: Carlson Publishing, 1995), 250–51.

[7] I thank Elly Green for her suggestions and corrections in this section.

[8] C. B. Alexander (letter to Eleanor Roosevelt, August 17, 1943), ER Papers Misc 1943, Franklin D. Roosevelt Library. For similar letters, see Cathy D. Knepper, ed., *Dear Mrs. Roosevelt: Letters to Eleanor Roosevelt through Depression and War* (New York: Carroll & Graf, 2004), 326–30.

[9] Eleanor Roosevelt, *My Day* (column), July 14, 1943. The full text of Eleanor Roosevelt's *My Day* columns can be found at the Eleanor Roosevelt Papers Project website, http://www.gwu.edu/~erpapers/myday/.

[10] Ibid.

[11] Joseph Lash, *Eleanor and Franklin: The Story of their Relationship, Based on Eleanor Roosevelt's Private Papers* (New York: W. W. Norton & Company, 1971), 675, quoting a letter from Eleanor Roosevelt to himself from July 11, 1943.

[12] Roosevelt, *My Day*, January 1, 1941.

[13] Ibid.

[14] "Universal Declaration of Human Rights Preamble," United Nations website, http://www.un.org/en/documents/udhr/index.shtml#ap (accessed August 14, 2009).

[15] Mary Ann Glendon, *A World Made New: Eleanor Roosevelt and the Universal Declaration of Human Rights* (New York: Random House, 2002), 4.

[16] Eleanor Roosevelt, "Albert Hall Speech: January 17, 1946," in *The Eleanor Roosevelt Papers*, ed. Black, 216.

[17] Elizabeth Borgwardt, *A New Deal for the World: America's Vision for Human Rights* (Cambridge: Harvard University Press, 2005), 4.

[18] "Text of the Atlantic Charter," Social Security Online, http://www.ssa.gov/history/acharter2.html (accessed August 14, 2009).

[19] Borgwardt, *A New Deal for the World*, 4.

[20] "Dumbarton Oaks and Yalta," the United Nations website, http://www.un.org/aboutun/charter/history/dumbarton.shtml (accessed on February 11, 2009).

[21] Eleanor Roosevelt, *The Autobiography of Eleanor Roosevelt* (USA: First Da Capo Press, 1992), 276.

22 Truman was especially interested in associating his new administration with Eleanor because of "her influence with Negro voters." See Joseph P. Lash, *Eleanor: The Years Alone* (New York: W. W. Norton & Company, 1972), 26.

23 Roosevelt, *Autobiography*, 299.

24 Roosevelt, *My Day*, May 2, 1945.

25 See, for example, letter from Eleanor Roosevelt to Harry S. Truman, August 12, 1959, Post-Presidential Files, Harry S. Truman Papers, Truman Library, http://www.trumanlibrary.org/eleanor/eleanordoctemplate.php?documentid=hst19590812&pagenumber=1 (accessed December 29, 2008).

26 Lash, *Eleanor: The Years Alone*, 29.

27 Roosevelt, *My Day*, December 22, 1945.

28 Ibid. Wendell Willkie, who ran against FDR in the 1940 election, later joined FDR as special ambassador to the world and as an advocate for war policies. In 1943, he published a book describing his goodwill travels and his plea for a united world after the war.

29 Eleanor Roosevelt, "Address by Eleanor Roosevelt to the Women's Joint Congressional Committee," in *The Eleanor Roosevelt Papers*, ed. Black, 274.

30 Roosevelt, *My Day*, May 7, 1946.

31 Lash, *Eleanor: The Years Alone*, 38.

32 Roosevelt, *Autobiography*, 302–03. The Third Committee was one of seven committees set up to deal with specific global issues, including legal, economic, and political matters.

33 Ibid., 302.

34 Ibid., 299.

35 A quote from the chief tormenter of Joan of Arc in George Bernard Shaw's *Saint Joan*. "Only by seeing we save ourselves from ignorance and from our own complacency," Eleanor said to her biographer and friend Joseph Lash (Lash, *Eleanor and Franklin*, 522).

36 Lash, *Eleanor and Franklin*, 522.

37 Edward Bliss, Jr., ed., *In Search of Light: The Broadcasts of Edward R. Murrow, 1939–1961* (New York: Alfred A. Knopf, 1967), 90–95.

38 Roosevelt, *My Day*, February 16, 1946. Emphasis added.

39 Eleanor Roosevelt, "Memorandum of Press Conference Held by Mrs. Eleanor Roosevelt," in *The Eleanor Roosevelt Papers*, ed. Black, 182.

40 Eleanor Roosevelt, "Address by Eleanor Roosevelt to the Women's Joint Congressional Committee," in *The Eleanor Roosevelt Papers*, ed. Black, 275.

41 Roosevelt, *My Day*, February 18, 1946.

42 Eleanor Roosevelt, "Speech before Women's Division of the United Jewish Appeal of Greater New York," in *The Eleanor Roosevelt Papers*, ed. Black, 258.

43 Ibid., 258.

44 Ibid., 255.

45 Roosevelt, *My Day*, February 16, 1946.

46 Dan Eshet, *Totally Unofficial: Raphael Lemkin and the Genocide Convention* (Brookline: Facing History and Ourselves National Foundation, 2007).

47 Address by Robert H. Jackson at the United Nations, April 15, 1947, St. John's University website, http://www.stjohns.edu/media/3/55b0a1b3050a46768c6647abc43ddb15.pdf (accessed August 25, 2009).

48 Quoted in John Q. Barrett, "The Unfinished Business of Humanity" (1947) (self-published paper, 2008), 3; Robert H. Jackson Papers, Library of Congress, Manuscript Division (Washington, DC, Box 44, Folder 10), 13.

49 Eleanor Roosevelt, "Speech before Women's Division of the United Jewish Appeal of Greater New York," in *The Eleanor Roosevelt Papers*, ed. Black, 258.

50 Black et al., *The Eleanor Roosevelt Papers*, 188.

[51] Roosevelt, "Speech before United Nations General Assembly 30th Plenary Session, February 12, 1946," in *The Eleanor Roosevelt Papers*, ed. Black, 246–48.

[52] Mary Ann Glendon, "Eleanor Roosevelt and the Universal Declaration of Human Rights," U.S. Diplomatic Mission to the United Nations in Geneva website, http://geneva.usmission.gov/graphics/2008/ERooseveltBook.pdf, 7 (accessed July 19, 2009).

[53] Black et al., *The Eleanor Roosevelt Papers*, 247.

[54] "Letter from Eleanor Roosevelt to Joseph Lash, February 13, 1946," in *The Eleanor Roosevelt Papers*, ed. Black, 28.

[55] When Polish Jews returned to their hometown of Kielce, Poland, 42 were massacred and more than 50 wounded by the local population. See the United States Holocaust Memorial Museum website, http://www.ushmm.org/wlc/article.php?lang=en&ModuleId=10005366 (accessed August 25, 2009).

[56] Roosevelt, *My Day*, November 7, 1945.

[57] Ibid.

[58] Roosevelt, *Autobiography*, 310.

[59] Eleanor Roosevelt, "The Universal Validity of Man's Right to Self-Determination" (1952), in *What I Hope to Leave Behind*, 603.

[60] Eleanor Roosevelt, "Speech before Women's Division of the United Jewish Appeal of Greater New York, February 20, 1946," in *The Eleanor Roosevelt Papers*, ed. Black, 258.

[61] The idea for a declaration of human rights would ultimately emerge from this small, temporary committee, which was to be replaced by the permanent Human Rights Commission in January 1947.

[62] Eleanor Roosevelt, *On My Own* (New York: Harper, 1958), 60.

[63] Roosevelt, *Autobiography*, 299–300.

[64] Lash, *Eleanor: The Years Alone*, 47. Cf. Eleanor Roosevelt to Joseph Lash, February 13, 1946, in *The Eleanor Roosevelt Papers*, ed. Black, 247–49.

[65] Roosevelt, "The Moral Basis of Democracy," in *What I Hope to Leave Behind*, 80–81.

[66] Roosevelt, *My Day*, January 1, 1941.

[67] Ibid.

[68] Ibid.

[69] Franklin D. Roosevelt, "Annual Message to Congress: The Four Freedoms Speech," January 6, 1941, Franklin D. Roosevelt Presidential Library and Museum website, (accessed April 6, 2009).

[70] Roosevelt, *My Day*, July 14, 1943.

[71] C. B. Alexander (letter to Eleanor Roosevelt, August 17, 1943), ER Papers Misc 1943, Franklin D. Roosevelt Library. For similar letters, see Cathy D. Knepper, ed., *Dear Mrs. Roosevelt: Letters to Eleanor Roosevelt through Depression and War* (New York: Carroll & Graf, 2004), 326–30.

[72] "Atlantic Charter," Yale Law School: the Avalon Project website, http://avalon.law.yale.edu/wwii/atlantic.asp (accessed August 14, 2009).

[73] "Charter of the United Nations Preamble," United Nations High Commission for Human Rights website, http://www.unhcr.ch/html/menu3/b/ch-pream.htm (accessed March 4, 2009).

[74] Black et al., *The Eleanor Roosevelt Papers*, 134–35.

[75] Roosevelt, *My Day*, November 7, 1945.

[76] In other camps, for example, survivors and refugees occupied barracks formerly used by Nazi detainees.

[77] Roosevelt, *My Day*, February 16, 1946.

[78] Roosevelt, *My Day*, February 18, 1946.

[79] Eleanor Roosevelt, "Speech before Women's Division of the United Jewish Appeal of Greater New York," in *The Eleanor Roosevelt Papers*, ed. Black, 255–58.

*[L]ack of standards for human
rights the world over was one
of the greatest causes of friction
among the nations, and that
recognition of human rights might
become one of the cornerstones
[on] which peace could eventually
be based.[1]*

– Eleanor Roosevelt, 1948

UNDERTAKING A NEW MISSION

In the spring of 1946, the newly formed "nuclear" committee began holding meetings in a room at New York's Hunter College. The group had been asked to outline the composition and agenda of a commission that would address human rights issues around the world. This idea—that a set of moral principles put on paper could ensure world peace—would guide Eleanor's work on human rights through the next two and a half years.

She and the committee quickly decided that the Human Rights Commission would proceed toward the goal of a declaration of rights in three stages. First, the commission would draft a preliminary, or nonbinding, declaration to promote consensus; then it would present a draft of a binding agreement, to be signed by all United Nations member states; finally, the commission would lay out how the rights listed in the treaty could be protected.[2]

"We also finally recommended," Eleanor recalled, "that the Human Rights Commission be composed of eighteen members, each of whom would represent one of the United Nations governments." The purpose of this change was to give many more countries the ability to influence the UN debates on human rights. The committee agreed that, as with the Security Council, five of the eighteen member states would be the great powers that had emerged from World War II—the United Kingdom, France, China, the Union of Soviet Socialist Republics, and the United States—and the balance of the seats would rotate. Eleanor would serve as chairwoman of the commission. The vice chairman was the Chinese delegate Zhang Peng. Charles Malik, the delegate from Lebanon, assumed a secretarial function and was known as the *rapporteur*. The group was assisted by John P. Humphrey, the director of the UN Secretariat's human rights division.[3]

As meetings began in January 1947, the commission set out to outline the predecessor to the Universal Declaration of Human Rights, then called the International Bill of Rights. The Declaration would answer one deceptively simple question: what rights should belong to every human being on earth?

To arrive at an answer, something like a small miracle would be necessary. The world had shifted over the course of World War II, and although the United States and the Union of Soviet Socialist Republics (the Soviet Union) were allies during the war, these former partners retreated to their corners and glowered once the common enemy of Germany was defeated. The world was divided between the capitalists and the socialists—and few could resist the pressure to choose a side.

The idea that a group of 18 representatives could come up with a moral code that would apply to everyone at a time when the globe appeared to be increasingly divided would have struck many as naïve. Yet because the commission was chaired by a master of behind-the-scenes negotiation, the goal stood a chance of being achieved. The Lebanese delegate Charles Malik made clear how important basic definitions would be:

> *Since you cannot promote what remains vague and undefined, the preliminary function of the Commission must be the precise definition of these rights. This is why the Economic and Social Council has asked it first to draw up the Bill of Human Rights. The present task of the Commission is therefore to give content and meaning to the pregnant phrase in the preamble of the Charter, "the worth and dignity of man." What is the worth of man? What constitutes his proper dignity? These are the basic initial challenges which the Commission on Human Rights must try to meet.*[4]

INDIVIDUAL AND SOCIETY

The delegates to the Human Rights Commission began with the single question of which to consider paramount: society or the individual. The ensuing debate revealed two fundamentally different views about the relationship between the individual, society, and the state.

To get a sense of what its task would involve, the commission reviewed many constitutions and legal treaties. In addition to the United States' Declaration of Independence and Bill of Rights, the commission examined the Atlantic Charter, speeches by Franklin Roosevelt, and similar wartime documents. To widen its perspective on individual and political rights, the group reviewed documents from Latin American countries, noting a series of differences from the European tradition.[5] The commission also reviewed the International Labor Organization's Declaration Concerning Aims and Purposes (1944), which included many provisions for the protection of working people. The group found that some countries were more committed than others to providing guarantees against unemployment, discrimination and exploitation in the workplace, child labor, and the sudden loss of income at retirement.[6]

The original caption for this political cartoon satirically states: Mrs. Roosevelt, to her class on human rights: "Now, children, all together: 'The rights of the individual are above the rights of the state.'"

Late in January 1947, the Yugoslav delegate, Vladislav Ribnikar, presented the Communist position.[7] (By this time, the Soviet Union had established firm dominance over Czechoslovakia, Byelorussia, Ukraine, and Yugoslavia; together, the five states were known as the Soviet Bloc.) Each of the declarations, codes, and bills the committee had reviewed, Ribnikar declared, reflected "middle class" values. According to classic socialist theory, to which all the delegates from the Soviet Bloc generally subscribed, capitalist countries adopted constitutions that favored the middle classes and exploited the working class. Socialists argued that all of the rhetoric about idealized individualism served to conceal oppression of the poor. Western individualism, they held, also unleashed unprecedented selfish competition and allowed a few individuals to amass huge fortunes while others were doomed to poverty. For the members of the Soviet Bloc, individualism did not promote social harmony; rather, it caused conflicts between society's competing elements and led to the abuse of human rights.

Claiming to represent all working people, the Soviet Bloc commissioners argued that they could not accept the individualistic assumptions made by the authors of the documents they reviewed. People rarely acted independently of others, they said, and, in fact, lives were largely determined by social class. Furthermore, Ribnikar continued, true liberty depended on "perfect harmony between the individual and the community." Only when individual interests were reconciled by the state could workers be protected from economic turmoil and competition, permitting them to achieve their full potential.[8]

The discussion was picked up a few days later at Lake Success, New York. Valentin Tepliakov, the member representing the USSR, reminded his colleagues of the socialist view: "One thing I would like you to keep in mind: at least I am right when I speak about the people of the Soviet Union; there are two hundred million people living and enjoying human rights, as they were proclaimed in [our] Constitution. Our principle . . . is that we cannot divide the individual from the society, from the group, the community."[9] If the people all shared in the project of creating a worker's paradise, then their group identity would serve as their guarantee of individual rights: the state and society were one and the same.

Malik, who believed that the individual is born, at least in principle, with a number of natural rights, challenged the "collectivist" view:

> The "human person" [comes before] any group to which he
> may belong, whether it be class, race, or nation; his "mind and
> conscience" were the "most sacred and inviolable things about
> him"; the group can be wrong, just as the individual can be.[10]

He would later add: "I'm not arbitrarily setting the state against the individual. But which, I ask, is for which? I say that the state is for the individual."[11] The danger is that the individual's mind, creativity, expression, and freedoms could be subsumed by the collective. The collectivist approach, he felt, granted the state the power of "snuffing out any real personal liberty."[12]

Malik's worries were not baseless. National Socialism, the ideology behind the Nazi regime (1933–1945), had called for individuals to sacrifice all their personal ambitions for the goals of the nation. The Nazis then violently suppressed any form of dissent and opposition. Hundreds of thousands of communists, socialists, and others dissidents died in Hitler's concentration camps. The Soviet Union, a government driven by totalitarian ideas, was guilty of similar crimes. Since the communist revolution of 1917, tens of millions had been imprisoned without trials, and millions more had died in a prolonged civil war that the regime conducted against its enemies, real and imagined, and in penal labor camps called gulags.

The clash between the Soviet Bloc delegates and those from Western democracies pushed a series of questions to the forefront. Are communities and social interaction crucial to the fulfillment of human potential? Does true freedom mean complete independence from others, or do humans thrive in collaboration with each other? The British delegate, a leftist named Charles Dukes, argued that

> *[t]here is no such thing as complete personal freedom. . . . If freedom*
> *or complete detachment from society were possible it would provide*
> *for a very poor life indeed. We must all pay the price for advantages*
> *resulting from [asking] the state to safeguard our liberties both*
> *in the sense of personal freedoms, and also in the direction of a*
> *minimum degree of economic security.*[13]

It was at this juncture that René Cassin jumped in. A French Jew who lost 29 members of his family in the Holocaust, Cassin became a legal consultant to the exiled French government during the war; later, he led the rebuilding of France's administrative system. His experience as the French delegate to the League of Nations made him a great asset to the Human Rights Commission. To accommodate two seemingly incompatible positions, he proposed a nuanced definition of the human being: "The human being is above all a social creature whose life and development and whose progress have been made possible only because he could lean on his neighbors." At the same time, only real freedom could give man "his value and dignity."[14]

Eleanor also took a conciliatory stand on the relationship between the individual and society:

> *Many of us believe that an organized society, in the form of a*
> *government, exists for the good of the individual; others believe*
> *that an organized society in the form of a government, exists for*
> *the benefit of a group. We may not have to decide this particular*
> *point, but I think we do have to make sure, in writing a bill of*
> *human rights, that we safeguard the fundamental freedoms of*
> *the individual. If you do not do that, in the long run, it seems to*
> *me, that you run the risk of having certain conditions which we*
> *have just tried to prevent at great cost to human life, paramount in*
> *various groups.*[15]

JANUARY 1946:

The first meeting of the Economic and Social Council is held.

The Economic and Social Council creates the "Nuclear Commission" to plan a permanent Human Rights Commission (London).

JANUARY 1947:

The first meeting of the full Human Rights Commission (HRC) is held.

The HRC names a drafting committee (Lake Success, NY).

JUNE 1947:

Drafting committee meets to create International Bill of Rights.

DECEMBER 1947:

The second full HRC meeting is held (Geneva); it breaks into three groups with the assignment of creating proposal for the Human Rights Declaration, covenant, and implementation.

MAY 1948:

The drafting committee meets for the last time in preparation for the full commission's meeting later that month.

The third and last full HRC meeting takes place to prepare the final draft.

DECEMBER 1948:

The General Assembly of the United Nations deliberates and adopts the Universal Declaration of Human Rights (December 10).

A TEA PARTY WITH A THEME: HOW UNIVERSAL IS UNIVERSAL?

The end of the Human Rights Commission's first session marked the beginning of work to draft an International Bill of Rights (February 1947). "Thinking that our work might be helped by an informal atmosphere," Eleanor recalled in her autobiography, "I asked a small group to meet in my apartment for tea." Chinese representative P. C. Chang, John Humphrey, a Canadian who also served as the permanent head of the United Nations Division of Human Rights, and Charles Malik of Lebanon comprised the group.

That night, in Eleanor's apartment, the discussion between the learned members became more abstract and philosophical, and Eleanor, amused, sat back and enjoyed the exchange. Humphrey later wrote that

> *Chang and Malik were too far apart in their philosophical approaches to be able to work together on a text. There was a great deal of talk, but we were getting nowhere. Then, after still another cup of tea, Chang suggested that I put my other duties aside for six months and study Chinese philosophy . . . [which] was his way of saying that Western influence might be too great, and he was looking at Malik as he spoke. There was some more discussion mainly of a philosophical character, Mrs. Roosevelt saying little and continuing to pour tea.[16]*

Rather than start a Confucian study group, it was decided that Humphrey would write a draft for the commission to discuss. Fluent in both Anglo-Saxon

Eleanor and Dr. P. C. Chang of China at the first session of the Drafting Committee on the International Bill of Rights at Lake Success, New York, on June 9, 1947.

and French legal traditions, and well versed in civil and common law, Humphrey and his staff were prepared to tackle this task. But they still had much to learn, and they embarked on a study of "all the world's existing constitutions and rights instruments, as well as suggestions that had poured in to the Secretariat from members of the Commission, outside organizations, and even from various interested individuals."[17]

Their work mirrored a concurrent study being conducted by the United Nations Educational, Scientific, and Cultural Organization (UNESCO). In June 1947, UNESCO set up a Committee on the Theoretical Bases of Human Rights to study the world's cultures, sending questionnaires to experts around the globe. Replies from scholars, philosophers, and political activists indicated that some rights were protected by all cultures. For example, a Confucian philosopher named Lo Zhongshu wrote:

> [t]he problem of human rights was seldom discussed by Chinese thinkers of the past, at least in the same way as it was in the West. There was no open declaration of rights in China, either by individual thinkers or by political constitutions, until this conception was introduced from the West. . . . [However], the idea of human rights developed very early in China. . . . A great Confucianist, Mencius (372–289 BC), strongly maintained that a government should work for the will of the people. He said: "The people are of primary importance. The [ruler] of least importance."[18]

Similarly, the Bengali Muslim poet Humayun Kabir argued that early Islam had "succeeded in overcoming distinction of race and color to an extent experienced neither before nor after." (According to Kabir, Western ideas about human rights had suffered from a gap between grand notions and less-than-grand practices.)[19]

While few challenged the UNESCO study's basic conclusion that the idea of human rights was universal, criticisms quickly arose. What was the basis for human rights? When and how did the concept of human rights originate? Some critics of the document began to suggest that any search for universal traits would obscure the diversity of cultures around the world.

It turned out that many anthropologists, and particularly the American Anthropological Association, feared that any discussion of human values would tend to be dominated by Western ideas, to the detriment of smaller and more

WHO WAS PENG-CHUN CHANG (ZHANG PENJUN)?

Chang served as a delegate of China and vice-chairman of the HRC during the drafting of the Declaration. A philosopher, playwright, and diplomat, Chang helped bridge conflicting views of human rights.

Peng-chun Chang represented China in the United Nations during the negotiation of the Declaration. Born in China in 1892, Chang was a playwright, educator, musician, and philosopher. He was educated in his home country, and in 1910 he traveled to the United States and attended Clark University in Worcester, Massachusetts, as an undergraduate student. He went on to study at Columbia University, where he eventually completed his doctoral degree under the supervision of progressive philosopher John Dewey. Chang made a name for himself as an expert on Confucianism and through his dramatic writings and productions. Before his selection for the Chinese delegation to the United Nations, he served as a diplomat in Turkey, Chile, and England. In his diplomatic career, he displayed a deep curiosity about the world's cultures and an almost "missionary zeal to promote understanding of Chinese culture abroad."

When the United Nations set up the Commission on Human Rights and its members elected Eleanor as the commission's chairperson, the organization also chose Chang as the vice-chairman. Well versed in both Asian and Western philosophy, Chung was able to bridge cultural gaps between various members of the commission. He promoted the Chinese idea of ren, or "two-man mindedness," which can be translated as sympathy or the understanding of another person's point of view without giving up on one's own.

Chang, who believed that the Declaration should be a unifying tool for the world's diverse cultures, proved a savvy negotiator. Drawing on his knowledge of Chinese philosophy, he often helped conflicting parties reach a satisfactory compromise, and in doing so, he greatly helped the Human Rights Commission complete its mission. Chang remained on the Chinese delegation during the communist takeover of the Chinese mainland and the establishment of the communist People's Republic of China. He retired from his work at the United Nations in 1952 and died in 1957.

vulnerable cultures. In their 1947 Statement on Human Rights, the association offered the following thought:

> *Because of the great number of societies that are in intimate contact*
> *in the modern world, and because of the diversity of their ways*
> *of life, the primary task confronting those who would draw up a*
> *Declaration on the Rights of Man is thus, in essence, to resolve the*
> *following problem: how can the proposed Declaration be applicable*
> *to all human beings, and not be a statement of rights conceived only*
> *in terms of the values prevalent in the countries of Western Europe*
> *and America?[20]*

For good reason, the American Anthropological Association suspected that the Declaration would be used by Western nations to justify colonialism. For centuries, the Europeans and Americans dominated Latin American, Asian, and African nations, imposing colonial and semi-colonial arrangements that injured local cultures. The association's report stated:

> *Definitions of freedom, concepts of the nature of human rights, and*
> *the like, have . . . been narrowly drawn. Alternatives have been*
> *decried, and suppressed where controls have been established over*
> *non-European peoples. . . . The consequences of this point of view*
> *have been disastrous for mankind. Doctrines of the "white man's*
> *burden"[21] have been employed to implement economic exploitation,*
> *and to deny the right to control their own affairs to millions of*
> *peoples over the world, where the expansion of Europe and America*
> *has not meant the literal extermination of whole populations.[22]*

The alleged inferiority of non-Western groups permitted colonialists to present themselves as benevolent guardians, a convenient fiction backed up by a dubious science known as eugenics. This hugely influential set of ideas about racial hierarchies was studied by schoolchildren from San Francisco to Prague, and many of the leading scientists of the day endorsed it.[23] Rather than embracing the unity of mankind, eugenics presented a picture of irreconcilable differences. Based on poor science and prejudices, those who believed the principles of eugenics imagined that some races were superior to others, at times resulting in violence against those deemed inferior. This outlook contributed to a worldview that divided humanity along lines of class, race, and ethnicity.

The anthropologists' statement explained that while all cultures confront similar challenges, "no two of them, however, do so in exactly the same way, and some of them employ means that differ, often strikingly, from one another."[24] Such striking differences should not be the basis for enmity or intolerance, but rather for an appreciation of the need to value all cultures equally.[25]

If the American Anthropological Association was correct, and human values depended on very specific cultural characteristics, could there ever be a universal human right? The association's response was that

> [o]nly when a statement of the right of men to live in terms of their own traditions is incorporated into the proposed Declaration...can the next step of defining the rights and duties of human groups as regards each other be set upon the firm foundation of the present-day scientific knowledge of Man.[26]

This concept that all ideas are of equal value, or cultural relativism, had won over many progressive thinkers in the 1920s and 1930s. Such an idea challenged the mission of Eleanor and her colleagues, since "standards and values are *relative* to the culture from which they derive." If the "beliefs or moral codes of one culture must to that extent detract from the applicability of any Declaration of Human Rights to mankind as a whole," then the commission might encounter a basic contradiction between respect for individual cultures and the search for overarching universal traits.[27]

However powerful these arguments were, World War II and the Holocaust had shown the danger of accepting one group's claim to superiority over others. Many held that in the aftermath of such events, the need to protect what individuals did share trumped the safeguarding of differences between cultures. Critics of the American Anthropological Association argued that at a time when the future of human civilization itself was threatened, the organization's position (known commonly as relativism) was untenable. In other words, cultural differences could be tolerated but not necessarily glorified, especially when they denied individuals' basic rights or threatened the life of groups and individuals.

In December 1948, a lively debate about this issue began as the Third Committee reviewed the Human Rights Commission's preliminary draft. The Chilean delegate, who had ceaselessly championed the rights of the poor, took on the role of mediator. Hernan Santa Cruz, a progressive judge, had previously presented Humphrey with his government's version of a human rights bill, but he was now working hard to bridge his colleagues' views.

The delegate from Uruguay held up the discussion, leveling objection after objection. Eleanor appealed to Santa Cruz, hoping he might convey to the Uruguayan delegate the importance of the Declaration. Santa Cruz "looked at me," she recalled, and he said,

> *"I have been on the Human Rights Committee for quite some time and have become accustomed to this document, and you must let him become accustomed to it because it is an Anglo-Saxon document."*

> *"But," I protested, "It is the result of eighteen nations and they were not all Anglo-Saxon nations."*

> *He insisted, "It is still an Anglo-Saxon document. In time, the delegate from Uruguay will grow accustomed to it, but just now he is very much shocked, just as I was when I first read it."*[28]

This conversation troubled Eleanor. It had never occurred to her that so many negotiations and compromises could produce a document that was one-sided. A veil had been pulled aside, and she saw that her fellow delegates had often felt left out of the discussions. It was imperative, she wrote, that "we should become accustomed to thinking in their terms, as well as having them thinking in our terms." This idea sat well with her vision of an international body designed to keep war at bay: "That flow backwards and forwards of ideas and understanding," she reflected, "is one of the great contributions of the United Nations."[29] She expressed this again years later, in a reflection on the labor involved in reconciling different perspectives:

> *Producing a meeting of the minds on what these rights ought to be was most difficult. That which a country or an individual considers a fundamental right depends much upon the history of freedom in that country, on the stage of political, economic, and social development, and on the political, economic, and social conditions of the moment. The Czarist Government of Russia failed to develop economic prosperity or social equality among the masses of people; it is not unnatural that Communist Russia should emphasize*

economic and social rights provided by the State. Our own experience was quite different: oppressed American Colonists formed a nation in which the emphasis was on individual rights with a minimum of government.[30]

Eleanor, in other words, argued that differences in human values reflected stages in society's struggle to achieve freedom and prosperity. In the course of these struggles, each society or culture tends to highlight or give priority to the rights it deems most important; however, in most cases, the goals remained largely the same. Framing the debate in terms of history and priorities allowed Eleanor much more flexibility and inclusiveness. After all, these were debates about emphasis, not about fundamental differences.

BEYOND NATIONAL SOVEREIGNTY: HOW TO PROTECT CITIZENS FROM THEIR OWN GOVERNMENT

To make the work more efficient, a smaller group immediately set to work on Humphrey's draft, a set of 48 articles that became known as the Humphrey Draft.[31] The drafting committee met for the first time in June 1947, and its first task was whittling down Humphrey's long list to something the permanent Human Rights Commission would approve.[32]

Not all issues were easily resolved. Consider, for instance, the right to freedom of movement. Those who live under democratic governments take for granted their ability to choose where to live, a freedom that also facilitates the movement of workers according to market shifts. But for the USSR delegate, Vladimir M. Koretsky, the inclusion of such a right would undermine a command economy, in which the state decided how labor was assigned. More importantly, telling workers they had a right to move from place to place as they wished, he argued, interfered with the principle of national sovereignty. In other words, it amounted to telling a sovereign state what to do inside its own borders, which he adamantly rejected. While national sovereignty in its ideal form was designed to protect the right of every nation to choose its own destiny, many states committed crimes against their citizens while essentially telling other states to mind their own business.

Still later, when the full Human Rights Commission met for the second time in Geneva late in November 1947, the idea of creating a United Nations

International Court of Human Rights upset those who feared that the human rights project would unsettle the authority of the states. The Yugoslav delegate, Ribnikar, warned against attempting to make the United Nations a world government that superseded national sovereignty.[33]

Humphrey later reflected that the Soviet delegate's complaints "had, of course, hit the nail right on the head. One purpose of both drafts was to protect individuals from their governments. If the protection of human rights did not mean that, it did not mean much." The struggle for human rights, he stressed, "has always been and always will be, a struggle against authority."[34]

Recent events had left no question that the power of the state had to be curbed. As Raphael Lemkin proved in his furious attempts to outlaw genocide and racial violence, the Nazis had not violated existing international laws when they stripped Jews of citizenship, confiscated their property, and sent them to concentration camps.[35] Even the prosecutors at the postwar Nuremburg trials, who worked with outdated international laws, were only able to determine that Nazi officials violated international law with the invasion of Poland and the outbreak of the war. So when USSR delegate Vladimir M. Koretsky complained that the commission threatened to interfere with the power of sovereign states, René Cassin's reply was sharp:

> I must state my thoughts very frankly: the right of interference is here; it is in the [United Nations] Charter . . . Why? Because we do not want a repetition of what happened in 1933, [when] Germany began to massacre its own nationals, and everybody . . . bowed, saying "Thou art sovereign and master in thine own house."[36]

This would remain the most sensitive question addressed by the commission. Even once the Universal Declaration of Human Rights was adopted, getting states to comply with its requirements would often prove impossible. Many states resisted, and eventually killed, efforts to monitor their human rights records. But what was the point of toiling over international agreements if the signatories all preserved the final say on human rights within their borders? Can internationalism mean anything if no one is willing to surrender some authority to the group?

CIVIL RIGHTS AS HUMAN RIGHTS

While the Human Rights Commission worked on drafting the Declaration, some of those leading the struggle for civil rights in America believed that bringing the case of segregation in America before the United Nations would help draw international attention to their plight. They felt that a change in terminology—from "civil rights" to "human rights"—would align their struggle with that of other oppressed groups and colonized nations around the world. They hoped that the shift would bring pressure on the United States to live up to the ideals and freedoms inscribed in the American Constitution.

Nearly one million black men and women served in World War II, many of whom believed that wartime patriotism would earn them full parity with white Americans upon their return. They also hoped that the struggle to defeat Nazi racism would transform racism on American soil. They were wrong on both counts.

> *During the war, blacks began more forcefully to demand their citizenship rights. . . . Weary of Jim Crow indignities, many Southern blacks refused to be segregated any longer on streetcars and buses, stood their ground when challenged, and thus provoked almost daily racial altercations. Blacks became less compliant with conventional rules of racial etiquette, finding small but symbolic ways to challenge the racial status quo. Black soldiers, frustrated by the constant racial abuse they suffered, began fighting back; the result was much interracial violence and many deaths.*[37]

The huge industrial boom, precipitated by military production, failed to benefit many black workers and factory owners. In the military, only a few black soldiers were allowed to assume combat roles or become officers. Enough was enough. Roosevelt's Executive Order 8802 (see Part II), which banned government contractors from discriminating according to race, religion, or national origin, made a big difference. Within three years, two million blacks were reportedly working in the defense industry.[38] Extraordinary as this presidential move was, however, the lives of black men and women were little improved when the war ended.

Moreover, hostility toward black veterans increased at the end of the war. The attacks and violence were neither accidental nor simple crimes of passion

Columbia, Tennessee, race riots of 1946. The riot in Columbia was incited by the failure of the United States to offer African Americans full equality after so many of them had fought the racist policies of Nazi Germany.

(although passionate mobs were often involved). They were carried out by whites who were determined to put loyal American veterans "back in their place" and to reinstate segregation. Eleanor was acutely aware of the explosive potential of this racial friction. But now that she was no longer a White House insider, how could she help? The return of these soldiers and their bitterly cold reception highlighted the need for uncompromising action. As the issue of civil rights was forced to the forefront, Eleanor used her popularity, connections, and influence to promote racial and social equality. She participated in conferences, fund-raisers, and public debates to raise awareness about America's racial problem. She also joined the board of directors of several organizations, including the NAACP.

Frustrated by a country that could demand sacrifice in its moment of need and then turn its back when the crisis passed, black veterans sometimes took direct action. The results could be chilling:

In Alabama, when an African American veteran removed the Jim Crow sign on a trolley, an angry street car conductor took aim and

*unloaded his pistol into the ex-Marine. As the wounded veteran
staggered off the tram and crawled away, the chief of police
hunted him down and finished the job . . . In South Carolina,
another veteran, who complained about the inanity of Jim Crow
transportation, had his eyes gouged out with the butt of the sheriff's
billy club. In Louisiana, a black veteran who defiantly refused
to give a white man a war memento was partially dismembered,
castrated, and blow-torched...In Columbia, Tennessee, when
African Americans refused to "take lying down" the planned
lynching of a black veteran who had defended his mother from a
beating, the sheriff's storm troopers . . . "drew up their machine
guns and tommy guns . . . fired a barrage of shots directly into the
black area of town, and then moved in."[39]*

The events in Columbia, Tennessee, were indicative. In this town of 5,000 whites and 3,000 blacks, racial tensions actually subsided during the war. But when the returning soldiers did not accept the daily humiliations of Jim Crow laws, many whites reacted violently. The events began on February 25, 1946, when a dissatisfied black customer, accompanied by her navy veteran son, got into a fight with a radio repair clerk who refused to address their concerns and became abusive. The clerk was pushed out the window, an act for which both the veteran and his mother were arrested. After pleading guilty and paying their fine, the two headed home. Later that day, the son was arrested again on more serious charges but was bailed out and released again.

That night, an angry white mob gathered near the black neighborhood. Blacks, including armed veterans, organized to protect themselves against possible attack. When four police officers attempted to disperse the crowd, they were shot and wounded. What followed was not uncharacteristic of the way law-enforcement agents reacted to racial tensions:

*Within hours, state highway patrolmen and the state safety
commissioner, Lynn Bomar, arrived in town. Together with some of
the town's whites, they surrounded the Mink Slide [black] district.
During the early morning of February 26, highway patrolmen first
entered the district. The officers fired randomly into buildings, stole
cash and goods, searched homes without warrants, and took any
guns, rifles, and shotguns they could find. When the sweep was over,
more than one hundred blacks had been arrested, and about three*

hundred weapons from the black community had been confiscated.
None of the accused were granted bail or allowed legal counsel.[40]

According to prisoners' testimonies, three of the black prisoners were later taken for interrogation. Shots followed; one was injured, and the other two were killed. While the police officers claimed it was self-defense, fellow prisoners claimed that the men were executed in retaliation for their actions during the riots. Thurgood Marshall, the NAACP's leading lawyer, who would be the first African American to sit on the Supreme Court, immediately flew in with Walter White. They built a national defense committee (representing various organizations) whose mission was to provide funds and protection for the prisoners. They demanded that the alleged violations of black residents' civil rights be investigated. Walter White then approached Eleanor to co-chair the committee with Channing Tobias, and she immediately agreed. Though occupied with her work for the United Nations, Eleanor participated in the committee's defense efforts. In a letter she wrote with Channing Tobias to prospective donors, she summarized her views on the events. The men who were arrested, she argued, more than half of whom were recently discharged servicemen, had been

> *the innocent victims of race hatred and violence. The events which*
> *took place in Columbia on February 25th and 26th rose out of a*
> *dispute between a white shopkeeper and a Negro customer. They*
> *culminated in lynch threats, an armed invasion of the Negro*
> *district, wanton destruction of Negro property and wholesale arrests*
> *and beatings of Negro citizens.*[41]

Thurgood Marshall's spectacular defense saved many of the prisoners the injustice of long prison terms. But when he and others forced Tennessee Attorney General Tom C. Clark to investigate the actions of the National Guard unit and highway patrolmen who raided the black neighborhood, the results were deeply disappointing. Despite the fact that dozens of people witnessed the actions of the National Guard unit and patrolmen, blacks were not allowed to testify, and the white officers did not cooperate. The record of this investigation, Marshall later wrote to Eleanor, showed "that none of the witnesses . . . could identify any person responsible for the property damage which occurred or for any other act prohibited by Federal laws."[42] When Marshall left town, the police followed him and his colleagues. He was arrested for alleged drunk driving and was almost lynched by white residents of Columbia.

Responding to the maelstrom of violence, representatives of the African American community turned to the United Nations. W. E. B. Du Bois, a highly accomplished scholar and activist (he was the first African American to receive a doctoral degree from Harvard), led a team of lawyers and scholars who submitted a brief to the human rights division in 1947. It was titled "An Appeal to the World: A Statement of Denial of Human Rights to Minorities in the Case of Citizens of Negro Descent in the United States of America and an Appeal to the United Nations for Redress."

How, asked Du Bois, could the leaders of the United States seek to lead the free world while refusing to confront the injustices of racism in every American town and city? A "disastrous" policy, segregation, he wrote, had

> *repeatedly led the greatest modern attempt at democratic government to deny its political ideals, to falsify its philanthropic assertions and to make its religion to a great extent hypocritical. A nation which boldly declared "That all men are created equal," proceeded to build its economy on chattel slavery; masters who declared race-mixture impossible, sold their own children to slavery and left a mulatto progeny which neither law nor science can today disentangle; churches which excused slavery as calling the heathen to god, refused to recognize the freedom of converts or admit them to equal communion. . . . [A] great nation, which today ought to be in the forefront of the march toward peace and democracy, finds itself continuously making common cause with race-hate, prejudiced exploitation, and oppression of the common man.*[43]

America's "high and noble words," Du Bois concluded, had been "turned against it, because they are contradicted in every syllable by the treatment of the American Negro for three hundred and twenty-eight years."[44]

"An Appeal to the World" was Du Bois's plea for the international community to take notice of the ongoing discrimination, segregation, and racial violence in America. In writing and submitting it to the United Nations, Du Bois and his colleagues tried to shift from national and internal debate to an international and universal one. When arguing in court and protesting on the street,

African Americans were fighting to receive their *civil* rights: rights granted to all the citizens of the United States but denied to them. Du Bois and the NAACP believed that the United Nations' discussion of human rights was an opportunity to mobilize international public opinion for their cause and to align their plight with that of other oppressed people. This was neither the first nor the last such attempt to "internationalize" the injustices suffered by blacks.

The brief was to be submitted on October 23, 1947, to Humphrey as the director of the human rights division and to Henri Laugier of the Secretariat. Walter White, a longtime civil rights activist and the executive director of the NAACP, asked Eleanor to be present.[45] She declined:

> As an individual I should like to be present, but as a member of the delegation, I feel that until this subject comes before us in a proper way, in a report to the Human Rights Commission or otherwise, I should not seem to be lining myself up in any particular way on any subject.[46]

She added: "It isn't as though everyone did not know where I stand."[47] For example, before taking up her duties at the United Nations, Eleanor had often identified racism directed at African Americans as intolerable. The situation had to change, and in 1942, she repeated demands she had made many times before—that every citizen of the United States should have the following rights:

- Equality before the law
- Equality of education
- Equality to hold a job according to his or her ability
- Equality of participation through the ballot in the government[48]

"We cannot force people to accept friends for whom they have no liking," she argued, "but living in a democracy, it is entirely reasonable to demand that every citizen of that democracy enjoy the fundamental rights of a citizen."[49]

In Eleanor's essay, "Abolish Jim Crow," she spoke about the need to align the ethical mission of the war with the struggle for justice at home, drawing parallels among the persecution of the European Jews, the Russian dissidents, and the American blacks.[50] Moreover, since the war, Eleanor had often warned against the hypocrisy of condemning the Nazis for their racial policies while allowing the free reign of white supremacy in many areas of the United Sates. In a response to a member of President Truman's commission on civil rights, she repeated the comparison: "We cannot look down too much on the Nazis or the Communists, when somewhere in our land things like this happen."[51] While Eleanor called for patience and for working within the system, but this did not mean that she went along with official decisions with which she disagreed: she knew how to dig in her heels and push back.

A case in point was the United States' support for the formation of the state of Israel. In the aftermath of the Holocaust, Eleanor became convinced that this was the only appropriate response to horrific actions that had left six million Jews dead and had turned those who survived into unwanted, stateless refugees.[52] So when the United States seemed as if it would withdraw its support for the formation of a Jewish state in Palestine, Eleanor threatened her resignation from the United Nations.[53]

But "The Appeal to the World" put Eleanor in a tough position. She believed that receiving petitions from anyone but a member state violated the guidelines for the Human Rights Commission. The commission had never been assigned any executive power at all. Both human rights standards and the institutions that would act to uphold them were yet to be created. Moreover, Eleanor anticipated complications. She knew that the Soviets would use "The Appeal to the World" for anti-American propaganda (which they later did). In that case, if Eleanor sided with the petitioners, she would be set against the government she represented, which was unthinkable.

Nevertheless, Eleanor continued to communicate with White and Du Bois. She also agreed to meet Du Bois in person to talk things over. In their conversation, recorded by Du Bois, Eleanor repeated her concern about the potential abuse of the petition by the Soviets, and she pointed out that if the Soviets and other countries continued to attack the United States for its racial policies, she would be forced to defend those policies—a situation she deeply resented. According to Du Bois's account, Eleanor said that the situation "might be so unpleasant that she would feel it necessary to resign from the United States Delegation to the United Nations."[54] Du Bois's uncompromising position eventually led to a crisis within the NAACP and to the termination of his service. In his place, on September 7, 1948, the NAACP sent Walter White to consult with the United States delegation. His close ties with Eleanor were well known, and the choice suggested that the NAACP expected that she would continue to support the organization's mission.[55]

THE POLITICS OF WORDS

When the drafting committee adjourned on June 25, 1947, it had produced a document that would serve as the starting point for many rounds of further talks and revisions, as well as many deadlocks, breakthroughs, hopes, and disappointments. The committee's work was done, but before the full Human Rights Commission could begin the sequel, delegates knew they had to make a strategic decision. Eleanor had observed with dismay as the American public and its elected officials turned away from the international affairs. It was unlikely that Congress—so dominated by isolationists and southern segregationists—would approve any declaration of human rights except in gradual stages. So she proposed that the work should be broken up: first a nonbinding declaration, then a treaty, and last an enforcement mechanism would be put forward.

This view prevailed, and the commission broke into three working groups: declaration, treaty, and implementation. Though it would take 19 years to complete social-economic and civic-political human rights treaties, the Human Rights Commission forged ahead. Its second session took place in Geneva, Switzerland. Many believed that setting the conference in Europe, where the war's atrocities had hardly faded, would give their work additional urgency.

The opening meeting took place on December 2, 1947. During the first session, Eleanor informed her colleagues at the HRC that the United States would not support the drafting of a legally binding "covenant" of human rights until the political conditions for its good-faith use materialized. She also said that "flagrant, prolonged, and repeated violations" of such conventions would certainly hurt the United Nations.[56] The United States' position was rejected, and the HRC broke up into the three working groups mentioned above. Charles Dukes (who became Lord Dukeston), of the United Kingdom, led the drafting of the covenant, and India's Hansa Mehta headed the group that debated the ways in which human rights would be enforced and their violations addressed. Eleanor was to chair the drafting of a human rights declaration.

And that she did. Wasting no time, she told her colleagues:

> *I want to be home for Christmas, and I assume everyone else does, too. . . . In fact, I have made reservations, and I hope to keep them.*

If we work night sessions from the beginning, instead of waiting until the last week as usual, we should get through in time.[57]

Although the delegates muttered that the chairwoman's schedule violated their human rights, they set to work and maintained a remarkable spirit of friendliness and cooperation over the ensuing weeks.[58]

If we look at the concerns that surrounded a single word, we get some idea of how cultural, political, and social ideals shaped the language of the Declaration. When the delegates opened their folders of the draft and took a look at Article 1, here is what they saw:

All men are brothers. They are endowed by nature with reason and conscience. They are born equal in dignity and rights.

The representative from India, Hansa Mehta, was concerned about use of the word "men." A freedom fighter during her country's recent struggle for independence, she imagined that the word would be interpreted in India and other countries to mean males alone. She questioned whether the word could be used to exclude women from enjoying the rights listed in the Declaration. Eleanor disagreed: the English term was inclusive of both men and women.[59] For now, the wording did not change.

But nothing had really been settled. In the fall of 1948, when the final draft was debated by the Third Committee before it was brought to the General Assembly for adoption, several female delegates insisted that the Declaration's language be "gender neutral." They refused to back down, and the final version of Article 1 finally read "All *human beings. . .*" Eleanor later described how she came to accept this change:

The women on Committee III—and remember there were 58 representatives of governments in Committee III, not 18—58—and the women said "'all men,' oh, no. In this document we are not going to say 'all men' because in some of our countries we are just struggling to recognition and equality. Some of us have come up to the top, but others have very little equality and recognition and freedom. If we say 'all men,' when we get home it will be 'all men.'" So you will find in this Declaration that it starts with "all human beings" in Article I, and in all the other Articles it says "everyone," "no one." In the body of the Article, it occasionally says "his,"

*because to say "his or hers" each time was a little awkward, but it is
very clearly understood that this applies to all human beings.*[60]

Our attitudes and our prejudices are often built into the language we use
every day. The twentieth century saw women gain voting rights, become wage
earners, and achieve a position comparable to men's in many nations around
the world. Language, therefore, also underwent a transformation. Women
were making forays into politics and public office—and the women sitting
around the commission's table were determined to use their new power to
refashion the world, one word at a time.

Greater challenges, however, lay ahead, as the delegates from the Soviet Bloc
and from the West retreated into hostile positions. In her memoirs, Eleanor
reflected:

> *Over the years, in one capacity or another, I saw a great deal of
> the Russian delegates, and not infrequently, felt I saw and heard
> too much of them, because of course they were usually the center of
> opposition to [the American delegation's] ideas.*[61]

She devoted many lines to the diatribes delivered by "a big, dramatic man
with flowing white hair and a bristling black beard—Dr. Alexei P. Pavlov."
She noted that Pavlov, a nephew of the famous physiologist, "was a brilliant
talker," but he often

> *arose with a flourish, shook his white locks angrily, and made a
> bitter attack on the United States on the basis of some report or
> even of some rumor that had to do with discrimination against
> Negroes, particularly in our southern states.*[62] *Of course, I always
> replied vigorously, pointing out that, despite discrimination of one
> kind of another, the United States had done a great deal to improve
> the social and economic status of the Negro, but Dr. Pavlov never
> admitted any such improvement. On one occasion I took pains to
> explain that I had spent a good part of my own life fighting against
> discrimination, and working for education and other measures for
> the benefit of Negro citizens of the United States. But to everything I
> said, Dr. Pavlov replied by sticking out his black beard and barking:
> "Yes, you worked. But where did it ever get you?"*

Eleanor believed that these attacks were calculated to derail the work of the commission while "publicizing the Communist point of view."[63] Keeping the commission's work on schedule while coping with a speaker whose "words rolled out of his black beard like a river" required all of Eleanor's political skills.

On one occasion, it seemed to me that the rash accusations he brought up against the United States. . . . were proving a real detriment to our work. . . . I banged the gavel so hard that the other delegates jumped in surprise and, before he could continue, I got in a few words of my own. "We are here," I said, "to devise ways of safeguarding human rights. We are not here to attack each other's governments and I hope when we return on Monday the delegate of the Soviet Union will remember that!" I banged the gavel again. "Meeting adjourned!"[64]

I can still see Dr. Pavlov staring at me in surprise. But this maneuver may have had some effect, because his orations were brief and to the point for about a week after that.[65]

While she rarely had to gavel delegates into silence, Eleanor did need to cope with the larger-than-life personalities in the Human Rights Commission, and her remarkable skill at doing so proved to be one of the keys to the group's success. She was a principled and disciplined negotiator, which ensured that work proceeded professionally and smoothly. But there was no dodging or finessing certain hard questions, and before the end of the commission's third and final session, the meeting room echoed with prolonged arguments.

During September 1948, supporters of the focus on civil and political rights argued with a newer generation committed to protecting social and economic rights. The first group drew its inspiration from British philosophers John Locke, James and John Stewart Mill, and other classical liberal thinkers. They supported these "old rights" and favored relatively weak government that did not interfere in the life of the common person. Precious to them were the right to hold property, the freedoms of expression, assembly, and protest, a legal system that proceeded rationally without any prejudice toward the accused, and the right to elect (and replace) government officials in accordance with the interest of the public.[66]

Social and economic rights, by contrast, became a fixture on national political agendas in the West with the rise of working-class politics in the late nineteenth century. During the Industrial Revolution, many of the rural poor moved to towns and cities where they labored in factories. Exposed to dangerous machinery, toxic chemicals, and the whims of managers, these workers began to unionize in the late nineteenth century. They demanded higher wages, safer surroundings, and protection against injury and unemployment. Workers also formed political parties and labor unions, and in a few decades, they managed to win a number of important new social and economic rights including child labor laws and workplace safety laws.[67]

The distinctions between old and new rights were not very pronounced at the early stages of the drafting process, and many delegates believed that both needed to be written into the Declaration. Not least among these delegates was Henri Laugier, the assistant secretary general responsible for the United Nations' social and economic affairs (as well as the human rights project). As early as April 1946, Laugier instructed the committee to address these new rights. He told them to

> *show that the political rights are the first condition of liberty, but that today the progress of scientific and industrial civilization has created economic organizations which are inflicting on politically free men intolerable servitude and that, therefore, in the future, the declaration of the rights of man must be extended to the economic and social fields.*[68]

But many American officials argued that guarantees of social and economic rights would interfere with the fundamentals of the American economy. Some raised the specter of communism in response to nearly every government-sponsored social program. One of the strongest opponents of the inclusion of social and economic rights in the Declaration was Undersecretary of State Robert Lovett. Indeed, Lovett opposed the creation of any international agreement on human rights; such agreements, he believed, ran contrary to the interests of the United States. These and other sentiments—isolationism and objection to international criticism of United States racial policies—account for the United States' failure to ratify the Genocide Convention and a number of later international treaties.[69]

In spite of Eleanor's best efforts, the delegates from the Soviet Union barraged the American and British delegates with criticism of their countries' "ruthless" exploitation of the working poor. Other delegates—Santa Cruz, for example—promoted social and economic rights with far less drama and antagonism. Moreover, having helped her husband forge the New Deal in the 1930s, Eleanor was not opposed to government playing a role in the economy; she believed that such intervention had helped pull the American people out of the Great Depression.

When news from Moscow indicated that vast numbers of Russian citizens were being sent to prison camps on suspicion of dissent, Eleanor, evidently frustrated by Soviet disparagement, presented her view on the commission's negotiations to a general audience. In a speech given at the Sorbonne University in Paris in 1948, she said,

> *I think the best example one can give of this basic difference of the use of terms is "the right to work." The Soviet Union insists that this is a basic right which it alone can guarantee, because it alone provides full employment by the government. But the right to work in the Soviet Union means the assignment of workers to do whatever task is given to them by the government, without an opportunity for the people to participate in the decision. . . .*
>
> *We in the United States have come to realize it means freedom to choose one's job, to work or not to work as one desires. We, in the United States, have come to realize, however, that people have a right to demand that their government will not allow them to starve because as individuals they cannot find work of the kind they are accustomed to doing. . . . But we would not consider in the United States that we had gained any freedom if we were compelled to follow a dictatorial assignment to work where and when we were told. The right of choice would seem to us an important, fundamental freedom.[70]*

Months later, when the Human Rights Commission's work was nearly done, Eleanor replied to yet another round of Soviet criticism by acidly demanding to know "if those in the USSR's forced labor camps enjoyed paid vacations."[71] More typically, though, she tried to find compromise:

> *A society in which everyone works is not necessarily a free society, and may indeed be a slave society; on the other hand, a society in which there is widespread economic insecurity can turn freedom into a barren and vapid right for millions of people.[72]*

That was why Eleanor insisted that labor rights, such as the right to organize without jeopardizing one's income, were perfectly legitimate and needed to be included in the Declaration. And, as one expert claimed, "contrary to what many suppose today, it was Santa Cruz, far more than any Soviet Bloc representative, who was the Commission's most zealous promoter of social and economic rights."[73]

If Eleanor found negotiations with the Soviet delegates "tough," she noted that she had "never felt any personal bitterness" toward them and that she was certain that, with time, the two camps would find common ground.[74] And there was common ground: she believed there were some things that, within a complicated social and economic system, private citizens could not handle alone. "It is basic in a democracy," she wrote, "that leadership for the welfare of the people as a whole must come from the government." Long after right-wing critics of the New Deal had targeted her and Franklin as undercover socialists, she soberly stated "that a democracy must meet the needs of its people."[75]

In the end, Article 23 read, "Everyone has the right to work, to free choice of employment, to just and favorable conditions of work, and to protection against unemployment." This practical formulation satisfied the vast majority of the delegates, regardless of their cultural and political backgrounds.

ADOPTION

The United Nations' Committee on Social, Humanitarian and Cultural Questions, known as the Third Committee, began its review of the Declaration on September 28, 1948, and spent almost the entire session debating the draft. In 85 meetings, it considered 170 amendments—but, fortunately, many members of the Human Rights Commission, including Eleanor, Malik, Chang, Cassin, and Pavlov, also served as delegates to the Third Committee, enabling the committee's work to continue smoothly.[76]

When the Third Committee began to discuss the preamble (or introduction), Father Beaufort of the Netherlands moved that it should mention the divine origin of human beings and the immortal destiny of man. Both suggestions were entirely in keeping with Beaufort's own faith, which taught that God had created human beings and endowed them with immortal souls. Non-believers, said Beaufort, could simply ignore the references to Christianity.

Of course, the declaration was not meant to speak only to Christians and non-believers; it was meant to speak to all people everywhere without regard to religious identities and beliefs. The first Human Rights Commission itself was comprised of 18 representatives of the world's main religions and cultures, including those that were Jewish, Muslim, Hindu, Christian, and secular.[80] "[W]hen it became clear to Father Beaufort that his amendment would not be supported by the majority of the committee, he withdrew it. The result was that the Universal Declaration of Human Rights mentioned neither God nor nature."[81] The passage in question, in the final version, stated plainly:

Whereas recognition of the inherent dignity and of the equal and inalienable rights of all members of the human family, is the foundation of freedom, justice, and peace in the world. . . . [82]

After a long struggle between those who could not imagine a foundational document about rights that did not mention God and those who rejected such a mention, Eleanor fully appreciated the extraordinary delicacy needed to achieve consensus:

Now, I happen to believe that we are born free and equal in dignity and rights because there is a divine Creator, and there is a divine spark in men. But, there were other people around the table who wanted it expressed in such a way that they could think in their particular way about this question, and finally, these words were agreed upon because they stated the fact that all men were born free and equal, but they left it to each of us to put in our own reason, as we say, for that end.[83]

She insisted on the necessity of finding "the words that most people can say and that will accomplish the ends you desire, and will be acceptable to practically everyone sitting around the table, no matter what their background, no matter what their beliefs may be." [84]

A similar conflict erupted over the first article in the Declaration. At a certain moment, months before, Article 1 had read:

All men are brothers. They are endowed by nature with reason and conscience. They are born equal in dignity and rights.

WHO WAS CHARLES MALIK?

Dr. Charles Malik, representative from Lebanon and successor to Eleanor Roosevelt as chairman of the seventh session of the Human Rights Commission at Geneva, Switzerland, on April 16, 1951.

Credited for his brilliant contribution in shaping the Universal Declaration of Human Rights, Charles Malik served as the influential rapporteur for the Human Rights Commission in 1947 and 1948.

Malik was born in 1906 in Lebanon and graduated with a degree in mathematics and physics from the American University of Beirut in 1927. He developed an interest in philosophy and studied in Freiburg, Germany, in 1932 before obtaining a PhD in philosophy from Harvard University in 1937.[77]

After teaching at Harvard University and other American universities, Malik returned to Lebanon and founded the philosophy department and a cultural studies program at his alma mater. In 1945 he was appointed to the position of Lebanese ambassador to the United Nations, and he signed the United Nations charter on behalf of his country. A defender of individual freedoms, Malik promoted the view that human rights were rooted in natural rights—rights belonging to every person before he or she gave some of them up to become a member of society. According to Malik, individual rights were more important than state rights. In his opinion, the UN Declaration was important for advocating individual rights: now, he argued in 1948, "I can agitate against my government, and if she does not fulfill her pledge, I shall have and feel the moral support of the entire world."[78]

As the drafting process continued, the question of national sovereignty became increasingly personal for Malik and other members of the drafting committee. At stake was the formation of the state of Israel, which Eleanor and Cassin supported and Malik didn't. Despite the disagreement, Malik, Cassin, and Eleanor were able to continue their work together cordially and effectively. Malik replaced Eleanor as chairperson of the Human Rights Commission in 1951, served as president of the 13th session of the General Assembly in 1958, and, in 1960, returned to his academic career in Beirut.

The first statement reflected the guiding ideals of the French Revolution: *liberté, égalité, fraternité* (liberty, equality, and brotherhood). This was the work of the French representative, Cassin, who had added it as part of the process of revising Humphrey's original. Now the Lebanese representative, Malik, suggested substituting the words "by their Creators" for "by nature" to echo a celebrated passage in the American Declaration of Independence. This would not do, said Cassin, because not all cultures believed that humans were created by a god or another higher power. In a subsequent account, Humphrey provided some background:

> *At the second session of the Human Rights Commission, and again at the second session of the drafting committee, Malik had unsuccessfully tried to bring a reference to the Creator into the article on the family. Now it was the Brazilian delegation which wanted Article 1 to say that human beings are created in the image of God. The article, as it then stood, said that human beings are endowed "by nature" with reason and conscience, and the Brazilians wanted this statement to be preceded by a reference to the deity.*[85]

Naturally, many of the delegates represented countries where a single creed accounted for the vast majority of the population; Brazil, for example, has been predominantly Roman Catholic since the sixteenth century. Other delegates, such as those from socialist states, had formally rejected all conventional religion. If one believed that God's creation of humans in his own image provided the foundation for all rights and principles, it would not be easy to sit on one's hands at such a moment.

After the long debate regarding Article 1, another major controversy over religion arose when the group began to review Article 18, which addressed religious liberty. As Humphrey acknowledged, "Something as important as religion, which is so intimately related to the life of the individual and which has played such a role, for good and for bad, in the long struggle for human rights, could not be ignored by the Declaration."[86] Malik, whose country was divided between Christians and Muslims, appealed to his colleagues to endorse the right to change religions.[87] But another Lebanese Christian, who represented Saudi Arabia, objected to this clause. Jamil Baroody, a colorful speaker, was concerned about the "proselytizing activities of missionaries who were often the precursors of foreign intervention; and to include the principle would also be an affront to Muslims, since the Koran forbade them to change their religion."[88] Despite the opposition of several Muslim-majority states, Malik's clause was approved.

The leader of the delegation from Pakistan worked to bridge the differences. Eleanor recalled, "Fortunately, we consulted with Sir Zafrulla Khan, who courageously rose during the final vote in Committee Three to defend the Declaration." Pakistan was the largest Muslim nation present, and Khan's position carried a lot of weight. "It is my opinion," he declared, "that our Pakistan delegate [who rejected Article 18] has misinterpreted the Koran. I understand the Koran to say: 'He who can believe shall believe; he who cannot believe shall disbelieve; the only unforgivable sin is to be a hypocrite.' I shall vote for acceptance of the Universal Declaration of Human Rights."[89] Article 18 therefore reads:

Everyone has the right to freedom of thought, conscience and religion; this right includes freedom to change his religion or belief, and freedom, either alone or in community with others and in public or private, to manifest his religion or belief in teaching, practice, worship and observance.

After almost a year of work, on December 10, 1948, just two days before the close of the Paris session, the General Assembly voted to adopt the Universal Declaration of Human Rights:

As the General Assembly rose to give her a standing ovation, a radiant smile illuminated Eleanor Roosevelt's weary face. In future years, she would always consider her chairmanship of the committee that drafted the Declaration as her most important achievement and a culmination of her life's work.[90]

Although no country voted against the Universal Declaration in the General Assembly—a remarkable success, particularly when one reflects on all of the disputes along the way—eight countries abstained. Among them were the Soviet Union and its allies—Czechoslovakia, Byelorussia, Poland, and the Ukraine. According to Eleanor, the Soviet delegation explained its vote by contending that the Declaration "put emphasis mainly on 'eighteenth-century rights' and not enough on economic, social, and cultural rights."[91]

Yugoslavia and Saudi Arabia also declined to vote. The delegate from the latter justified his abstention as a rejection of Zafrulla Khan's interpretation of the Koran. South Africa was the final abstention, explaining that though "they hoped to give their people basic human rights . . . the Declaration went too far."[92] This was to be expected, since an aggressively racist party had won the general election in South Africa some months earlier and would soon pass a vast collection of laws reinforcing the racial discrimination that was long the norm in that nation. This system, called apartheid, greatly restricted the human rights of black South Africans as well as other racial minorities.

But Eleanor did not dwell on the abstentions:

Despite these difficulties, despite these variations in attitudes and customs and historic precedents, we have produced a document of very great intrinsic worth. The United States has not always won its points. The Declaration is not exactly as we would have written it; on the other hand, no two Americans would have written it in the same way. But it is a sure guide. It is not unlikely that it will be of historic importance.[93]

Despite the claims of her early critics, she had risen above the narrow interests of her country and culture, inspiring other members of the commission to do the same. Even Humphrey, whose diaries are filled with critical remarks about her (and just about everybody else), called her "a symbol that stood above this quarrel"—he meant the Cold War.[94]

After the General Assembly adopted the Universal Declaration of Human Rights, Eleanor finally resigned from her position as chairwoman of the Human Rights Commission. "It seemed to me," she later wrote,

that the United States had held the chairmanship of the Commission on Human Rights long enough. So at the 1951 meeting of the Commission in Geneva, I nominated Charles Malik of Lebanon, with the consent of my government. He was elected, and from then on I was just a member, but a most interested member, for I believed the Human Rights Commission was one of the very important parts of the foundation on which the United Nations might build a peaceful world.[95]

DOCUMENTS REVIEWED BY THE DRAFTING COMMITTEE

In this reading, we present three documents that the drafters of the Universal Declaration of Human Rights studied. They appear in chronological order, beginning with the United States Declaration of Independence of 1776. Other documents reviewed by the Human Rights Commission, including Franklin Delano Roosevelt's "four freedoms" speech and the Atlantic Charter, are presented in Part II. By perusing these three documents, the reader can get a good sense of what sorts of rights were debated during the drafting process. As with all historical texts, students may need to research the context in which these documents were written.

The United States Declaration of Independence, July 4, 1776 (excerpt)

This statement by America's thirteen original colonies marked a formal break from Britain. It declared in firm, clear language that the colonies were no longer part of the British Empire. Among the grievances with which the Declaration begins were several "self-evident" truths and "unalienable" rights. These included the equality of all human beings in the eyes of their creator, and their rights to "life, liberty, and the pursuit of happiness." In claiming the rights to choose or replace their government and to dispose of a king who proved cruel and arbitrary, the Americans were echoing the philosophy of the Englishman John Locke (1632–1704) and other Enlightenment thinkers.

> *We hold these truths to be self-evident, that all men are created equal, that they are endowed by their Creator with certain unalienable Rights, that among these are Life, Liberty and the pursuit of Happiness. That to secure these rights, Governments are instituted among Men, deriving their just powers from the consent of the governed, that whenever any Form of Government becomes destructive of these ends, it is the Right of the People to alter or to abolish it, and to institute new Government, laying its foundation on such principles and organizing its powers in such form, as to them shall seem most likely to effect their Safety and Happiness.*

The Declaration of the Rights of Man and of the Citizen (1789) (excerpt)

This document, entitled *Déclaration des droits de l'homme et du citoyen* in French, was adopted during the early stages of the French Revolution as a preliminary effort at a new constitution. During the revolution, the "third estate" (the common people) overturned the French monarchy and established a revolutionary government based on democratic principles. With "liberty, equality, and fraternity" as its slogan, the French Revolution became an inspirational model for future democratic revolutions. Indeed, many of the basic assumptions of today's democratic governments—including the idea that all people are equal, free, and deserve the full protection of the law—are spelled out in the *Déclaration des droits de l'homme et du citoyen*. Moreover, a large number of the civic and political rights listed in the Universal Declaration of Human Rights can be traced to this document.

Articles:

1. Men are born and remain free and equal in rights. Social distinctions may be founded only on the common good.

2. The aim of all political association is the preservation of the natural and imprescriptible rights of man. These rights are liberty, property, security, and resistance to oppression.

3. The principle of all sovereignty resides essentially in the nation. No body nor individual may exercise any authority which does not proceed directly from the nation.

4. Liberty consists in the freedom to do everything which injures no one else; hence the exercise of the natural rights of each man has no limits except those which assure to the other members of the society the enjoyment of the same rights. These limits can only be determined by law.

5. Law can only prohibit such actions as are hurtful to society. Nothing may be prevented which is not forbidden by law, and no one may be forced to do anything not provided for by law.

6. Law is the expression of the general will. Every citizen has a right to participate personally, or through his representative, in its foundation. It must be the same for all, whether it protects or punishes. All citizens, being equal in the eyes of the law, are equally eligible to all dignities and to all public positions and occupations, according to their abilities, and without distinction except that of their virtues and talents.

7. No person shall be accused, arrested, or imprisoned except in the cases and according to the forms prescribed by law. Any one soliciting, transmitting, executing, or causing to be executed, any arbitrary order, shall be punished. But any citizen summoned or arrested in virtue of the law shall submit without delay, as resistance constitutes an offense.

8. *The law shall provide for such punishments only as are strictly and obviously necessary, and no one shall suffer punishment except it be legally inflicted in virtue of a law passed and promulgated before the commission of the offense.*

9. *As all persons are held innocent until they shall have been declared guilty, if arrest shall be deemed indispensable, all harshness not essential to the securing of the prisoner's person shall be severely repressed by law.*

10. *No one shall be disquieted on account of his opinions, including his religious views, provided their manifestation does not disturb the public order established by law.*

11. *The free communication of ideas and opinions is one of the most precious of the rights of man. Every citizen may, accordingly, speak, write, and print with freedom, but shall be responsible for such abuses of this freedom as shall be defined by law.*

12. *The security of the rights of man and of the citizen requires public military forces. These forces are, therefore, established for the good of all and not for the personal advantage of those to whom they shall be intrusted.*

14. *All the citizens have a right to decide, either personally or by their representatives, as to the necessity of the public contribution; to grant this freely; to know to what uses it is put; and to fix the proportion, the mode of assessment and of collection and the duration of the taxes.*

15. *Society has the right to require of every public agent an account of his administration.*

17. *Since property is an inviolable and sacred right, no one shall be deprived thereof except where public necessity, legally determined, shall clearly demand it, and then only on condition that the owner shall have been previously and equitably indemnified.*

The International Labor Organization Declaration Concerning
Aims and Purposes, May 10, 1944

The International Labor Organization (ILO) was founded in Philadelphia in 1919 as part of the League of Nations. The constitution presented below was adopted, with the blessings of Franklin Roosevelt, in 1944. Two years later, in 1946, at the demise of the League of Nations, it became a special agency of the United Nations. The organization's mission states that the ILO is

devoted to advancing opportunities for women and men to obtain decent and productive work in conditions of freedom, equity, security and human dignity...In promoting social justice and internationally recognized human and labor rights, the organization continues to pursue its founding mission that labor peace is essential to prosperity.[96]

These goals, codified in some of the articles below, are part of what were termed "new rights" during discussion of the Declaration of Human Rights. This document shows that many who served on the Human Rights Commission—not just the Soviets—were deeply interested in the rights of workers.

Believing that experience has fully demonstrated the truth of the statement in the Constitution of the International Labor Organization that lasting peace can be established only if it is based on social justice, the Conference affirms that:

(a) all human beings, irrespective of race, creed or sex, have the right to pursue both their material wellbeing and their spiritual development in conditions of freedom and dignity, of economic security and equal opportunity;

. . .

The Conference recognizes the solemn obligation of the International Labor Organization to further among the nations of the world programs which will achieve:

(a) full employment and the raising of standards of living;

(b) the employment of workers in the occupations in which they can have the satisfaction of giving the fullest measure of their skill and attainments and make their greatest contribution to the common wellbeing;

. . .

(f) the extension of social security measures to provide a basic income to all in need of such protection and comprehensive medical care;

(g) adequate protection for the life and health of workers in all occupations;

(h) provision for child welfare and maternity protection;

(i) the provision of adequate nutrition, housing and facilities for recreation and culture;

(j) the assurance of equality of educational and vocational opportunity.

CONNECTIONS

1. Compare the three documents. What rights do each of these documents emphasize? What rights are guaranteed in each of the documents? How do you explain the differences between each?

2. What do these documents suggest about the values held by those who wrote them? If you created a document laying out your own foundational values, what would you include?

3. What are rights? Who gives people rights? Who protects these rights? Are there rights that human beings possess everywhere, at any time?

THE INDIVIDUAL OR SOCIETY: THE HUMAN RIGHTS COMMISSION DEBATES

During the first session of the Human Rights Commission, which began late in January 1947, its members debated the relationship between the individual and society. The debate was not an abstract one. On one side, countries whose delegates believed in the liberal democratic model placed individuals at the center and sought to ensure their freedoms from government interference. The United Kingdom and the United States are two examples of such countries. Those who supported this model often drew on the philosophy of such thinkers as John Locke and John Stuart Mill, who had presented compelling arguments for an almost limitless individual liberty. Historically, liberal political theory was embraced most enthusiastically in countries with a robust capitalist economy—the United States being the most obvious example. Very often, political rhetoric in liberal democracies combines the championing of personal liberties with advocacy of free economic competition.

On the other side of the debate were representatives from socialist states. They insisted on the importance of society over the individual. If the interests of individuals conflicted, then society would help each of them achieve greater things through solidarity and cooperation. In many socialist countries, the state assumed the duties traditionally handled by society, while coordinating national production and eliminating economic competition. In between the two camps were delegates, including Eleanor, who endorsed a compromise between these seemingly opposing views.

Simply stated, while the liberal model argued that the individual needs the greatest freedom to realize her or his potential, the socialist model argued that people need to combine with other individuals for real success. With the outbreak of the Cold War, the two sides adopted inflexible positions and became determined to discredit each other's political systems. Below are remarks made during a debate among members of the Human Rights Commission on February 4, 1947. The speakers were Charles Malik of Lebanon, Valentin Tepliakov of the Soviet Union, Hansa Mehta of India, and Eleanor Roosevelt.

MR. MALIK (Lebanon): *What interests me most concerning this question of the Bill of Rights is the whole problem of personal liberty. Now, we are wont usually to use such phrases as personal liberty and freedom of speech and opinion, freedom of information and of the press, and freedom of religious worship, etc.—we are wont to use these phrases, I think, many a time glibly, without full appreciation of the infinite importance of what these phrases really mean. I say this because, I think, if we fail in the formulation of our International Bill of Rights, it is not going to be on the grounds of failing to state explicitly the rights of the individual for food and housing and work and migration, and this, and that, but rather on the grounds of our failing to allow sufficiently for this all-fundamental problem of personal liberty.*

So, on the one hand, we have the definition of liberty as the perfect harmony between the individual and society, and on the other the affirmation that society comes first. . . . If I understand the present age correctly, this is our problem; the struggle between the human person …and freedom on the one hand, and the endless pressure of groups on the other, including, of course, his own nation.

For one must belong to a group today. He must have his identification papers. He must have social loyalties. He must belong to some association.

The claims of groups today—and especially the political group, the nation embodying itself in the institution called the state—are becoming increasingly dominant. These claims have a tendency to dictate to the person what he ought to think, what he ought to do, what even he ought to believe and hope for, concerning himself and the nature of things. The political state is becoming increasingly determinant of the very being of the person, and it does it by its laws, by psychological pressure, by economic pressure, by every possible means of propaganda and social pressure.

In my opinion, there is here involved the deepest danger of the age…the disappearance of real freedom of choice.

MR. TEPLIAKOV (USSR): *Madam Chairman, in connection with the remarks just made, may I say that I have to make a short observation in regard to the four principles [personal liberty, freedom of speech and opinion, freedom of information and of the press,*

and freedom of religious worship] presented by the representative of
Lebanon. . . . *I would say I oppose such principles or the adoption
of such principles for the Bill of Human Rights. . . .*

*First of all, these principles are wrong from the point of view that
we are living as individuals in a community and a society, and we
are working for the community and the society. The community has
provided the material substance for our existence.*

MRS. MEHTA (India): *Madam Chairman, this question should
not be a matter of dispute. The Charter of the United Nations has
already said that we are to uphold the dignity and worth of the
human person. We are here to reaffirm faith in fundamental human
rights, whether the human person comes first or the society. . . .
Our object should be to uphold the dignity and worth of the human
person. What are the rights which we should recognize, which will
carry out this purpose? I think we should not enter into this maze of
ideology at this stage. . . .*

CHAIRMAN [Eleanor Roosevelt]: *I think perhaps I would like to
say a word about what was said by the representative from Lebanon.
It seems to me that in much that is before us, the rights of the
individual are extremely important. It is not exactly that you set the
individual apart from his society, but you recognize that within any
society, the individual must have rights that are guarded. And while
we may, many of us, differ on exact interpretations, I think that is
something, in writing a bill of human rights, that you have to think
of rather carefully.*

*Many of us believe that an organized society in the form of a
government, exists for the good of the individual; others believe
that an organized society in the form of a government, exists for
the benefit of a group. We may not have to decide that particular
point, but I think we do have to make sure, in writing a bill of
human rights, that we safeguard the fundamental freedoms of the
individual. If you do not do that, in the long run, it seems to me,
that you run the risk of having certain conditions which we have
just tried to prevent, at great cost in human life.*[97]

DOCUMENT ❷ (continued)

CONNECTIONS

1. What are the different approaches to protecting rights of the individual? Which countries would have supported Malik's argument? Who would have supported Tepliakov? Why?

2. According to Malik, what fundamental freedoms are essential to the exercise of human rights? What do you see as fundamental freedoms?

3. Do you agree with Malik in that people are increasingly pressured to belong to a group? Can individuals exist without belonging to groups? How does belonging to a group shape the way you think and behave?

4. Do you think it is ever necessary for a person to give up certain rights for the welfare of her or his community? What happens when one person's individual liberties impose on those of other people? What rights might you be willing to give up for the benefit of a group to which you belong?

5. What does Mehta suggest is the goal of the discussion? She argues that "ideology" is getting in the way of the discussion. What is an ideology? When might ideologies get in the way of achieving a goal?

STATEMENT ON HUMAN RIGHTS BY THE AMERICAN ANTHROPOLOGICAL ASSOCIATION

Critics of the attempts to write a human rights declaration suggested that such a document did not (or could not) represent the diversity of cultures around the world. When UNESCO invited the American Anthropological Association to present its view, the organization issued an official statement.

The problem faced by the Commission on Human Rights of the United Nations in preparing its Declaration on the Rights of Man must be approached from two points of view. The first . . . concerns the respect for the . . . individual as such, and his right to its fullest development as a member of his society. In a world order, however, respect for the cultures of differing human groups is equally important. . . .

How can the proposed Declaration be applicable to all human beings, and not be a statement of rights conceived only in terms of the values prevalent in the countries of Western Europe and America? . . .

The consequences of this point of view have been disastrous for mankind. Doctrines of the "white man's burden"[98] have been employed to implement economic exploitation and to deny the right to control their own affairs to millions of peoples over the world. . . .

Religious beliefs that for untold ages have carried conviction . . . have been attacked as superstitious, immoral, untrue . . .

Ideas of right and wrong, good and evil, are found in all societies, though they differ in their expression among different peoples. What is held to be a human right in one society may be regarded as antisocial by another people, or by the same people in a different period of their history. The saint of one epoch would at a later time be confined as a man not fitted to cope with reality. Even the nature of the physical world, the colors we see, the sounds we hear, are conditioned by the language we speak, which is part of the culture into which we are born.

The problem of drawing up a Declaration of Human Rights was relatively simple in the Eighteenth Century, because it was not a matter of human rights, but of the rights of men within the framework of the sanctions laid by a single society. Even then, so noble a document as the American Declaration of Independence, or the American Bill of Rights, could be written by men who themselves were slave-owners in a country where chattel slavery was a part of the recognized social order. . . .

Only when a statement of the right of men to live in terms of their own traditions is incorporated into the proposed Declaration, then, can the next step of defining the rights and duties of human groups, as regards each other, be set upon the firm foundation of the present day scientific knowledge of Man.

CONNECTIONS

1. The American Anthropological Association feared that the Universal Declaration of Human Rights would be used to impose Western values on other countries. Considering what you have read in this chapter, how would you respond?

2. When should cultural differences matter? When should those differences be disregarded or criticized?

3. Can you rely upon national laws and cultural norms to protect human rights? How should people of one nation or culture respond when people of another country or culture abuse the rights of their own members?

4. Are rights universal and timeless? Do rights change? What does it mean for rights to be universal?

5. What are the potential consequences if the world cannot agree on universal rights? What are the dangers in codifying one set of rights to apply to every nation?

6. Is it possible to create a document that represents a universal view?

7. Does every culture have the right to determine its own rights and wrongs? What are the consequences of moral relativism—that is, when all rights and wrongs are defined only within a particular culture? How might your understanding of the Holocaust influence your understanding of moral relativism?

THE HUMAN RIGHTS COMMISSION AND BLACKS IN AMERICA

While the HRC worked on drafting the Declaration, some of those leading the struggle for civil rights in America believed that bringing their case before the United Nations would draw helpful international attention. They felt that a change in terminology—from "civil rights" to "human rights"—would align their struggle with that of other oppressed groups and colonized nations around the world.

This was the strategy employed by W. E. B. Du Bois, who served as the director of research at the NAACP. He gathered a team of lawyers and scholars, and the group drew up a brief explaining the status of blacks in America. The comprehensive document—"An Appeal to the World: A Statement of Denial of Human Rights to Minorities in the Case of Citizens of Negro Descent in the United States of America and an Appeal to the United Nations for Redress"— was submitted to the human rights division of the United Nations in 1947.

Eleanor refused to participate in the meeting when "An Appeal to the World" was presented. She claimed that, among other things, the appeal would be used by the Soviets to condemn America, which would force her, in her position as a representative of the United States, to defend America's racial policies. Eleanor, by this time a well-known critic of racial discrimination in the United States, felt that if she were to be put in this awkward position, she would have to resign from the United Nations. As a compromise, Eleanor referred the issue of racial discrimination in the United Nations to a Human Rights Commission subcommittee. While Du Bois continued to press the issue, the NAACP changed its tactic. The organization decided that Walter White, not Du Bois, should be its representative to the delegation. In his introduction to the document below, Du Bois questioned how a government determined to lead the free world could turn a blind eye to daily acts of racist terror. He argued that segregation—a practice taken for granted by most white Americans—led to a gross violation of the human rights of African Americans.

There were in the United States of America, 1940, 12,865,518 native-born citizens, something less than a tenth of the nation, who form largely a segregated caste, with restricted legal rights, and many illegal disabilities. They are descendants of the Africans brought to America during the sixteenth, seventeenth, eighteenth,

*and nineteenth centuries, and reduced to slave labor. This group
has not complete biological unity, but varies in color from white
to black, and comprises a great variety of physical characteristics,
since many are the offspring of white European-Americans as well
as of Africans and American Indians. There are a large number
of white Americans who also descend from Negroes but who are
not counted in the colored group, nor subjected to caste restrictions
because the preponderance of white blood conceals their descent.*

*The so-called American Negro group . . . has . . . a strong,
hereditary cultural unity, born of slavery, of common suffering,
prolonged proscription and curtailment of political and civil rights;
and especially because of economic and social disabilities. Largely
from this fact, have arisen their cultural gifts to America—their
rhythm, music and folk-song; their religious faith and customs;
their contribution to American art and literature; their defense
of their country in every war, on land, sea and in the air; and
especially the hard, continuous toil upon which the prosperity and
wealth of this continent has largely been built. . . .*

*If however, the effect of the color caste system on the North American
Negro has been both good and bad, its effect on white America has
been disastrous. It has repeatedly led the greatest modern attempt
at democratic government to deny its political ideals, to falsify its
philanthropic assertions and to make its religion to a great extent
hypocritical. A nation which boldly declared "That all men are
created equal," proceeded to build its economy on chattel slavery;
masters who declared race mixture impossible, sold their own
children into slavery and left a mulatto progeny, which neither law
nor science can today disentangle; churches which excused slavery
as calling the heathen to God, refused to recognize the freedom of
converts, or admit them to equal communion . . .*

*But today the paradox again looms after the Second World War. We
have recrudescence of race hate and caste restrictions in the United
States, and of these dangerous tendencies not simply for the United
States itself, but for all nations. When will nations learn that their
enemies are quite as often within their own country as without? It is
not Russia that threatens the United States so much as Mississippi;*

*not Stalin and Molotov, but Bilbo[99] and Rankin[100]; internal injustice
done to one's brothers is far more dangerous than the aggression of
strangers from abroad . . .*

*It may be quite properly asked at this point, to whom a petition
and statement such as this should be addressed? Many persons say
that this represents a domestic question which is purely a matter of
internal concern; and that therefore it should be addressed to the
people and government of the United States and the various states.*

*It must not be thought that this procedure has not already been
taken. From the very beginning of this nation, in the late eighteenth
century, and even before, in the colonies, decade by decade, and
indeed year by year, the Negroes of the United States have appealed
for redress of grievances, and have given facts and figures to support
their contention.*

*It must also be admitted that this continuous hammering upon
the gates of opportunity in the United States has had [an] effect,
and that because of this, and with the help of his white fellow
citizens, the American Negro has emerged from slavery and*

Demonstration against Jim Crow segregation laws, 1944. In an essay entitled "Abolish Jim Crow," Eleanor spoke of the need "to align the ethical mission of the war abroad and the struggle for justice at home."

attained emancipation from chattel slavery, considerable economic independence, social security, and advance in culture.

But manifestly this is not enough; no large group of a nation can lag behind the average culture of that nation, as the American Negro still does, without suffering not only itself but becoming a menace to the nation.

In addition to this, in its international relations, the United States owes something to the world; to the United Nations of which it is part, and to the ideals which it professes to advocate. Especially is this true since the United Nations has made its headquarters in New York. The United States is honor bound not only to protect its own people and its own interests, but to guard and respect the various peoples of the world who are its guests and allies. Because of caste custom and legislation along the color line, the United States is today in danger of encroaching upon the rights and privileges of its fellow nations. Most people of the world are more or less colored in skin; their presence at the meetings of the United Nations as participants, and as visitors, renders them always liable to insult and to discrimination; because they may be mistaken for Americans of Negro descent . . .

This question, then, which is without doubt primarily an internal and national question, becomes inevitably an international question, and will in the future become more and more international, as the nations draw together. In this great attempt to find common ground and to maintain peace, it is therefore fitting and proper that thirteen million American citizens of Negro descent should appeal to the United Nations, and ask that organization in the proper way to take cognizance of a situation which deprives this group of their rights as men and citizens, and by so doing makes the functioning of the United Nations more difficult, if not in many cases impossible.[101]

CONNECTIONS

1. What main concerns does Du Bois raise? What argument does he make to support his assertion that civil rights issues are, indeed, human rights issues?

2. Why would Du Bois want to submit this document to the human rights division of the United Nations? What did he hope to accomplish?

3. As a board member of the NAACP *and* a member of the United States delegation to the United Nations, this petition created a dilemma for Eleanor. What dilemma did this raise for her? How do you evaluate her response? What do you think is the right thing to do with a petition like this in that situation?

4. Why do you think that Eleanor said that she would resign from the United Nations if she were forced to defend America's racial policies?

SOCIAL AND ECONOMIC RIGHTS: ELEANOR'S SPEECH AT THE SORBONNE

As the work of the Human Rights Commission wound down, the Western delegations and the Soviet Bloc members quarreled over social and economic rights. Would the final document address the right and responsibility of the state to provide health care, employment, and education? In this excerpt from a speech delivered at the University of Paris (the Sorbonne), Eleanor tackled the differences between the Americans and the Soviets regarding the right to work:

There are basic differences that show up even in the use of words between a democratic and a totalitarian country. For instance "democracy" means one thing to the U.S.S.R. and another to the U.S.A. and, I know, in France.

The U.S.S.R. representatives assert that they already have achieved many things which we . . . cannot achieve because their government controls the accomplishment of these things. Our government seems powerless to them because, in the last analysis, it is controlled by the people. They would not put it that way—they would say that the people in the U.S.S.R. control their government by allowing their government to have certain absolute rights. We, on the other hand, feel that certain rights can never be granted to the government, but must be kept in the hands of the people . . .

I think the best example one can give of this basic difference of the use of terms is "the right to work." The Soviet Union insists that this is a basic right which it alone can guarantee because it alone provides full employment by the government. But the right to work in the Soviet Union means the assignment of workers to do whatever task is given to them by the government without an opportunity for the people to participate in the decision that the government should do this. A society in which everyone works is not necessarily a free society, and may indeed be a slave society; on the other hand, a society in which there is widespread economic insecurity can turn freedom into a barren and vapid right for millions of people. We in the United States have come to realize it means freedom to choose one's job, to work or not to work as one desires. We, in the United

*States, have come to realize, however, that people have a right
to demand that their government will not allow them to starve
because as individuals they cannot find work of the kind they are
accustomed to doing . . . but we would not consider in the United
States that we have gained any freedom if we were compelled
to follow a dictatorial assignment to work where and when we
were told. The right of choice would seem to us an important,
fundamental freedom. . . .*

*Long ago in London during a discussion with Mr. Vyshinsky [the
Soviet representative to the United Nations], he told me there was no
such thing as freedom for the individual in the world. All freedom
of the individual was conditioned by the rights of other individuals.
That, of course, I granted. I said: "We approach the question from a
different point of view; we here in the United Nations are trying to
develop ideals which will be broader in outlook, which will consider
first the rights of man, which will consider what makes man more
free: not governments, but man."*

*The totalitarian state typically places the will of the people second
to decrees promulgated by a few men at the top. . . .*

*Freedom for our peoples is not only a right, but also a tool. Freedom
of speech, freedom of the press, freedom of information, freedom of
assembly—these are not just abstract ideals to us; they are tools
with which we create a way of life, a way of life in which we can
enjoy freedom. . . .*

*Among free men, the end cannot justify the means. We know the
patterns of totalitarianism—the single political party, the control
of schools, press, radio, the arts, the sciences, and the church, to
support autocratic authority. . . .*

*The place to discuss the issue of human rights is in the forum
of the United Nations. The United Nations has been set up as
the common meeting ground for nations, where we can consider
together our mutual problems and take advantage of our differences
in experience. It is inherent in our firm attachment to democracy
and freedom that we stand always ready to use the fundamental
democratic procedures of honest discussion and negotiation.*

It is now as always our hope that despite the wide differences in approach we face in the world today, we can with mutual good faith in the principles of the United Nations Charter, arrive at a common basis of understanding.[102]

CONNECTIONS

1. What is a democracy? What does Eleanor mean when she says that democracy is interpreted differently around the world?

2. How did the Soviets interpret the right to work? How does Eleanor interpret this same right? How does she try to integrate the two perspectives?

3. How might the Great Depression have influenced Eleanor's thinking in addressing the right to work?

4. Eleanor says, "A society in which everyone works is not necessarily a free society, and may indeed be a slave society." What does she mean by this? What is the difference between the right to work and the opportunity to work?

5. What does Eleanor mean when she says, "Freedom for our peoples is not only a right, but also a tool"? For what is it a tool? Do you agree with her? What does this statement suggest about what Eleanor believes is the purpose of a human rights document?

6. What is a "common basis of understanding," and how do you arrive at one? How does Eleanor herself try to model a common basis of understanding?

MAGNA CARTA FOR MANKIND

On December 10, 1948, the General Assembly voted to adopt the Universal Declaration of Human Rights. In her memorable speech, "On the Adoption of the Universal Declaration of Human Rights," Eleanor notes that this was not a binding international treaty. Such a treaty was still in the making. Like the Atlantic Charter, the Declaration was "to serve as a common standard of achievement for all peoples of all nations." She went on to say that it "may well become the international Magna Carta of all men everywhere." Human beings, she reminded the audience, are primarily moral beings and can thrive only in a world where freedom and justice are secured. Eleanor hoped that the Declaration of Human Rights would guide the world toward a freer, more just, and more humane future.

The long and meticulous study and debate of which this Universal Declaration of Human Rights is the product means that it reflects the composite views of the many men and governments who have contributed to its formulation. Not every man nor every government can have what he wants in a document of this kind. There are of course particular provisions in the Declaration before us with which we are not fully satisfied. I have no doubt this is true of other delegations, and it would still be true if we continued our labors over many years. Taken as a whole the Delegation of the United States believes that this is a good document—even a great document—and we propose to give it our full support. . . .

In giving our approval to the Declaration today, it is of primary importance that we keep clearly in mind the basic character of the document. It is not a treaty; it is not an international agreement. It is not, and does not purport to be, a statement of law or of legal obligation. It is a Declaration of basic principles of human rights and freedoms, to be stamped with the approval of the General Assembly by formal vote of its members, and to serve as a common standard of achievement for all peoples of all nations.

We stand today at the threshold of a great event both in the life of the United Nations and in the life of mankind. This Universal Declaration of Human Rights may well become the international Magna Carta of all men everywhere. We hope its proclamation by the General Assembly will be an event comparable to the proclamation of the Declaration of the Rights of Man by the French people in 1789, the adoption of the Bill of Rights by the people of the United States, and the adoption of comparable declarations at different times in other countries.

At a time when there are so many issues on which we find it difficult to reach a common basis of agreement, it is a significant fact that 58 states have found such a large measure of agreement in the complex field of human rights. This must be taken as testimony of our common aspiration, first voiced in the Charter of the United Nations, to lift men everywhere to a higher standard of life and to a greater enjoyment of freedom. Man's desire for peace lies behind this Declaration. The realization that the flagrant violation of human rights by Nazi and Fascist countries sowed the seeds of the last world war has supplied the impetus for the work which brings us to the moment of achievement here today. . . .

This Declaration is based upon the spiritual fact that man must have freedom in which to develop his full stature and through common effort to raise the level of human dignity. We have much to do to fully achieve and to assure the rights set forth in this Declaration. But having them put before us with the moral backing of 58 nations will be a great step forward.

As we here bring to fruition our labors on this Declaration of Human Rights, we must at the same time rededicate ourselves to the unfinished task which lies before us. We can now move on with new courage and inspiration to the completion of an international covenant on human rights, and of measures for the implementation of human rights.[103]

CONNECTIONS

1. What does Eleanor say was the motivation for writing the Universal Declaration of Human Rights?

2. What do you think is involved in making a document that reflects "composite views"? Does such a document tend to be less or more universal? What does "universality" mean in this case?

3. Eleanor emphasizes that the Declaration is not a treaty, an international agreement, or a statement of law or of legal obligation. What are the differences? What is the purpose of the Declaration?

4. Eleanor compared the Universal Declaration of Human Rights to the Magna Carta (1215), the Declaration of the Rights of Man (1789), and the Bill of Rights (1791). Research when and why these documents were written. Why do you think Eleanor chose to mention them? What is the purpose of her comparison?

5. Why do you think Eleanor mentioned that the United States delegation did not agree with every aspect of the Declaration? What is she trying to suggest is necessary when working with a diverse group of people?

1 Allida M. Black, ed., *Courage in a Dangerous World: The Political Writings of Eleanor Roosevelt* (New York: Columbia University Press, 1999), 157.

2 For a concise *procedural* history of the creation of the Declaration, see the United Nations Audiovisual Library of International Law, http://untreaty.un.org/cod/avl/ha/udhr/udhr.html (accessed December 23, 2009).

3 Eleanor Roosevelt, *On My Own* (New York: Harper, 1958), 74.

4 Speech by Dr. Charles Malik (Lebanon), "The Basic Issues of the International Bill of Human Rights," delivered before a conference of American educators in Lake Success, NY, February 26, 1948, available at United Nations Publications, Eleanor Roosevelt, box 4580, folder UN Publications, 5.

5 Documentation for International Bill of Rights, 1946, Franklin Delano Roosevelt Library, vol. 1, box 4575.

6 John Peters Humphrey, who wrote the first draft of the Universal Declaration of Human Rights, borrowed heavily from the American Law Institute's "Statement of Essential Human Rights" (1943), which was presented to the drafting committee by Panama. See Johannes Morsink, *The Universal Declaration of Human Rights: Origins, Drafting, and Intent* (Philadelphia: University of Pennsylvania Press, 1999), 6.

7 Born into a family that owned a respected liberal newspaper in Belgrade, Ribnikar joined local communist forces during the war.

8 Mary Ann Glendon, *A World Made New: Eleanor Roosevelt and the Universal Declaration of Human Rights* (New York: Random House, 2001), 39.

9 "Commission on Humans Rights Verbatim Record, Fourteenth Meeting (February 4, 1947)," in *The Eleanor Roosevelt Papers: Human Rights Years: Vol. 1, 1945–48*, (Farmington Hills: Thomson Gale, 2007), eds. Allida Black, John F. Sears, and Mary Jo Binker, 508.

10 Joseph P. Lash, *Eleanor: The Years Alone* (New York: W. W. Norton & Company, 1972), 52.

11 Lash, *The Years Alone*, 53.

12 Glendon, *A World Made New*, 39, 41.

13 Lash, *The Years Alone*, 53.

14 Glendon, *A World Made New*, 41.

15 "Commission on Humans Rights Verbatim Record, Fourteenth Meeting (February 4, 1947)," in *The Eleanor Roosevelt Papers*, ed. Black, 508–09.

16 Morsink, *The Universal Declaration of Human Rights*, 5.

17 Glendon, *A World Made New*, 56.

18 Ibid., 73–74.

19 Ibid., 74.

20 American Anthropological Association, "Statement on Human Rights," *American Anthropologist* 49, no. 4 (1947): 539. In June 1999, the American Anthropological Association issued a "Declaration on Human Rights and Anthropology" reconciling its position with the Universal Declaration of Human Rights. It reads, in part, "Thus, the AAA founds its approach on the anthropological principles of respect for concrete human differences, both collective and individual, rather than the abstract legal uniformity of Western tradition. In practical terms, however, its working definition builds on the Universal Declaration of Human Rights . . . and other treaties which bring basic human rights within the parameters of international written and customary law and practice. The AAA definition thus reflects a commitment to human rights consistent with international principles but not limited by them." See American Anthropological Association, "Declaration on Anthropology and Human Rights," available at the American Anthropological Association website, http://www.aaanet.org/stmts/humanrts.htm (accessed December 19, 2009).

[21] "The White Man's Burden" was the title of a poem written by Rudyard Kipling in 1899, at the height of European colonialism. It calls on Westerners to take up the challenge of civilizing the primitive peoples of the world, opening with the following lines:

> Take up the White Man's burden—
> Send forth the best ye breed—
> Go, bind your sons to exile
> To serve your captives' need;
> To wait, in heavy harness,
> On fluttered folk and wild—
> Your new-caught sullen peoples,
> Half-devil and half-child.

For more on Kipling and the poem, see the Facing History and Ourselves resource book *Race and Membership in American History: The Eugenics Movement* (Brookline: Facing History and Ourselves National Foundation, 2002), 113–15.

[22] American Anthropological Association, "Statement on Human Rights," 540.

[23] The issue of eugenics is extensively discussed in Facing History and Ourselves, *Race and Membership in American History* (Brookline: Facing History and Ourselves National Endowment, 2002).

[24] American Anthropological Association, "Statement on Human Rights," 540.

[25] Karen Engle, "From Skepticism to Embrace: Human Rights and the American Anthropological Association from 1947–1999," *Human Rights Quarterly* 23, no. 3 (2001): 346–47.

[26] American Anthropological Association, "Statement on Human Rights," 543.

[27] Ibid., 542.

[28] Eleanor Roosevelt, *What I Hope to Leave Behind* (New York: Carlson Publishing, 1995), 567.

[29] Roosevelt, *What I Hope to Leave Behind,* 567–68.

[30] Eleanor Roosevelt, "Statement by Mrs. Franklin D. Roosevelt, United States Representative on the Commission on Human Rights, June 18, 1948," Eleanor Roosevelt Papers, United Nations Publications, box 4580, 1948, 1.

[31] Humphrey recalled that his draft led to "a long debate lasting through six meetings during which the Secretariat draft declaration was discussed and compared with the United Kingdom draft convention. I was put on the spot at the very first meeting. Colonel Hodgson [representing Australia] wanted to know what principles the Secretariat had used in the preparation of its draft and what was the philosophy behind it. He should have known that any answer that I could give to his question would, in that ideologically divided group, get me and my draft into hot water. I therefore replied that the draft was not based on any particular philosophy; it included rights recognized by various national constitutions and also a number of suggestions that had been made for an international bill of rights." See John Peters Humphrey, *Human Rights and the United Nations: A Great Adventure* (Dobbs Ferry: Transnational Publishers, 1984), 39.

[32] Ibid., 29–30.

[33] Glendon, *A World Made New,* 95.

[34] Humphrey, *Human Rights,* 41. Humphrey went on to concede that "there was perhaps something paradoxical about what the United Nations was trying to do; for the international bill of rights was being drafted by the representatives of governments."

[35] Even as the Universal Declaration of Human Rights was being drawn up, Lemkin was lobbying the United Nations to adopt the Convention for the Prevention and Punishment of Genocide. The Convention for the Prevention and Punishment of Genocide would ultimately be signed on December 9, 1948, one day before the Universal Declaration of Human Rights.

[36] Glendon, *A World Made New,* 60.

[37] Michael J. Klarman, *From Jim Crow to Civil Rights: The Supreme Court and the Struggle for Racial Equality* (Oxford: Oxford University Press, 2004), 177.

[38] "The United States from 1920 to 1945," *Encyclopaedia Britannica* online, http://www.britannica.com/EBchecked/topic/616563/United-States/77877/World-War-II#ref=ref613139 (accessed March 10, 2009).

[39] Carol Anderson, *Eyes Off the Prize: The United Nations and the African American Struggle for Human Rights, 1944–1955* (Cambridge: Cambridge University Press, 2003), 58–59.

[40] "Columbia Race Riots, 1946," the Tennessee Encyclopedia of History and Culture website, http://tennesseeencyclopedia.net/imagegallery.php?EntryID=C128 (accessed October 16, 2009). We thank Elly Green and Allida Black for drawing our attention to Eleanor's involvement in the Columbia riots.

[41] Eleanor Roosevelt and Channing H. Tobias, fund-raising letter for the National Committee for Justice in Columbia, TN, May 29, 1946, available at the Eleanor Roosevelt Papers Project website, http://www.gwu.edu/~erpapers/documents/correspondence/doc042556.cfm#sdendnote1anc (accessed October 16, 2009).

[42] "Tom Clark to Eleanor Roosevelt, November 26, 1946," in *The Eleanor Roosevelt Papers*, ed. Black, 149.

[43] W. E. B. Du Bois et al., "Statement on the Denial of Human Rights to Minorities in the Case of Citizens of Negro Descent in the United States of America and an Appeal to the United Nations for Redress" (1948), 5–6, Eleanor Roosevelt Papers, United Nations Publications, box 4581.

[44] Du Bois et al., "Statement on the Denial of Human Rights to Minorities in the Case of Citizens of Negro Descent in the United States of America and an Appeal to the United Nations for Redress," 6.

[45] Lash, *The Years Alone*, 57–58.

[46] Black et al., *The Eleanor Roosevelt Papers*, 634.

[47] Ibid. In her important book, historian Carol Anderson also criticized Eleanor for siding with the Truman administration in suppressing the "Appeal to the World." Anderson argued that despite Eleanor's reputation for protecting minorities' rights, she was unsupportive of NAACP leadership and blocked the petition in the Human Rights Commission. Anderson concludes her book about the failure of the United Nations to address the rights of America's blacks between 1945 and 1955 by saying that Eleanor's actions "spoke volumes about her priority." Eleanor, she continued, "was in complete agreement with the State Department," which, Anderson argued, was deeply racist. Eleanor's work at the HRC, Anderson contended, was designed to "erect a formidable barrier between the oversight abilities of the UN and the horrific conditions in the African America communities." See Anderson, *Eyes Off the Prize*, 96–98, 112, 175.

[48] Roosevelt, "Race, Religion and Prejudice," *New Republic* 106 (May 11, 1942): 630, available at the Eleanor Roosevelt Papers Project website, http://www2.gwu.edu/~erpapers/documents/articles/racereligionprejudice.cfm. (accessed October 19, 2009).

[49] Ibid.

[50] Eleanor Roosevelt, "Abolish Jim Crow," *New Threshold*, August 1943; reprinted in *Courage in a Dangerous World*, ed. Black, 139–40.

[51] Black et al., *The Eleanor Roosevelt Papers*, 593.

[52] Historian Michelle Mart explained that in Eleanor's mind, an independent state was "the one place where they will have a status where they will feel again that sense of belonging to a community which gives most of us security." She argued that Americans as a nation must respond to the needs of the refugees, "the greatest victims of this war": "[O]ur consciences can hardly be clear at the news of their suffering." Eleanor Roosevelt's quotes are from her *My Day* column from November 7, 1945. See Michelle Mart, "Eleanor Roosevelt, Liberalism, and Israel," *Shofar* 24 (2006): 68.

[53] "Eleanor Roosevelt to George Marshall, March 22, 1948," and "Eleanor Roosevelt to Harry Truman, March 22, 1948," Eleanor Roosevelt Papers, UN Pubilcations, 774–75. Truman did not accept Eleanor's resignation. In her letter to Truman, Eleanor also criticized his attempt to restore the prewar "balance of power" rather than engage the Soviet Union in an open political dialogue. She felt that this policy undermined the role of the United Nations and could very well lead to another war, adding: "No one won the last war, and no one will win the next war." See ibid., 775.

[54] "W. E. B. Du Bois to Walter White, July 1, 1948," in *The Eleanor Roosevelt Papers*, ed. Black, 863. On December 8, Eleanor informed White, who traveled with the United States delegation as a consultant, that Jonathan Daniels was going to present a new proposal to the United Nations Sub-Commission on the Prevention and the Protection of Minorities. When the Soviets demanded that this subcommission accept the NAACP's "Appeal to the World," Daniels voted against it. White continued to argue that only an independent international court of human rights could make a difference in cases where states refused to investigate and improve the treatment of minorities. The United States delegation did not accept his position at that time. Ibid., 681–83.

[55] Black et al., *The Eleanor Roosevelt Papers*, 863–64.

56 "Commission on Human Rights Summary Record, Second Session, December 2, 1947," in *The Eleanor Roosevelt Papers*, ed. Black, 685. Eleanor faced a new Secretary of State–William Lovett–who objected to the writing of both a human rights declaration and an international agreement to enforce it. She fought back, and the compromise was to give priority to the drafting of a moral declaration of human rights.

57 Roosevelt, *On My Own*, 80–81.

58 Eleanor added that hers "was a rather grueling schedule for everybody and within a few days I was being denounced–mostly in fun, I hope–as a merciless slave driver." Eleanor Roosevelt, *The Autobiography of Eleanor Roosevelt* (New York: Da Capo Press, 2000), 319.

59 Glendon, *A World Made New*, 89–90.

60 Roosevelt, *What I Hope to Leave Behind*, 560.

61 Roosevelt, *Autobiography*, 311.

62 Segregation was the rule in much of the country during the years after World War II. This system prohibited blacks and whites from sharing public facilities such as schools, swimming pools, restaurants, water fountains, libraries, and even zoos. Whites enjoyed vastly superior facilities than those provided for black citizens. In addition, blacks faced discrimination in all areas, including the political sphere and the workplace. Soviet delegates, whose constitution emphasized the equal rights of all citizens regardless of race or gender, attacked America's racist laws.

63 Roosevelt, *Autobiography*, 320.

64 Ibid.

65 This part of the quotation was removed from the later version of Eleanor's autobiography.

66 These rights are especially celebrated by proponents of the American and British democratic models, and critics argue that workers' rights and job security are often compromised in both countries.

67 In some cases–the Russian Revolution (1917) is a prime example–parties representing workers seized power by force and attempted to take control of the economy. It is now widely acknowledged that in many cases–especially in the Soviet Union–these attempts not only stifled economic progress but also served the interests of a small group of leaders. In most cases, working-class politics were influenced by socialist and communist thinkers, including Karl Marx, Friedrich Engels, and Vladimir Lenin. In the eyes of many, the deplorable human rights record of the Soviet Union has permanently tarnished socialist claims to champion workers' rights.

68 Morsink, *Universal Declaration of Human Rights*, 223.

69 Black et al., *The Eleanor Roosevelt Papers*, 711–13, 754–55.

70 Eleanor Roosevelt, "The Struggle for Human Rights Speech at the Sorbonne, Paris (September 28, 1948)," in *The Eleanor Roosevelt Papers*, ed. Black, 902.

71 Roosevelt, *My Day* (column), November 24, 1948," in *The Eleanor Roosevelt Papers*, ed. Black, 950.

72 Roosevelt, "Struggle for Human Rights Speech," 902.

73 Mary Ann Glendon, "The Forgotten Crucible: The Latin American Influence on the Universal Human Rights Idea," *Harvard Human Rights Journal*, vol. 16 (2003): 35.

74 Eleanor Roosevelt, "The Russians Are Tough," *Look*, February 18, 1947, in *The Eleanor Roosevelt Papers*, ed. Black, 511–13.

75 Roosevelt, in *Courage in a Dangerous World*, ed. Black, 270.

76 Black et al., *The Eleanor Roosevelt Papers*, 921. As Humphrey recalled, "With their full knowledge of the commission's draft and of the difficulties that had to be overcome preparing it, they provided the leadership which made it possible for the Third Committee to produce a text which was very similar to the one that had been prepared by the commission." See Humphrey, *Human Rights*, 65.

77 For a short biography of Malik, see "Dr. Charles Malik," Chahadatouna website, http://www.chahadatouna.com/2006/2006-12/Dr.%20Charles%20Malik/Dr%20Charles%20Malik%20Bio.htm (accessed November 2009).

78 United States Mission to the United Nations in Geneva in Celebration of the Sixtieth Anniversary of the UDHR, *Eleanor Roosevelt and the Universal Declaration of Human Rights* (Geneva: United States Mission to the United Nations in Geneva in Celebration of the Sixtieth Anniversary of the UDHR, 2008), 39.

79 Roosevelt, *My Day*, June 17, 1958.

[80] The first HRC included, among other states, China, Egypt, India, Lebanon, and Iran, alongside Chile, Panama, the Ukraine, the Soviet Union, France, the United Kingdom, and the United States. Excepted were countries that were still under European colonial rule; these weren't represented in the United Nations.

[81] Humphrey, *Human Rights*, 65.

[82] "Human Rights for All: Fiftieth Anniversary of the Universal Declaration of Human Rights, United Nations," http://www.un.org/Overview/rights.html (accessed June 20, 2008).

[83] Roosevelt, *What I Hope to Leave Behind*, 560–61.

[84] Ibid.

[85] Humphrey, *Human Rights*, 67.

[86] Ibid., 67–68.

[87] Ibid.

[88] Ibid., 68.

[89] Roosevelt, *Autobiography*, 322.

[90] Mary Ann Glendon, *A World Made New,* 16.

[91] Roosevelt, *Autobiography*, 322.

[92] Ibid.

[93] Eleanor Roosevelt, "Statement by Mrs. Franklin D. Roosevelt, United States Representative on the Commission on Human Rights, June 18, 1948," Eleanor Roosevelt Papers, United Nations Publications, box 4590, 1948, 2.

[94] John P. Humphrey, *On the Edge of Greatness: The Diaries of John Humphrey, First Director of the United Nations Division of Human Rights,* ed. A. J. Hobbins (Montreal: McGill University Libraries, 1994), 1: 50. In this entry from September 28, 1948, Humphrey criticized Eleanor for speaking too harshly about the Russians in her speech at the Sorbonne.

[95] Roosevelt, *Autobiography*, 322.

[96] International Labor Organization website, http://www.ilo.org/global/About_the_ILO/lang--en/index.htm (accessed May 7, 2009).

[97] "Commission on Human Rights, Verbatim Record, Fourteenth Meeting [excerpt], February 4, 1947," in *The Eleanor Roosevelt Papers*, ed. Black, 506–509.

[98] See note 21, above, for the text of this poem and more information about it.

[99] Theodore G. Bilbo was a two-time governor of Tennessee and later served as a Democrat senator (1935–1947). Known for his fiery rhetoric, Bilbo devoted his time to protecting white supremacy. While supporting the New Deal, he was one of the main obstacles to anti-lynching legislation. Late in his career, he confessed to his membership in the Ku Klux Klan.

[100] John Elliott Rankin was a congressman from Mississippi for 16 consecutive terms (1921–1953) who was known for his anti-black and antisemitic statements. Part of a group of sothern Democrats, he fought civil rights legislation and sought to defend Jim Crow in the South. Rankin was also a vocal member of the House Un-American Activities Committee (HUAC), which investigated alleged communist leanings of leading artists and intellectuals in the United States.

[101] NAACP, "An Appeal to the World: A Statement on the Denial of Human Rights to Minorities in the Case of Citizens of Negro Descent in the United States of America and an Appeal to the United Nations for Redress" (New York: National Association for the Advancement of Colored People, 1947), 4–23.

[102] Eleanor Roosevelt, "Struggle for Human Rights," quoted in *The Eleanor Roosevelt Papers,* ed. Black, 901–05.

[103] Eleanor Roosevelt, "On the Adoption of the Universal Declaration of Human Rights," December 9, 1948, American Rhetoric website, http://www.americanrhetoric.com/speeches/eleanorrooseveltdeclarationhumanrights.htm (accessed March 27, 2009).

"We stand today at the threshold of a great event both in the life of the United Nations and in the life of mankind."

– Eleanor Roosevelt, 1948

THE UNIVERSAL DECLARATION OF HUMAN RIGHTS

The Universal Declaration of Human Rights can be broken down into several parts, each of which contributes to its overall structure and meaning. The chart below shows one way to understand this breakdown.

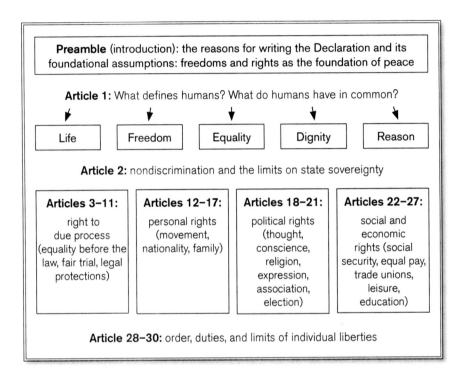

The preamble, or introduction, to the Declaration describes why the document was written. It states that recognizing human dignity and human rights is the foundation of lasting peace. Failure to protect basic rights, and spreading pain and injustice around the world, can only contribute to international violence and instability: "[I]t is essential, if man is not to be compelled to have recourse, as a last resort, to rebellion against tyranny and oppression, that human rights should be protected by the rule of law." In order to prevent such outbreaks of violence, the preamble argues, the world must formulate laws that protect human rights. Finally, the text reaffirms the faith of all signatories "in fundamental human rights, in the dignity and worth of the human person, and in the equal rights of men and women."

Article 1 establishes the tone for what follows, balancing an assertion of essential rights against the duties of the individual. We all start out in life free—no human being should be considered a slave or in any sense inferior to others at birth. The article adds that all humans are "endowed with reason" and are obligated to treat each other fairly.

Article 2 emphasizes that the equal rights of all people are not altered by biological, cultural, or political differences. It states:

> *Everyone is entitled to all the rights and freedoms set forth in this Declaration, without distinction of any kind, such as race, color, sex, language, religion, political or other opinion, national or social origin, property, birth or other status.*

Having surveyed the history of discrimination, the authors of the Declaration explicitly rejected past grounds on which one group claimed it should enjoy higher status than another; even a sovereign state has no right to rank its citizens. This article places human rights not in opposition to the laws of a given country but over and above them. After the Germans deprived Europe's Jews of their freedoms during World War II—a process legal under Nazi laws—states should no longer be permitted, this article maintains, to trample on basic rights.

Article 3 establishes three basic rights, echoing the American Declaration of Independence's identification of "life, liberty, and the pursuit of happiness"—only the third was changed, to "security of person." When individuals choose to enter society, they do so on the premise that their government will not deprive them of these fundamental rights—indeed, the state is expected to do its utmost to guarantee them.

The next few articles set forth a number of important legal rights. They declare slavery and torture to be direct violations of human rights; they lay out the process of charging human beings with crimes and bringing them to trial (the right to "due legal process"); and they proclaim everyone "innocent until proved guilty," which places the responsibility of proving guilt in the hands of their prosecutors.

Articles 12 through *17* address the rights to move freely, to possess a nationality, to form a family, and to own property. Before and during the war, Jews and other minorities had been deprived of all of these rights. They lost their right to nationality and became a stateless people with no government to represent them or hear their grievances. Other societies had done the same to certain classes of human beings, including slaves, servants, and dissenters who held minority views about politics and religion.

Articles 18 to *21* relate to a category some call "old rights": those rights and liberties defined by classical liberal theory. Won after a long struggle against European monarchies and religious oppression, these rights long defined free society in the West. They declare that "Everyone has the right to freedom of thought, conscience and religion"; "Everyone has the right to freedom of opinion and expression"; "Everyone has the right to freedom of peaceful assembly and association"; and "Everyone has the right to take part in the government of his country, directly or through freely chosen representatives." They range from freedom of speech to basic political rights. In addition, Article 21 upholds the principle of popular sovereignty, namely, the idea that all legitimate governments reflect the wishes and aspirations of the people:

The will of the people shall be the basis of the authority of government; this will shall be expressed in periodic and genuine elections which shall be by universal and equal suffrage, and shall be held by secret vote or by equivalent free voting procedures.

Articles 22 to *27* protect what are often called "new rights," because they reflect the struggles and needs of a modern industrial society, a place where people long for fair employment, economic security, health care, and education. The security of these rights is "indispensable" for the "dignity and the free development" of the individual.

Article 23, which prompted a long debate among members of the Human Rights Commission, declares that everyone has the right "to just and favorable conditions of work and to protection against unemployment." Moreover, everyone, "without any discrimination, has the right to equal pay for equal work." The right to form trade unions is also declared, meaning that workers may form a group to negotiate with owners.

Article 24, complementing Article 23, protects workers with leisure time: "Everyone has the right to rest and leisure, including reasonable limitation of working hours and periodic holidays with pay."

Article 26 declares that "Everyone has the right to education." The article demands that education be universally available and that every child receive schooling. The article also grants parents the right to decide what education their children receive.

Articles 28 through *30* take a step back, adding a few broad, framing principles to the Declaration. As a practical matter, people are "entitled to a social and international order in which the rights and freedoms set forth in this Declaration can be fully realized." Disrupting peace and order would therefore violate the article. Not only do all human beings have duties they must perform so that their community can continue to thrive, they must surrender a measure of freedom to honor the rights of others; everyone must respect "the just requirements of morality, public order and the general welfare in a democratic society."

The Universal Declaration of Human Rights (1948)

Preamble

Whereas recognition of the inherent dignity and of the equal and inalienable rights of all members of the human family is the foundation of freedom, justice and peace in the world,

Whereas disregard and contempt for human rights have resulted in barbarous acts which have outraged the conscience of mankind, and the advent of a world in which human beings shall enjoy freedom of speech and belief and freedom from fear and want has been proclaimed as the highest aspiration of the common people,

Whereas it is essential, if man is not to be compelled to have recourse, as a last resort, to rebellion against tyranny and oppression, that human rights should be protected by the rule of law,

Whereas it is essential to promote the development of friendly relations between nations,

Whereas the peoples of the United Nations have in the Charter reaffirmed their faith in fundamental human rights, in the dignity and worth of the human person, and in the equal rights of men and women, and have determined to promote social progress and better standards of life in larger freedom,

Whereas Member States have pledged themselves to achieve, in cooperation with the United Nations, the promotion of universal respect for and observance of human rights and fundamental freedoms,

Whereas a common understanding of these rights and freedoms is of the greatest importance for the full realization of this pledge,

---

Now, Therefore THE GENERAL ASSEMBLY proclaims THIS UNIVERSAL DECLARATION OF HUMAN RIGHTS as a common standard of achievement for all peoples and all nations, to the end that every individual and every organ of society, keeping this Declaration constantly in mind, shall strive by teaching and education to promote respect for these rights and freedoms and by progressive measures, national and international, to secure their universal and effective recognition and observance, both among the peoples of Member States themselves and among the peoples of territories under their jurisdiction.

Article 1. *All human beings are born free and equal in dignity and rights. They are endowed with reason and conscience and should act towards one another in a spirit of brotherhood.*

Article 2. *Everyone is entitled to all the rights and freedoms set forth in this Declaration, without distinction of any kind, such as race, color, sex, language, religion, political or other opinion, national or social origin, property, birth or other status. Furthermore, no distinction shall be made on the basis of the political, jurisdictional or international status of the country or territory to which a person belongs, whether it be independent, trust, non-self-governing or under any other limitation of sovereignty.*

Article 3. *Everyone has the right to life, liberty and security of person.*

Article 4. *No one shall be held in slavery or servitude; slavery and the slave trade shall be prohibited in all their forms.*

Article 5. *No one shall be subjected to torture or to cruel, inhuman or degrading treatment or punishment.*

Article 6. *Everyone has the right to recognition everywhere as a person before the law.*

Article 7. *All are equal before the law and are entitled without any discrimination to equal protection of the law. All are entitled to equal protection against any discrimination in violation of this Declaration and against any incitement to such discrimination.*

Article 8. *Everyone has the right to an effective remedy by the competent national tribunals for acts violating the fundamental rights granted him by the constitution or by law.*

Article 9. *No one shall be subjected to arbitrary arrest, detention or exile.*

Article 10. *Everyone is entitled in full equality to a fair and public hearing by an independent and impartial tribunal, in the determination of his rights and obligations and of any criminal charge against him.*

Article 11. *(1) Everyone charged with a penal offence has the right to be presumed innocent until proved guilty according to law in a public trial at which he has had all the guarantees necessary for his defense. (2) No one shall be held guilty of any penal offence on account of any act or omission which did not constitute a penal offence, under national or international law, at the time when it was committed. Nor shall a heavier penalty be imposed than the one that was applicable at the time the penal offence was committed.*

Article 12. *No one shall be subjected to arbitrary interference with his privacy, family, home or correspondence, nor to attacks upon his honor and reputation. Everyone has the right to the protection of the law against such interference or attacks.*

Article 13. *(1) Everyone has the right to freedom of movement and residence within the borders of each state. (2) Everyone has the right to leave any country, including his own, and to return to his country.*

Article 14. *(1) Everyone has the right to seek and to enjoy in other countries asylum from persecution. (2) This right may not be invoked in the case of prosecutions genuinely arising from non-political crimes or from acts contrary to the purposes and principles of the United Nations.*

Article 15. *(1) Everyone has the right to a nationality. (2) No one shall be arbitrarily deprived of his nationality nor denied the right to change his nationality.*

Article 16. *(1) Men and women of full age, without any limitation due to race, nationality, or religion, have the right to marry and to found a family. They are entitled to equal rights as to marriage, during marriage and at its dissolution. (2) Marriage shall be entered into only with the free and full consent of the intending spouses. (3) The family is the natural and fundamental group unit of society and is entitled to protection by society and the State.*

Article 17. *(1) Everyone has the right to own property alone as well as in association with others. (2) No one shall be arbitrarily deprived of his property.*

Article 18. *Everyone has the right to freedom of thought, conscience and religion; this right includes freedom to change his religion or belief, and freedom, either alone or in community with others and in public or private, to manifest his religion or belief in teaching, practice, worship and observance.*

Article 19. *Everyone has the right to freedom of opinion and expression; this right includes freedom to hold opinions without interference and to seek, receive and impart information and ideas through any media and regardless of frontiers.*

Article 20. *(1) Everyone has the right to freedom of peaceful assembly and association. (2) No one may be compelled to belong to an association.*

Article 21. *(1) Everyone has the right to take part in the government of his country, directly or through freely chosen representatives. (2) Everyone has the right of equal access to public service in his country. (3) The will of the people shall be the basis of the authority of government; this will shall be expressed in periodic and genuine elections which shall be by universal and equal suffrage, and shall be held by secret vote or by equivalent free voting procedures.*

Article 22. *Everyone, as a member of society, has the right to social security and is entitled to realization, through national effort and international cooperation and in accordance with the organization and resources of each State, of the economic, social and cultural rights indispensable for his dignity and the free development of his personality.*

Article 23. *(1) Everyone has the right to work, to free choice of employment, to just and favorable conditions of work and to protection against unemployment. (2) Everyone, without any discrimination, has the right to equal pay for equal work. (3) Everyone who works has the right to just and favorable remuneration ensuring for himself and his family an existence worthy of human dignity, and supplemented, if necessary, by other means of social protection. (4) Everyone has the right to form and to join trade unions for the protection of his interests.*

Article 24. *Everyone has the right to rest and leisure, including reasonable limitation of working hours and periodic holidays with pay.*

Article 25. *(1) Everyone has the right to a standard of living adequate for the health and well-being of himself and of his family, including food, clothing, housing and medical care and necessary social services, and the right to security in the event of unemployment, sickness, disability, widowhood, old age or other lack of livelihood in circumstances beyond his control. (2) Motherhood and childhood are entitled to special care and assistance. All children, whether born in or out of wedlock, shall enjoy the same social protection.*

Article 26. *(1) Everyone has the right to education. Education shall be free, at least in the elementary and fundamental stages. Elementary education shall be compulsory. Technical and professional education shall be made generally available, and higher education shall be equally accessible to all on the basis of merit. (2) Education shall be directed to the full development of the human personality and to the strengthening of respect for human rights and fundamental freedoms. It shall promote understanding, tolerance, and friendship among all nations, racial or religious groups, and shall further the activities of the United Nations for the maintenance of peace. (3) Parents have a prior right to choose the kind of education that shall be given to their children.*

Article 27. *(1) Everyone has the right freely to participate in the cultural life of the community, to enjoy the arts and to share in scientific advancement and its benefits. (2) Everyone has the right to the protection of the moral and material interests resulting from any scientific, literary or artistic production of which he is the author.*

Article 28. *Everyone is entitled to a social and international order in which the rights and freedoms set forth in this Declaration can be fully realized.*

Article 29. *(1) Everyone has duties to the community in which alone the free and full development of his personality is possible. (2) In the exercise of his rights and freedoms, everyone shall be subject only to such limitations as are determined by law solely for the purpose of securing due recognition and respect for the rights and freedoms of others and of meeting the just requirements of morality, public order and the general welfare in a democratic society. (3) These rights and freedoms may in no case be exercised contrary to the purposes and principles of the United Nations.*

Article 30. *Nothing in this Declaration may be interpreted as implying for any State, group, or person any right to engage in any activity or to perform any act aimed at the destruction of any of the rights and freedoms set forth herein.*[1]

THE IRON CURTAIN

While the Human Rights Commission labored to complete the Declaration, tensions between the Soviet Bloc and the West were steadily mounting. Although the Soviet Union and the United States had fought as allies in World War II, the alliance disintegrated as the Soviets solidified their control over large areas of Eastern Europe (and East Asia).[2] Even before Germany had been defeated, the Soviets sought to extend their sphere of influence to match the advance of the Red Army. Eastern Europe, East Germany, the Baltic states, and the Balkans all became aligned with Moscow and together constituted the Soviet or Eastern Bloc (courtiers with communist governments that fell under the USSR's influence). By the middle of the 1950s, the Soviet Bloc included 16 states.[3]

The United States and its allies countered Soviet strength by developing economic ties with Western Europe and by creating the North Atlantic Treaty Organization (NATO), which in 1949 included 12 states from Western and Central Europe and North America. The hostility between the competing alliances worried many small nations and contributed to a growing cynicism about the prospects for international cooperation.[4]

Soon after the Allies prevailed in Europe, Winston Churchill, the British prime minister, lost his bid for reelection. Now a private citizen, Churchill gave a memorable speech on March 5, 1946, at Westminster College in Fulton, Missouri. "From Stettin in the Baltic to Trieste in the Adriatic," he declared,

> *an iron curtain has descended across the Continent. Behind that line lie all the capitals of the ancient states of Central and Eastern Europe . . . in what I must call the Soviet sphere, and all are subject, in one form or another, not only to Soviet influence but to a very high and in some cases increasing measure of control from Moscow.[5]*

He then went on to announce that the Soviets posed an immediate threat to Christian civilization: "Except in the British Commonwealth and in the United States where Communism is in its infancy, the Communist parties or fifth columns constitute a growing challenge and peril to Christian civilization."[6] With President Truman in the audience, Churchill urged the creation of a strong alliance between Britain and the United States in order to protect democracy:

> *If the population of the English-speaking Commonwealth be added to that of the United States, with all that such cooperation implies in the air, on the sea, all over the globe, and in science and in industry, and in moral force, there will be no quivering, precarious balance of power to offer its temptation to ambition or adventure. On the contrary, there will be an overwhelming assurance of security.[7]*

Churchill believed that such an alliance would be more effective than the United Nations in maintaining a global balance of power and limiting the spread of communism.

Two days later, Eleanor responded:

> *I think the time has come for us as a nation . . . to decide what really offers us the best chance for peace in the future. Mr. Churchill's speech in Missouri indicates his belief . . . that the future peace of the world can best be guaranteed by a military alliance*

between Great Britain and the United States. . . . I think he pays the
English-speaking people of the world a very high compliment.
I hope that we could be trusted to have no selfish desires, not
to think of our own interests first, and therefore never to take
advantage of our strength at the expense of other peoples. We must,
however, it seems to me face the fact that were such an alliance
formed, other nations in the world would certainly feel that they
must form independent alliances too. . . .

The situation does not seem to me to differ very greatly from the
old balance of power politics that have been going on in Europe for
hundreds of years. . . . Almost invariably it led sooner or later to
wars and more wars. The alternative to this old political game was
what Woodrow Wilson dreamed of in the League of Nations. Then
my husband and many other great statesmen planned the United
Nations organization as a result of this last war. Instead of running
an armament race against each other and building up trade cartels
and political alliances, we the nations of the world should join
together, each contributing a certain amount of military strength to
be used only against an aggressor. We would use the forum of the
United Nations to discuss our difficulties and our grievances using
our diplomatic machinery to adjust such things as we could among
ourselves, but bringing questions that individual governments
disagreed on before the bar of the United Nations as a whole.
Difficult machinery to work out, but it aims at the nations of the
world living under law, using an international court of justice and
only resorting to force to curb an aggressor.[8]

Eleanor then alluded to Churchill's speech: "I do not wonder that the elderly statesmen think this a new and revolutionary move in the international situa-

---

Description of map on next page: Following the victory in World War II, the former Allied Powers broke apart along ideological and socio-political lines. Tensions rose before the war was entirely over, and they began to divide their areas of influence. The communist Soviet Union annexed several countries it liberated from the Nazis and made others satellite states that created the Eastern Bloc. Fearing the expansion of communism, the West—including Britain, France, and the United States—reacted by establishing its own sphere of control, known as the Western Bloc, and by creating the North Atlantic Treaty Organization (NATO). Between 1947 and 1991, the two leading powers, the U.S. and the Soviet Union, engaged in what became known as the Cold War. It involved an atomic arms race, clandestine operations, and direct and indirect involvement in wars whose goal was to undermine each other's influence. Countries not directly involved in the Cold War in Asia, Latin America, and the former European colonies were often called the "Third World."

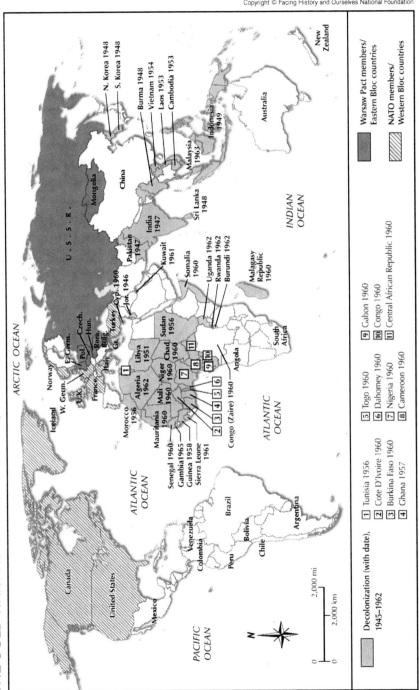

THE COLD WAR AND DECOLONIZATION, 1945–1962

Decolonization (with date), 1945–1962

1 Tunisia 1956	5 Togo 1960
2 Cote D'Ivoire 1960	6 Dahomey 1960
3 Burkina Faso 1960	7 Nigeria 1960
4 Ghana 1957	8 Cameroon 1960

9 Gabon 1960	
10 Congo 1960	
11 Central African Republic 1960	

Warsaw Pact members/
Eastern Bloc countries

NATO members/
Western Bloc countries

tion." But, she continued, the world now faces "two possibilities here, the old way and the new way. We have seen the results of the old way . . . in war and destruction. . . . Might it be wise to try the new way?"[9]

Such was the increasing international pressure when the organizing, or "nuclear," committee began its preliminary meetings at Hunter College in New York in April and May 1946; it would be more than two years before the Universal Declaration of Human Rights was approved by the General Assembly, by which time many world leaders would embrace the strategy of the elderly statesman Churchill. International cooperation lost its luster, and the world witnessed the dawn of a new era of international conflict. The postwar superpowers, the United States and the Soviet Union, rushed into a nuclear arms race and relied on propaganda, espionage, and secret operations to gain the edge. The Cold War yielded an atomic arsenal so huge that it had the potential to destroy human civilization many times over. Vast resources were devoted to this arms race, a project at odds on every level with the goals of the United Nations. The work of the Human Rights Commission inevitably suffered.

Against this background, national sovereignty became even more important. As Eleanor and her colleagues discussed the Declaration, some states insisted on their unqualified right to decide their own laws and policies. French jurist and member of the Declaration's drafting committee René Cassin responded. Cassin, who had lost many members of his family in the Holocaust, warned against this renewed emphasis on national sovereignty. Years later, with Cold War tensions on the rise, he wrote:

> The Great Powers are still saying "Every man is master in his own house. You have no right to know what I am doing with my own citizens." You can see how difficult it is to uproot a principle which derives undeniably from practical reality, since the independence of States is in itself a desirable thing, something people will fight for. The right of nations to govern themselves is accepted as the natural order of things. Why should we fear that any country protects its interests too vigorously? Our anxiety is justified in that there comes a moment when the State says: for the purpose of my development, I propose to set my own rules, as I think fit, and if I destroy men in the process, that is no concern of yours.[10]

"But it is very much our concern," Cassin argued. "World progress cannot be built on the ashes of human suffering. That is the aim of Human Rights."[11]

Cassin's concern was justified. In the years that followed the adoption of the Declaration, governments often used the idea of national sovereignty as a shield against legitimate international criticism. News of political repression in the Soviet Union appeared almost daily in the West. Many activists, intellectuals, and human rights groups adopted the Universal Declaration of Human Rights and began to apply it routinely to call attention to these abuses. In a few years, it became the moral yardstick for measuring individual freedom and security around the world.[13]

Cartoon depiction of Winston Churchill peering under the figurative "Iron Curtain" that separated the Soviet Bloc from the Western world, March 6, 1946.

Leslie Gilbert, 1946. Courtesy of the British Cartoon Archive, University of Kent

While the United States enthusiastically supported the United Nations during and immediately after the war, it began very shortly thereafter to reject the idea that an international body had the power to dictate policy to individual states.[14] The change of stance was due, in part, to pressure from a growing anticommunist movement in the United States, which reached its heyday in the early 1950s. During the infamous "Second Red Scare," Senator Joseph McCarthy inflamed national paranoia by claiming that communists had infiltrated the State Department and were controlling American foreign policy.[15] During the 1940s and 1950s, thousands of activists, politicians, intellectuals, artists, and entertainers were blacklisted, investigated, and interrogated in public hearings by the House Un-American Activities Committee (HUAC). Outraged when many of her friends and advisors came under scrutiny, Eleanor spoke out against this "extra-curricular Congressional activity" for silencing legitimate criticism of America's policies and questioning the patriotism of many decent citizens.[16] Notoriously, in 1947, HUAC investigated communist infiltration of the motion-picture industry in Hollywood. The commit-

WHO WAS RENÉ CASSIN?

UN Photo/Yutaka Nagata

René Cassin in 1944. Cassin was one of the most influential members of the Declaration's drafting committee. During World War II, he worked for General Charles de Gaulle, the leader of the French resistance in exile. Cassin was entrusted with the task of reorganizing France's administrative structure after the war.

Cassin was one of the most influential members of the drafting group. Born in 1887 to a merchant family in the town of Bayonne (near the border with Spain), Cassin was deeply influenced by his father's renunciation of religion and his loyalty to France. A brilliant student in law, economics, and the humanities, Cassin received his doctoral degree in 1914. Drafted to serve in the French army during World War I, he was severely injured. After taking a post as a professor of law, he founded an international organization for disabled veterans committed to peace.

In 1924, Cassin was selected to represent France in the League of Nations—the organization that preceded the United Nations. When World War II broke out and the German army invaded France, Cassin fled to England. Many of his relatives were deported to concentration camps by the collaborationist French government.

In England, Cassin worked for the leader of the French resistance in exile, Charles de Gaulle. A long collaboration between the two ensued. Cassin became the chief legal advisor to the Free French Forces, and, when the war ended and de Gaulle became the president of the new French republic, Cassin was entrusted with the task of reorganizing France's administrative structure. He worked on human rights in the United Nations for many years. In 1968 he won a Nobel Prize for his humanitarian work.[12]

tee targeted a list of several hundred members of the entertainment business (including the famous actor/director Charlie Chaplin). Those who were called to testify before the committee were almost automatically blacklisted (except for those who named friends and colleagues, and there were many who did just that). Often they lost their jobs and friends and were unable to find new jobs in the United States.

Isolationism, fostered by conservative Republicans and southern Democrats, dealt another blow to the spirit of international cooperation. The isolationists refused to consider any agreements that did not cater to a narrow definition of American interests. As the powerful southern Democrats, led by South Carolina's Strom Thurmond, fought to preserve segregation and white supremacy, they withheld crucial votes from treaties that might have allowed international bodies to criticize the United States' discriminatory policies against African Americans. They had allies in the executive branch, including the conservative under secretary of state, Robert A. Lovett. Lovett closely followed the drafting of the Universal Declaration of Human Rights, to which he objected because of his isolationist stance and deep suspicion of international agreements. Although Eleanor and other supporters of the project prevailed, Lovett was able to weaken the Declaration's authority. He did so by convincing

United Nations International Nursery School students look at a poster of the Declaration.

Eleanor that she and her colleagues should rework the preamble so that "it called upon members to 'promote' rather than to 'enforce' the rights enumerated in the draft Declaration."[17] Later, he opposed and slowed down the creation of a legally binding human rights covenant.

The Cold War and southern anxieties weakened Eleanor's position as the chairperson of the Human Rights Commission. Had conditions been different, she might have witnessed in her lifetime the completion not only of the Declaration but also of an international human rights treaty and a series of international institutions and rules for its enforcement.

"WHERE DO HUMAN RIGHTS BEGIN?"

What, then, did the authors of the Declaration achieve? What did *they* think was their primary achievement? Soon after the Universal Declaration of Human Rights was adopted, critics spoke up. Why had no binding legal agreement or covenant been created? Were prospects for completion of a successful covenant and its enforcement bright or dim? Eleanor was aware of some of the problems. For the time being, she explained, the document was

> *simply a declaration that sets standards and puts down things for which we want to strive. It has no legal binding value, but it is a preparation for the coming bill of rights. When the [legal] Covenant is written, then we will have to be prepared to ask our various nations to ratify that Covenant and to accept the fact that the Covenant has legal binding value.*[18]

As early as April 1948 (several months before the Declaration was finally adopted), Eleanor published an article entitled "The Promise of Human Rights." She wrote: "It seems to me most important that the Declaration be accepted by all member nations, not because they will immediately live up to all of its provisions, but because they ought to support the standards toward which the nations must henceforward aim." In a speech before the United Nations General Assembly, Eleanor fearlessly suggested that the Declaration "may well become the international Magna Carta of all men everywhere."[19] Still, she knew that it would take years to create the treaties and courts needed to enforce the Declaration.

It was impossible to dispute, Eleanor acknowledged, that no article in the document could be legally enforced. But to place the emphasis on that fact was to understimate the Declaration's power. Eleanor made it clear that she and her colleages had "great belief . . . in the force of documents which do express ideals." They were aware that while words, ideas, and ideals may mean little by themselves, they hold great power when properly disseminated and embraced: "They carry no weight unless the people know them, unless the people understand them, unless the people demand that they be lived."[20] This is where education mattered. Once those ideas come to life in the public mind, they could bring about real change.[21]

Moreover, as events teach us nearly every day, it takes much more than documents, agreements, and courts to ensure that rights are respected. When political will is lacking, the international community routinely fails to defend the downtrodden. So it was crucial that the human rights enterprise expanded beyond the confines of politics and the legal system. Eleanor understood this well: "I . . . think," she said in 1948, "that the Declaration will help forward

Eleanor at the United Nations General Assembly building. She served as a delegate to the United Nations from 1945 until 1952. Eleanor wrote in her daily column that every person "has a deep and solemn obligation" to create a peaceful world.

very largely the *education* of the peoples of the world."[22] The next year, she appealed to leaders worldwide to

> *make the Declaration a living document, something that is not just words on paper, but something which we really strive to bring to the lives of all people, all people everywhere in the world.*
>
> *Now to do that we, all of us, will have to study this document. We will have to understand how it came to be written, why certain things are in it. . . . M. Laugier, out of his wisdom, said, 'This is very valuable. People who discuss as much as this over ideas are going home to talk about them afterwards.' I hope that he was right, because that is the way this document will come to mean something in the lives of people all over the world.*[23]

A few years later, Eleanor gave a speech at the United Nations which she called "Where Do Human Rights Begin?" In her view, human rights began

> *in small places, close to home—so close and so small that they cannot be seen on any map of the world. Yet they are the world of the individual person: The neighborhood he lives in; the school or college he attends; the factory, farm, or office where he works. Such are the places where every man, woman, and child seeks equal justice, equal opportunity, equal dignity without discrimination. Unless these rights have meaning there, they have little meaning anywhere. Without concerted citizen action to uphold them close to home, we shall look in vain for progress in the larger world.*[24]

Fortunately, such change began right away. Three years after the Universal Declaration of Human Rights was adopted by the General Assembly, Eleanor announced that "the language of that Declaration has been written into the constitution of a number of states."[25] John Humphrey, who directed the human rights division until 1966, agreed. "I was happy," Humphrey recalled in his memoir,

> *about the [Human Rights Commission's initial] decision to concentrate on the Declaration. . . . The Declaration, even though it might not be technically binding, would apply to all states and would have the great authority of the United Nations behind it. It would also be a catalyst of national and international*

legislation. . . . Even in 1948, my instinct told me that eventually it would become part of international law whatever the intentions of its authors, or the form in which it was adopted.[26]

Indeed, in a diary entry from November 20, 1948, Humphrey described a conversation with Eleanor in which he anticipated the importance of the Declaration for future generations. "On Friday evening," he wrote,

I talked with Mrs. Roosevelt while she had some tea and sandwiches (having missed her dinner). I told her that I now think that the Declaration will prove to be more important than the [Convention], that the distinction between moral force and legal binding force means little in the present state of international organization, and that the Declaration will develop its own implementation. I am firmly convinced . . . that this Declaration will prove to be a tremendously important instrument.[27]

As more countries acknowledged the claims of the United Nations (and its emphasis on internationalism), some began to question the universality of its tenets. Had Western values prevailed, and were they about to be forced upon all other cultures? Many feared that they were. But the very diversity of world cultures did not, according to Eleanor, rule out the possibility that people from different backgrounds could come to an agreement that satisfied them all.

A shared moral framework for all cultures was, after all, the true goal of the Declaration. "The really important thing," said Eleanor,

was to get down on paper, for people all over the world, with different backgrounds, customs, and stages of development, the basic idea that every individual had certain rights and freedoms that could not be taken away from him. It gave respect and importance to the individual, which is, of course, a basic tenet of democracy.[29]

Could people who came from different cultures really agree on their future moral goals, as Eleanor hoped that they would? "Some people feel," Eleanor had argued in 1940,

that human nature cannot be changed, but I think when we look at what has been achieved by the Nazi and Fascist dictators, we have

WHO WAS JOHN HUMPHREY?

John Humphrey in Geneva in 1947. Entrusted by Eleanor Roosevelt with the task of producing a first sketch for the Declaration, Humphrey made evident his concern for the welfare of working people in many articles he inserted into the first draft of the document.

The Canadian scholar and activist John Peters Humphrey (1905–1995) was entrusted by Eleanor with the task of producing a first sketch for the Universal Declaration of Human Rights. Humphrey's childhood—remarkably like Eleanor's—bore deep marks of tragedy. One biographer wrote:

Humphrey's childhood had been a painful one. He was the third child of Frank Monmouth Humphrey, a St. John shoe manufacturer. . . . Frank died of cancer when John was only thirteen months old. At age six, John's left arm was amputated at the shoulder after an accident in which his clothes caught fire. Finally, when he was eleven, his mother also died of cancer.[28]

Humphrey went on to spend four years at boarding school, the Rothesay Collegiate School. His years there, in contrast to Eleanor's experience at Allenswood, were almost uniformly unpleasant and humiliating. Scholars argue that the abuse he suffered at the hands of his teachers made him acutely sensitive to cruelty in general. From there, he went on to study accounting and law.

After practicing law privately between 1929 and 1936, he eventually became a professor at McGill University. During the Great Depression, Humphrey became a socialist. His interest in the welfare of working people was manifested in many articles he inserted into his draft of the Declaration. Many of these "social and economic" rights made it into the final Declaration.

to acknowledge the fact that we do not live in a static condition,
but that the influences of education, of moral and physical training
have an effect upon our whole beings. If human beings can be
changed to fit a Nazi or Fascist pattern or a Communist pattern,
certainly we should not lose heart at the thought of changing
human nature to fit a Democratic way of life.[30]

In the end, she believed, the imperfections of the Declaration were not so important. If it had managed to suggest how human beings could be truly free, that was sufficient. In the speech she gave before the General Assembly just as the Declaration was being approved, Eleanor made that point:

The central fact is that man is fundamentally a moral being,
that the light we have is imperfect does not matter so long as we
are always trying to improve it. . . . We are equal in sharing the
moral freedom that distinguishes us as men. Man's status makes
each individual an end in himself. No man is by nature simply the
servant of the state or of another man. . . . The ideal and fact of
freedom—and not technology—are the true distinguishing marks
of our civilization.[31]

The Declaration was designed to define and ensure the freedoms for which all human beings yearn. For Eleanor, the classic demands for freedom and equal opportunities had been voiced in the historical struggle for democracy.[32] That struggle was far from over, and the Declaration would help move it toward its climax. In her earlier wartime essay "The Moral Basis of Democracy," Eleanor stated this point plainly: if we provide all citizens with basic rights and freedoms,

we have paved the way for the first hope for real peace the world has
ever known. All people desire peace, but they are led to war because
what is offered them in this world seems to be unjust, and they are
constantly seeking a way to right that injustice.[33]

Elsewhere she suggested that the people's desires could be satisfied by honoring the Universal Declaration of Human Rights:

Everywhere many people will feel more secure. And as the Great
Powers tie themselves down by their ratifications, the smaller

nations which fear that the great may abuse their strength, will
acquire a greater sense of assurance.[34]

Her sentiments were echoed in the Declaration's first articles, as well as in the words of her colleague Charles Malik. Speaking on February 26, 1948, Malik asserted that

the question of human rights is second only to the question of the
maintenance of peace and security. In fact, the violation of human
rights is one of the causes of war, so that to achieve the first aim of
the United Nations, namely the maintenance of international peace
and security, you must first guarantee the observance of human
rights.[35]

While the Declaration's legal status remained a topic of debate, its moral authority did not. Humphrey later commented:

Its impact on world public opinion has been as great as [if not
greater than] that of any contemporary international instrument,
including the Charter of the United Nations. . . . In the United
Nations, where the Declaration is constantly invoked, it has become
the criterion for judging the conduct of states in their relations
with individuals and groups. . . . It has inspired or influenced so
many resolutions in various organs of the United Nations and the
specialized agencies that it would be difficult to count them. It has
also inspired a growing body of treaties.[36]

But Humphrey knew that the true test was yet to come: "The final judgment of history will be determined by the impact which the Declaration has and will have on the actual conduct of states and of individual men and women everywhere." Still, even if there was "little reason for thinking that human rights . . . are better respected now than they were before 1948 . . . the international community now possesses 'a common standard of achievement' by reference to which the conduct of these governments can be and is judged."[37]

The Universal Declaration of Human Rights has proven to be remarkably influential. Scholars agree that it has been "the foundation of much of the post-1945 codification of human rights, and the international legal system is replete with global and regional treaties based, in large measure, on the Declaration."[38] Johannes Morsink, a scholar of political theory, recently concluded that "fifty international human rights instruments . . . can be said to have been inspired by the Universal Declaration of Human Rights."[39] For better or worse, the Declaration is now routinely cited in legal cases around the world—it has come to have the legal force of a law. Many national constitutions formally recognize that the rights enshrined in the Declaration take priority over any national laws. In addition, hundreds of organizations arose to protect the principles of the Declaration. Those organizations, inspired by the principles laid out in the Declaration, work to mobilize public opinion and monitor the human rights records of countries around the world.[40]

HUMAN RIGHTS AT HOME

When adopted in 1948, the Declaration became a formal code by which observers could measure the rights allotted to citizens. The United States, in Eleanor's eyes, needed it just like everyone else. In the draft of her 1948 Sorbonne speech, she wrote:

> *In the United States we are old enough not to claim perfection. We recognize that our minorities have not yet achieved the full rights which this Bill will make essential rights for every human being. . . . Discrimination against minorities is caused by bigotry and frequently is the result of ignorance and illiteracy. Economic inequality also makes for discrimination against minorities . . . [If] the Covenant [of human rights] is agreed upon and our leaders can achieve its ratification throughout the United States, then this International Act will have helped to speed the education fight now being made to achieve rights for all.[41]*

The State Department objected to this open discussion of discrimination and made her change her final draft.[42] But in the decade after the war, notwithstanding her work with the United Nations, Eleanor made the question of equal civil rights her number one priority. "As opponents of [equal] civil rights became more shrill in their resistance," wrote Allida Black, "and black demands for redress became more assertive, Eleanor Roosevelt increased her support of demonstrations and public protests. . . . [S]he now refused to back away from endorsing confrontational demands for racial equality."[43] Eleanor believed that segregation, discrimination, and racial prejudices had to be confronted out in the open.

Elizabeth Eckford entering the newly desegregated Little Rock Central High School. In response to white students' hostile reactions to the desegregation of public schools, Eleanor noted that ". . . [the United States has] the responsibility to give an example of how nations can live together in peace and unity."

In the 1950s, the civil rights movement began to crystallize, and people began to organize for a more direct confrontation—in the courts and on the streets. Eleanor, whose friendship with Walter White and other black activists grew stronger than ever, became an important partner in this struggle. Now an official board member of the NAACP, she helped raise funds, provided a place to instruct young activists and demonstrators, fought for improved housing conditions and slum clearing, provided strategic advice, and made endless appeals to legislators and state representatives. Among the main issues she fought for was equality in education. For example, in 1947, Eleanor addressed the NAACP's annual convention at the Lincoln Memorial in Washington, DC. Before a crowd of 100,000, she called for overturning the existing law that allowed for segregated schools across the United States. Later, in 1954, after years of legal battles, the NAACP saw the successful defeat of segregation in public schools. In possibly the most significant legal ruling of the civil rights era, *Brown v. Board of Education*, the Supreme Court declared separated all-white and all-black schools unconstitutional—the inferior education provided to black students was a violation of their civil rights. This court ruling renewed the struggle for civil rights, ushering in a period of new tactics, new goals, and many new challenges. In 1957, seeking to comply with the new Supreme Court ruling, the board of education in Little Rock, Arkansas, developed a desegregation plan: nine black students would be admitted to Little Rock Central High School. The decision was opposed by the governor of Arkansas, Orval E. Faubus, a segregationist who was courting votes. He responded by calling in the Arkansas National Guard to stop the "Little Rock Nine" from entering the school. Fueled by the governor's inflammatory rhetoric, a mob gathered at the school, threatening to lynch the students. One of the nine, Elizabeth Eckford, narrowly escaped with her life. For Eleanor, the hatred and anger on the streets of Little Rock highlighted the very issues to which she had dedicated her life:

Grown women wanted to kill one . . . girl, one of the [black] children going into the Little Rock school. The cold fact is hard to believe that anywhere in our country women would be screaming for the death of a child because she was going into a white school. Yet this is what happened. This was the result of mass fear and mass psychology.[44]

Eleanor warned about the consequences of resisting integration:

I only hope that before too long the people of my race in my country will wake up to the fact that they are endangering the peace of the world. The world is made up of people of many races and many colors. They must be accepted as people and treated with the same dignity and respect wherever they are. Until we do this with our own citizens at home, we will be suspect to the world, our leadership will have little value and we will endanger the peace of the world, because we have the responsibility to give an example of how nations can live together in peace and unity.[45]

A year later, Eleanor's own life was threatened. When she agreed to teach a workshop on integration at the Highlander Folk School, a training ground for generations of civil rights activists, the Ku Klux Klan put a price on her head. Eleanor could not be stopped from speaking her mind. Now elderly, she was not always on the movement's front lines, but she was a keen witness to the nonviolent civil rights revolution. She used her celebrity to support the efforts of the moment, speaking out in print, on the radio, and on television.

Eleanor did not live to see many of the key events of what we now call the civil rights movement, but at the end of her life, she was fully aware that the country had reached a turning point. Three months after her death, her book *Tomorrow Is Now* was published. In one of its chapters titled "The Social Revolution," she spoke of a nascent "revolution of equality, the assertion by men and women of their human dignity, and their demand for its recognition and acceptance by others." Referring to the Puritans, who had fled religious persecution in Europe, she drew a comparison. The United States was founded on the principle of religious freedom; the time for a broader toleration, which would ignore the color of someone's skin, had come.

If we are going to belong to our world, we must take into account the fact that the majority of the peoples of the world are non-whites. We must learn to surmount this deep-seated prejudice about color. Certainly we much face the evidence that the color of the skin does not regulate the superiority or inferiority of the individual.[46]

The essay ended with an assessment of the cultural transformation she had witnessed over the course of her life. The revolution was not about "modern transportation and electrical gadgets and all the scientific inventions" that had transformed the world. "No, the basic change in the social revolution has been the change in values," she contended, citing a personal example.

To my mother-in-law there were certain obligations that she, as a privileged person, must fulfill. She fed the poor, assisted them with money, helped them with medical expenses. This was a form of charity required of her.

The point of view that she simply could not accept was my husband's. He believed—as I trust most civilized people believe now—that human beings have rights as human beings: a right to a job, a right to education, a right to health protection, a right to human dignity, a right to a chance of fulfillment.

This is the inevitable growth in our thinking as a nation.[47]

Eleanor died on November 7, 1962, at the age of 78. In a eulogy delivered ten days later, her friend and United States ambassador to the United Nations Adlai E. Stevenson sought to define the person who had worked so long to make America and the world better for all:

Her life was crowded, restless, fearless. Perhaps she pitied most not those whom she aided in the struggle, but the more fortunate who were preoccupied with themselves and cursed with the self-deceptions of private success. She walked in the slums and the ghettos of the world, not on a tour of inspection, nor as a condescending patron, but as one who could not feel complacent while others were hungry, and who could not find contentment while others were in distress. This was not sacrifice; this, for Mrs. Roosevelt, was the only meaningful way of life.[48]

"What rendered this unforgettable woman so extraordinary," he continued, "was not merely her response to suffering; it was her comprehension of the complexity of the human condition." He recalled Eleanor's words: "Within all of us there are two sides. One reaches for the stars, the other descends to the level of the beast."

Born to great privilege, Eleanor had wrestled with her own prejudices. This combination of personal striving and professional dedication endowed her with the qualities needed to win over even the most skeptical and to lay foundations for future generations to build upon. Her recognition that humans are neither completely bad nor wholly good shaped much of this legacy. Not only did it allow her to accept others' shortcomings, it drove her to pursue support and freedom for that part of mankind that "reaches for the stars." For at the heart of her activism—and at the core of the Universal Declaration of Human Rights—was the belief that as humans, we must choose the kind of world we wish to live in so as never to descend "to the level of the beast."

DRAFTING THE PREAMBLE

The Declaration underwent many revisions between the establishment of the human rights "nuclear" commission on February 15, 1946, and the document's adoption on December 10, 1948, by the United Nations. Each version that was created emphasized different assumptions. The preamble (or introduction) to these drafts usually reflected those assumptions, which is why we selected three versions of that opening part of the Declaration. Humphrey's draft was the first document the commission worked on (it was prepared between February and June 1947). Cassin's was the second, and it represents an attempt to shorten and organize the articles laid out by Humphrey (he completed the draft in mid-June 1947). The last excerpt in this reading is the actual preamble to the Declaration (December 10, 1948).

Humphrey's First Draft

The Canadian scholar and activist John Peters Humphrey (1905–1995) was entrusted by Eleanor with the task of producing a first sketch of the Universal Declaration of Human Rights six months after he became the first director of the United Nations Division of Human Rights. As he prepared to write a document that would define the rights of all human beings, Humphrey studied many existing treaties, agreements, declarations, and proposals.[49]

Preamble

The Preamble shall refer to the four freedoms and to the provisions of the Charter relating to human rights and shall enunciate the following principles:

1. That there can be no peace unless human rights and freedoms are respected;

2. That man does not have rights only; he owes duties to the society of which he forms part;

3. That man is a citizen both of his State and of the world;

4. That there can be no human freedom or dignity unless war and the threat of war are abolished.

The "Cassin Draft"

Once the drafting committee had reviewed Humphrey's draft, it called for a revision: something more clearly organized and simpler. This task was given to the French jurist René Cassin (1887–1976), who, over a weekend in mid-June 1947, produced a version structured around a series of themes—personal freedoms, political freedoms, and social, economic, and cultural rights. Below is the preamble of the "Cassin Draft" as well as the final text of the Declaration's preamble.

Preamble

1. Ignorance and contempt of human rights have been among the principal causes of the sufferings of humanity and particularly of the massacres which have polluted the earth in two world wars;

2. There can be no peace unless human rights and freedoms are respected and, conversely, human freedom and dignity cannot be respected as long as war and the threat of war are not abolished;

3. It was proclaimed as the supreme aim of the recent conflict that human beings should enjoy freedom of speech and worship, and be free from fear and want;

4. In the Charter of 26 June 1945 we reaffirmed our faith in fundamental human rights, in the dignity and worth of the human person and in the equal rights of men and women;

5. It is one of the purposes of the United Nations to achieve international cooperation in promoting and encouraging respect for human rights and fundamental freedoms for all, without distinction as to race, sex, language, or religion;

6. The enjoyment of such rights and freedoms by all persons must be protected by the community of nations and guaranteed by international as well as municipal law . . .

Now, therefore, we the Peoples of the United Nations have resolved to define in a solemn Declaration the essential rights and fundamental freedoms of man, so that this Bill, being constantly present in the minds of all men, may unceasingly remind them of their rights and duties and so that the United Nations and its Members may constantly apply the principles hereby formulated;

And we have therefore adopted the following Bill . . .[51]

The Universal Declaration of Human Rights

The final text of the Declaration was adopted by the United Nations General Assembly on December 10, 1948:

Preamble

Whereas recognition of the inherent dignity and of the equal and inalienable rights of all members of the human family is the foundation of freedom, justice and peace in the world,

Whereas disregard and contempt for human rights have resulted in barbarous acts which have outraged the conscience of mankind, and the advent of a world in which human beings shall enjoy freedom of speech and belief and freedom from fear and want has been proclaimed as the highest aspiration of the common people,

Whereas it is essential, if man is not to be compelled to have recourse, as a last resort, to rebellion against tyranny and oppression, that human rights should be protected by the rule of law,

Whereas it is essential to promote the development of friendly relations between nations,

Whereas the peoples of the United Nations have in the Charter reaffirmed their faith in fundamental human rights, in the dignity and worth of the human person and in the equal rights of men and women and have determined to promote social progress and better standards of life in larger freedom,

Whereas Member States have pledged themselves to achieve, in cooperation with the United Nations, the promotion of universal respect for and observance of human rights and fundamental freedoms,

Whereas a common understanding of these rights and freedoms is of the greatest importance for the full realization of this pledge,

Now, Therefore THE GENERAL ASSEMBLY proclaims THIS UNIVERSAL DECLARATION OF HUMAN RIGHTS as a common standard of achievement for all peoples and all nations, to the end that every individual and every organ of society, keeping this Declaration constantly in mind, shall strive by teaching and education to promote respect for these rights and freedoms and by progressive measures, national and international, to secure their universal and effective recognition and observance, both among the peoples of Member States themselves and among the peoples of territories under their jurisdiction.

CONNECTIONS

1. Compare the drafts. What are some of the things they have in common? What are some of the differences?

2. Why, according to the texts above, are human rights necessary? What goals do these drafts set for a declaration (or bill) of human rights?

3. Humphrey's draft declares that "man is a citizen both of his State and of the world." What does he mean by that? How can a declaration of human rights serve citizens of the world?

4. What does the word "universal" mean? Why do you think the word is used in the name and aims of the Universal Declaration of Human Rights?

5. How can individuals help the United Nations' mission of creating a peaceful world?

6. Language often reflects the values and habits of the people who use it. The first draft talks about the rights and duties of "man." The final text talks about "all members of the human family" (people who study the use of language call this a "gender neutral" phrase). What is the difference? How can "gender neutral" language affect the equal treatment of men and women?

7. Why, according to the final version of the Declaration, is education central to the human rights mission? How can human rights become effective?

8. According to these documents, who grants human rights to people? What happens when human rights conflict with the laws of a nation? Whose role it is to defend human rights?

REFLECTIONS ON HUMAN RIGHTS

A few months before the General Assembly voted on the Universal Declaration of Human Rights, Eleanor published the essay from which the excerpts below were drawn. She discussed the process of drafting the Declaration and then addressed in detail the sections of the document that she deemed most important. (Eleanor occasionally refers to "the convention," a legally binding agreement that was supposed to be written following the Declaration. It took many more years to write such a human rights convention.)

Eleanor Roosevelt's "The Promise of Human Rights"

> The real importance of the Human Rights Commission which was created by the Economic and Social Council lies in the fact that throughout the world there are many people who do not enjoy the basic rights which have come to be accepted in many other parts of the world as inherent rights of all individuals, without which no one can live in dignity and freedom. . . .

> If the Declaration is accepted by the Assembly, it will mean that all the nations accepting it hope that the day will come when these rights are considered inherent rights belonging to every human being, but it will not mean that they have to change their laws immediately to make these rights possible. . . .

> As I look back at the work thus far of our Human Rights Commission, I realize that its importance is twofold.

> In the first place, we have put into words some inherent rights. Beyond that, we have found that the conditions of our contemporary world require the enumeration of certain protections which the individual must have if he is to acquire a sense of security and dignity in his own person. The effect of this is frankly educational. Indeed, I like to think that the Declaration will help forward very largely the education of the peoples of the world.

> It seems to me most important that the Declaration be accepted by all member nations, not because they will immediately live up to all of its provisions, but because they ought to support the standards toward which the nations must henceforward aim. Since the objectives have been clearly stated, men of good will everywhere

will strive to attain them with more energy and, I trust, with better hope of success.

As the Convention is adhered to by one country after another, it will actually bring into being rights which are tangible and can be invoked before the law of the ratifying countries. Everywhere many people will feel more secure. And as the Great Powers tie themselves down by their ratifications, the smaller nations which fear that the great may abuse their strength will acquire a sense of greater assurance.

The work of the Commission has been of outstanding value in setting before men's eyes the ideals which they must strive to reach. Men cannot live by bread alone.[52]

Charles Malik's "Talk on Human Rights"

Charles Malik served as *rapporteur* (secretary or organizer) of the Human Rights Drafting Committee (he also served as the president of the Economic and Social Council and as chairman of the Third Committee of the United Nations). When Eleanor retired as chairperson of the Human Rights Commission in 1951, Malik was chosen as her successor.

The excerpts below are taken from a speech Malik gave before a subcommittee of the United States Chamber of Commerce in New York on November 4, 1949. Serving as the Lebanese ambassador to the United States and to the United Nations, Malik encouraged American representatives to lead the way toward global human rights protections. In this talk, he argued that the debates about human rights offered the United Nations a unique opportunity to discuss two interrelated dilemmas: what a human being is, and what expectations all human beings have for their lives. "Here," he said, "you have the exciting drama of man seeking to grasp himself." That this debate proved divisive did not surprise Malik: "For man," he argued, "isn't only an ape: he does not only mimic the good example of others. Man is also a rational being who is moved and fired by ideas."[53]

The work on human rights is the one point in the total activity of the United Nations where the ultimate ideological issues are sharpest. . . . Today men fight precisely because they disagree on their own interpretation of themselves. Man, you and I in person, our origin, our nature, our rights, our destiny: these are the great questions of the age. And these questions are nowhere more dramatically discussed than in the United Nations debate on human rights. For here responsible representatives of all the effective cultures of the world vigorously contend every comma and every shade of meaning. Nothing is more repaying to the thoughtful student of the present ideological situation than to read and ponder, in all their prolonged, dramatic richness, the records of our debates on this question. Here you have the exciting drama of man seeking to grasp himself. . . . Now that we have completed and proclaimed the Universal Declaration of Human Rights, namely the determination of what belongs to the nature of man, the Commission on Human Rights has turned its attention to the elaboration of actual conventions, or international treaties, which will be signed by States and therefore be binding on them. This is obviously a much more difficult step, because it involves definite international obligations in this field. For many people agree with you in theory, but when it comes to actually putting that theory into practice in their own country, they speedily lose heart. And so it seems we are still at the barest beginning of a long and difficult historical process. The challenge of human rights is still very great. What is supremely needed is vigorous moral leadership convinced and therefore convincing. . . .[54]

René Cassin's "The Fight for Human Rights"

As the Cold War spread anxiety and uncertainty around the world, Cassin was called upon to reassess the importance of the Universal Declaration of Human Rights. Twenty years after the General Assembly had endorsed that ambitious document, Cassin spoke to a group of Jewish leaders, dwelling on connections between the history of the Jews, France, and the struggle for human rights. In Cassin's view, it was the Jews, the group most subjected to the human rights crimes of the recent past, who had to play a leadership role in securing rights for everyone. He presented a case for a strong international approach to human rights: too often, the greatest obstacle to the enforcement of human rights was the insistence of nations on preserving absolute power over what happened in their territory. Cassin also connected the issue of human rights to the creation of the state of Israel. For him, as for Eleanor,

Israel was a human rights issue—a response to the persecution of Jews in Europe.

It was the fundamental aim of Hitlerism to stamp out the Jews, but their destruction was also part of an attack on all that the French Revolution stood for: Liberty, Equality, Fraternity and Human Rights. Hitler's racialism was essentially an attempt to destroy the principles of the French Revolution. . . .

I would like to consider defense of Human Rights from a legal point of view. This is not by any means the most important aspect; educational and technical aid come first, as we have seen. But the legal side is enormously important, though it cannot show results overnight. . . . For example, one of the great stumbling blocks in the way of Human Rights is the question of national sovereignty. I was at the League of Nations in 1933 for the Bernheim case. Bernheim, a Jew, had been the victim of a violation of the Treaty of Upper Silesia. How did Germany, how did Hitler and Goebbels justify this? Germany's defense was "Every man is master in his own house. You have no business to inquire what we do with our socialists, our pacifists or our Jews. You have no right to pry into our affairs. This is a sovereign State."

That was the situation which led to the Second World War. The same is true today: the Great Powers are still saying "Every man is master in his own house. You have no right to know what I am doing with my own citizens." You can see how difficult it is to uproot a principle which derives undeniably from practical reality, since the independence of States is in itself a desirable thing, something people will fight for. The right of nations to govern themselves is accepted as the natural order of things. Why should we fear that any country protects its interests too vigorously? Our anxiety is justified in that there comes a moment when the State says: for the purpose of my development, I propose to set my own rules, as I think fit, and if I destroy men in the process, that is no concern of yours.

But it is very much our concern. World progress cannot be built on the ashes of human suffering. That is the aim of Human Rights. We must acknowledge at this point that resistance to an international system of controls is very strong. . . .[55]

CONNECTIONS

1. What do Eleanor Roosevelt, Charles Malik, and René Cassin see as the main challenges of implementing the Universal Declaration of Human Rights?

2. What is sovereignty? What is the importance of national sovereignty? How does the issue of sovereignty come up in these three reflections?

3. Do human rights complement national laws? Do they undermine them?

4. In their comments, how did the document's drafters anticipate discussions of the Universal Declaration of Human Rights, and human rights in general, that take place today?

MAKING HISTORY

Shortly after Eleanor's death, her last book was published. In it, Eleanor discussed the transformation her contemporaries experienced. She called this transformation a "revolution" because, in her mind, this change was so vast that at its end, the world was going to be radically different from the one in which she and her peers grew up. The book was permeated with a sense of endless possibilities and choices. It was, she claimed, "a reminder that we do make our history, that we are making it now—today—by the choices that shape our course."[56] Those choices, Eleanor argued, were what tomorrow was going to be made of: "The world of the future is in our making," she exclaimed. "*Tomorrow is now.*"[57]

The revolution, Eleanor suggested, was marked by the emergence of several challenges on the world stage: the need for international economic cooperation; the need to combat apathy and to educate the citizens of a future world; the need to control the destructive forces of science and technology; the need to diffuse the threat of the atomic bomb and the Cold War; and the need to get to know the cultures of other nations, including those of peoples who were recently liberated from European colonialism.

In the United States, this revolution took most visible shape in the struggle of African Americans for equal civil rights. Eleanor called this struggle a "social revolution." Disturbed by the reaction of whites to desegregation, she believed that the struggle for racial equality was one of the most important challenges American society faced. The excerpt below is from the chapter "The Social Revolution" from *Tomorrow is Now*.

"We know," Barbara Ward[58] wrote recently, "that the passionate desire of men to see themselves as the equals of other human beings without distinctions of class or sex or race or nationhood is one of the driving forces of our day." We know—yes. But what are we doing about it? We are dealing today with millions upon millions of people of diverse religions. That should be easy for us. This country, after all, was founded upon the principle of religious freedom. But how is it working out in actual practice?

. . .

In a very real sense, the United States is the world's show window of the democratic processes in action. We know, too well, what people see when they look in that window. They see [the race riots in] Little Rock and Baton Rouge and New Orleans. . . . They see the deep-rooted prejudice, the stubborn ignorance of large groups of our citizens, which have led to injustice, inequality, and, sometimes, even brutality. I think what most of us remember most vividly about the riots and the cruelty of Little Rock . . . is the pictures we saw in our newspapers, pictures which gave us a tremendous shock when we realized what ugliness and degradation mass fear could bring out in human beings.

Grown women wanted to kill one . . . girl, one of the children going into the Little Rock school. The cold fact is hard to believe that anywhere in our country women would be screaming for the death of a child because she was going into a white school. Yet this is what happened. This was the result of mass fear and mass psychology. . . . If we can learn to subdue the emotions arising from prejudice, if we can learn that the social revolution in which we are engaged should, among other things, provide all our people with an equal opportunity to enjoy the benefits that have been the privileges of a few, we are going to be astonished to discover that many whom we considered incapable of development were only underprivileged; that given the opportunity for education, there are latent endowments which will be valuable not only to these people in themselves but to their country and the world as well.

. . .

If we are going to belong to our world we must take into account the fact that the majority of the peoples of the world are non-whites. We must learn to surmount this deep-seated prejudice about color. Certainly we must face the evidence that the color of the skin does not regulate the superiority or inferiority of the individual. . . . The world cannot be understood from a single point of view. . . .

The revolution in our social thinking appears, in capsule form, to my eyes, in one family I know well—my own. My mother-in-law belonged to the established world of the last century. She accepted its shibboleths without questioning. To her these things were true.

When she died, in September, 1941, my husband felt strongly this ending of an unshakable world behind him. And yet, he told me, it *was probably as well for his mother to leave us at that time. She was immersed in her old world and the new one was alien to her. The adjustment for her would have been impossible.*

In using the term, I do not mean adjustment merely to the dramatic and obvious physical changes. . . . No, the basic change in the social revolution has been the change in values. To my mother-in-law, for instance, there were certain obligations that she, as a privileged person, must fulfill. She fed the poor, assisted them with money, helped them with medical expenses. This was a form of charity required of her.

The point of view that she simply could not accept was my husband's. He believed—as I trust most civilized people believe now—that human beings have rights as human beings: a right to a job, a right to education, a right to health protection, a right to human dignity, a right to a chance of fulfillment.

This is the inevitable growth in our thinking as a nation—the practical application of democratic principles. No one today would dare refer to the mass of the people, as Alexander Hamilton once did, as "that great beast." And that, perhaps, is a minor victory in the long battle for human rights.[59]

CONNECTIONS

1. Compare Eleanor's statements about race in this document to those she makes in Part I, Document 3 ("The Basic Thing We Must Do Is to Stop Generalizing About People"). What changed over these years in her analysis of America's racial problems? In her language? In her advice?

2. Eleanor describes a revolution. What does she see as the revolution? What characterizes this revolution?

3. What did Eleanor see as the main challenges facing citizens of the world at the time she wrote her last book? As you look at the world you live in, what do you see as the main challenges facing citizens today? What are some differences between the world Eleanor writes about and your world? What are some similarities?

4. How do people learn to live with new realities? What makes this difficult? What can make it easier?

5. What are the differences between the way Eleanor saw the world and the way her mother-in-law did?

1 The Universal Declaration of Human Rights," the United Nations website, http://www.un.org/en/documents/udhr/ (accessed August 25, 2009).

2 In 1947, the Guomindang forces of Chiang Kai-shek—backed by the United States—were losing ground to Mao Zedong's communist forces. Once the communists were in power, they threatened many American policies.

3 In June 1948, as work on the Universal Declaration of Human Rights drew to a close, the Soviets imposed a blockade on the areas of Berlin controlled by Western forces. This was the first of many open confrontations between the superpowers, and it greatly strained the relationship between them. In addition to Russia, the republics formally belonging the USSR, and the Baltic states (Estonia, Latvia, Lithuania, and Finland), the Soviet Bloc included East Germany, Hungary, Poland, Czechoslovakia, Yugoslavia (until 1948), Armenia, Bulgaria, and Romania.

4 Mary Ann Glendon, A World Made New: Eleanor Roosevelt and the Universal Declaration of Human Rights (New York: Random House, 2001), 14.

5 Winston S. Churchill, "Iron Curtain Speech" (March 5, 1946), the Internet Modern History Sourcebook website, http://www.fordham.edu/halsall/mod/churchill-iron.html (accessed August 22, 2009).

6 Churchill, "Iron Curtain Speech."

7 Ibid.

8 Eleanor Roosevelt, My Day (column), March 7, 1946, available at http://www.gwu.edu/~erpapers/myday/displaydoc.cfm?_y=1946&_f=md000280 (accessed March 31, 2009).

9 Ibid.

10 René Cassin, "The Fight for Human Rights," World, January 1969; see http://www.udhr.org/history/cassin1.htm (accessed June 2, 2009).

11 Cassin, "The Fight for Human Rights."

12 For a short biography of Cassin, see "René Cassin: The Nobel Peace Prize 1968," Nobel Prize website, http://nobelprize.org/nobel_prizes/peace/laureates/1968/cassin-bio.html (accessed June 2009).

13 A. J. Hobbins, ed., On the Edge of Greatness: The Diaries of John Humphrey, First Director of the United Nations Division of Human Rights, vol. 1 (Montreal: McGill University Library, 1994), 249.

14 This became particularly apparent when the United States refused to sign several important international agreements, including the Convention on the Prevention of Genocide (1948), which it ratified only in 1984. To this day the United States is among the few countries that refuse to endorse the International Criminal Court (set up by the Rome Statute of 1998), whose goal is to prosecute the most egregious human rights violations and war crimes.

15 David Halberstam, The Fifties (New York: Villard Books, 1993), 50.

16 Allida M. Black, ed., The Eleanor Roosevelt Papers, Volume 1: The Human Rights Years, 1945–1948 (New York: Thomson Gale, 2007), 849.

17 Joseph P. Lash, Eleanor: The Years Alone (New York: W. W. Norton & Company, 1972), 59. In contrast to Lovett, Eleanor thought that including an antidiscrimination clause would alleviate some of the concerns of African Americans and shield the United States from Soviet propaganda. See Black et al., The Eleanor Roosevelt Papers, 711.

18 Eleanor Roosevelt, "Making Human Rights Come Alive," in What I Hope to Leave Behind: The Essential Essays of Eleanor Roosevelt, ed. Allida M. Black (Brooklyn: Carlson, 1995), 559.

19 Eleanor Roosevelt, "The Promise of Human Rights," in Courage in a Dangerous World: The Political Writings of Eleanor Roosevelt, ed. Allida M. Black (New York: Columbia University Press, 1999), 558.

20 Roosevelt, "Making Human Rights Come Alive," in What I Hope to Leave Behind, ed. Black, 563.

[21] Roosevelt, "Promise of Human Rights," in *Courage in a Dangerous World*, ed. Black, 162. Emphasis added.

[22] Ibid., 162. Emphasis added.

[23] Roosevelt, "Making Human Rights Come Alive," in *What I Hope to Leave Behind*, ed. Black, 559–60. Emphasis added. Henri Laugier of France was the Assistant Secretary-General in the United Nations Department of Social Affairs, which oversaw the work of the Human Rights Commission. Laugier was a good friend of Eleanor Roosevelt's.

[24] Eleanor Roosevelt, "Where Do Human Rights Begin?" in *Courage in a Dangerous World*, ed. Black, 190.

[25] Eleanor Roosevelt, "Statement on Draft Covenant on Human Rights," in *What I Hope to Leave Behind*, ed. Black, 585.

[26] John P. Humphrey, *Human Rights and the United Nations: A Great Adventure* (New York: Transnational Publishers, 1984), 64–65.

[27] Hobbins, ed., *On the Edge of Greatness*, 81–82.

[28] A. J. Hobbins, "John Humphrey's Schooldays: The Influence of School Experience on the Canadian who Drafted the Universal Declaration of Human Rights," *McGill Journal of Education*, Spring 2002, available at http://findarticles.com/p/articles/mi_qa3965/is_200204/ai_n9030808/ (accessed May 29, 2009).

[29] Roosevelt, "Making Human Rights Come Alive," in *What I Hope to Leave Behind*, ed. Black, 571.

[30] Eleanor Roosevelt, "The Moral Basis of Democracy," in *What I Hope to Leave Behind*, ed. Black, 85.

[31] "Adoption of the Declaration of Human Rights, December 9, 1948," http://www.udhr.org/history/ergeas48.htm.

[32] Eleanor sketched a short history of democracy that started in medieval England and ended with the Declaration of Independence. See Roosevelt, "The Moral Basis of Democracy," in *What I Hope to Leave Behind*, ed. Black, 70–79.

[33] Ibid., 89.

[34] Roosevelt, "Promise of Human Rights," in *Courage in a Dangerous World*, ed. Black, 558.

[35] Dr. Charles Malik (Lebanon), "The Basic Issues of the International Bill of Human Rights," (speech delivered before a conference of American educators in Lake Success, NY, Feb. 26, 1948), United Nations Publications, box 4580, folder UN Publications, 4.

[36] Humphrey, *Human Rights and the United Nations*, 64–65.

[37] Ibid

[38] Hurst Hunnum, "The Status of the Universal Declaration of Human Rights in National and International Law," *Georgia Journal of International and Comparative Law* 25 (1995/1996): 289, quoted in Johannes Morsink, *The Universal Declaration of Human Rights: Origins, Drafting, and Intent* (Philadelphia: University of Pennsylvania Press, 1999), xi.

[39] Morsink, *The Universal Declaration of Human Rights*, xi.

[40] Amnesty International website, http://www.amnesty.org/en/united-nations (accessed August 21, 2009).

[41] Eleanor Roosevelt, "The Struggle for Human Rights," in *The Eleanor Roosevelt Papers*, ed. Black, 909–10. Eleanor was made to cut much of her language. We thank Allida Black for drawing our attention to Eleanor's original text.

[42] The State Department was concerned that any admission of guilt on the issue of discrimination would be exploited by the Soviets to criticize the United States. The formal speech said: "In the United States we are old enough not to claim perfection. We recognize that we have some problems of discrimination." Ibid., 903.

[43] Allida M. Black, *Casting Her Own Shadow: Eleanor Roosevelt and the Shaping of Postwar Liberalism* (New York: Columbia University Press, 1996), 105.

[44] Eleanor Roosevelt, "The Social Revolution" (1963), in *Courage in a Dangerous World*, ed. Black, 301.

45 Roosevelt, "Foreword to The Long Shadow of Little Rock by Daisy Bates," in *What I Hope to Leave Behind*, ed. Black, 182.

46 Eleanor Roosevelt, "The Social Revolution," in *Courage in a Dangerous World*, ed. Black, 306.

47 Roosevelt, "The Social Revolution," in *Courage in a Dangerous World*, ed. Black, 309.

48 Adlai E. Stevenson, "Eulogy for Eleanor Roosevelt," in *In Tribute: Eulogies of Famous People*, ed. Ted Tobias (Bushky Press, 2001), 151.

49 Glendon, *A World Made New*, 58.

50 Ibid., 271–274.

51 Glendon, *A World Made New*, 275–79.

52 Roosevelt, "Promise of Human Rights," in *Courage in a Dangerous World*, ed. Black, 553–58.

53 Charles Malik, "Talk on Human Rights," available at http://www.udhr.org/history/default.htm (accessed June 3, 2009).

54 Malik, "Talk on Human Rights."

55 Cassin, "The Fight for Human Rights."

56 Eleanor Roosevelt, *Tomorrow Is Now* (New York: Harper & Row, 1963), xvi.

57 Ibid., 134.

58 Barbara Ward was a celebrated foreign correspondent, economist, and activist who dedicated her career to humanitarian and environmental causes, to the problems faced by African nations, and to international cooperation. The two had met in the past (see Eleanor Roosevelt, *My Day*, March 9, 1960, and August 17, 1942), and Ward, who received the British title of baroness, wrote the text on the back cover of Eleanor's autobiography.

59 Roosevelt, *Tomorrow Is Now*, 49–65.

TIMELINE

1884

Eleanor Roosevelt is born to Anna Hall Roosevelt and Elliot Roosevelt on October 11 in New York City. The Roosevelts are a very wealthy and well-established American family.

1892

Eleanor's mother, Anna Hall Roosevelt, dies of diphtheria at the age of 29. Eleanor's maternal grandmother, Mary Ludlow Hall, assumes custody of Eleanor and her brothers.

1894

Eleanor's father, Elliot Roosevelt, dies at the age of 34 when he suffers a seizure related to alcoholism.

1899–1902

Eleanor enters Allenswood Academy, an elite English boarding school, at the age of 15. There she is educated by Headmistress Marie Souvestre, with whom she develops a close personal relationship.

Eleanor returns to New York in 1902 as a young debutante.

1903

Eleanor becomes engaged to Franklin Delano Roosevelt (FDR), a distant cousin.

Eleanor volunteers for the Junior League of New York, where she teaches impoverished immigrants at the Rivington Street Settlement House. She also joins the Consumers' League and investigates the working conditions of poor women and children.

1905

Eleanor marries Franklin on March 17 in New York City. President Theodore Roosevelt, Eleanor's uncle, accompanies her down the aisle.

1906–1916

Eleanor gives birth to six children, five of whom survive infancy.

1913

FDR is appointed assistant secretary of the navy by President Woodrow Wilson. Eleanor and Franklin move to Washington, DC.

1918

Eleanor volunteers with the American Red Cross and the United States Department of the Navy to help American servicemen during World War I.

1919

The League of Nations is formed. It is created under the Treaty of Versailles. Eleanor supports Woodrow Wilson's attempts to win approval of the League of Nations in the United States. Congress, however, votes not to join the peacekeeping organization.

1920

Eleanor joins the League of Women Voters, where she chairs the Legislative Affairs Committee. She joins FDR in his bid for the vice presidency. During the campaign, she also begins a close friendship with FDR's advisor, Louis Howe, who helps her develop her political career.

1921

FDR is diagnosed with polio. Eleanor nurses her husband back to health (although he remains in a wheelchair) and encourages him to resume his involvement in public life.

1922–1924

Eleanor becomes increasingly involved in politics and the Democratic Party, mobilizing women voters and campaigning for Democratic politicians. She joins the Women's Trade Union League and the Women's Division of the Democratic State Committee. Eleanor also supports Al Smith's campaign for New York governor and twice appears at the state Democratic convention.

1925

Eleanor and FDR build the Val-Kill cottage retreat in Hyde Park. Co-owned by Democratic activists Nancy Cook and Marion Dickerman, the estate serves as a furniture factory with the mission of providing a source of employment and additional income for local men and women. Val-Kill becomes Eleanor's home and a center of her social and political activity.

1927

Eleanor befriends Mary McLeod Bethune, an African American civil rights activist and educator. Bethune will later become an important voice in the Roosevelt administration and will lead FDR's "Black Cabinet," a group of African American intellectuals who inform FDR's social policy.

1928

With Louis Howe's help and Eleanor's encouragement, FDR returns to politics, runs for the position of New York governor, and wins.

1929

The United States' stock market crashes, signaling the beginning of an economic crisis that would continue through the 1930s, known as the Great Depression.

1931

Eleanor mobilizes voters to support FDR in the 1932 presidential election.

1932

FDR is elected president for the first of four terms.

1933

FDR and Eleanor enter the White House.

In the United States, FDR launches a series of economic policies to combat the financial crisis and to restore jobs and economic safety for millions of Americans. These policies will lay the foundation for what is known as the New Deal.

Following FDR's election as president, Eleanor holds regular press conferences to which only female reporters are admitted. She also starts a monthly column called *Mrs. Roosevelt's Page* in the widely read *Woman's Home Companion.*

Eleanor contributes to the founding of Arthurdale, a rural resettlement community in West Virginia. Developed during the New Deal era, the community is designed to promote economic self-sufficiency among impoverished miners.

Eleanor travels over 40,000 miles throughout the United States, investigating the country's economic and social conditions. She reports her experiences and observations in numerous essays, speeches, and letters.

Adolf Hitler gains dictatorial power in Germany, and his Nazi Party enacts a series of discriminatory laws (codified in the Nuremberg laws) that target people of Jewish ancestry as well as other "undesirable" groups.

1934

Eleanor convinces FDR to create the National Youth Administration (NYA), a student work program under the Works Progress Administration (WPA).

Eleanor arranges a meeting between NAACP leader Walter White and FDR to discuss anti-lynching legislation. This meeting is ultimately a failure due to the tense political climate, which prevents FDR from taking a public stance on the issue.

1935

Eleanor begins writing *My Day*, a daily newspaper column, which continues to be published until shortly before her death in 1962.

1936

Eleanor helps secure Bethune's appointment as the director of the Division of Negro Affairs at the NYA.

FDR wins a second term as president in a landslide victory.

1938

Eleanor attends the Southern Conference for Human Welfare in Birmingham, Alabama. Accompanied by Bethune, Eleanor attempts to defy state segregation laws by sitting in the section for blacks.

1939

The MS *St. Louis*, a German ocean liner carrying 900 Jewish refugees trying to escape Nazi persecution in Europe, sails to Cuba and the United States. The refugees are refused entry to both countries, and the ship returns to Europe, where many passengers will be killed in the Holocaust.

World War II begins when Germany attacks Poland on September 1.

Eleanor resigns from the Daughters of the American Revolution when the organization refuses to allow Marian Anderson, an African American opera singer, to perform in its Constitution Hall. Eleanor helps arrange for Anderson to perform a concert in front of 75,000 people at the Lincoln Memorial.

Eleanor addresses the NAACP national convention, strengthening her ties to the organization.

1940

Eleanor establishes the U.S. Committee for the Care of European Children. The committee relocates children fleeing from bombing in Britain and Nazi persecution in Western Europe.

Eleanor publishes "The Moral Basis of Democracy."

1941

FDR delivers his famous "four freedoms" speech during the State of the Union address. FDR states that all people around the world should possess four fundamental freedoms: freedom of speech and expression, freedom of religion, freedom from want, and freedom from fear. This speech echoes Eleanor's commitment to social development and her interest in human rights.

Eleanor helps European refugees relocate to America. Eleanor's assistance allows the SS *Quanza*, a Portuguese freight ship, to bring refugees from Nazi-occupied France to safety in the United States.

A. Philip Randolph organizes a march on Washington to protest discrimination in the booming defense industry. FDR asks Eleanor to try to stop the march. Randolph refuses to back down. As a result, FDR issues Executive Order 8802, which prohibits discrimination in the defense industry and federal bureaus. Randolph calls off the march.

The United States and Great Britain sign the Atlantic Charter. President Roosevelt and Prime Minister Churchill meet aboard a ship off the coast of Newfoundland to discuss British and American involvement in the war, as well as a vision for the postwar world order. The Atlantic Charter declares that "all the men in all the lands" share certain rights, establishing a precedent for the Universal Declaration of Human Rights.

The Japanese bomb the American naval base at Pearl Harbor, Hawaii, prompting the United States' entrance into World War II.

Eleanor speaks out against anti-Japanese sentiment in the United Nations after the attack on Pearl Harbor and tries to prevent the internment of Japanese Americans.

1942

Despite Eleanor's opposition, FDR issues Executive Order 9066 on February 19, authorizing the internment of nearly 120,000 innocent Japanese Americans.

1943

Despite the anti-discrimination ordinance of 1941, conflicts over housing between blacks and whites in Detroit reach a boiling point. Race riots finally break out in the summer. Eleanor is blamed by her opponents for inciting the violence.

Eleanor visits Gila River internment camp in Arizona and praises the resourcefulness of the Japanese American community interned there.

FDR, Winston Churchill, and Joseph Stalin, or the "Big Three," attend the Tehran Conference. The three discuss cooperation between the powers, the location of the Allied forces' invasion, and the opening of a second front in the fight against the German army in Western Europe. Also, at this conference, the three powers agree to form the United Nations organization after the war. The term *united nations*, which FDR coined to describe the alliance of anti-Nazi forces, receives its current meaning as a peace organization.

1944

In the Bretton Woods Accord, the leaders of the 44 Allied nations establish a system of international economic relations for the postwar world.

The United Nations Charter is drafted and negotiated at the Dumbarton Oaks Conference in Washington, DC.

1945

FDR, Winston Churchill, and Joseph Stalin attend the Yalta Conference. At Yalta, the Soviet Union commits to joining the United Nations and agrees on the structure of the UN Security Council.

FDR dies on April 12 in Warm Springs, Georgia.

Eleanor joins the NAACP board of directors.

The United Nations is formally established at the United Nations Conference on International Organization in San Francisco. One of the charter's main purposes is the promotion and encouragement of "respect for human rights and for fundamental freedoms for all without distinction as to race, sex, language, or religion."

Eleanor accepts President Harry Truman's offer to serve as a United States delegate to the United Nations.

In the spring, the war ends in Europe. After the war ends and the Nazi labor and death camps are liberated, the full extent of the Holocaust comes to light.

Allied forces decide to put individuals responsible for the Holocaust on trial. At the Nuremberg Trials, the Allied powers prosecute Nazi leaders for war crimes and crimes against humanity.

In the summer, World War II finally ends after the United States drops atomic bombs on two Japanese cities.

The Cold War begins between the United States and the Soviet Union.

1946

Eleanor visits displaced persons camps in Germany. The misery and desperation she witnesses at the camps convince her of the need for an international guarantee of civil and human rights. Eleanor also becomes committed to the establishment of a Jewish homeland in Israel.

Race riots break out in Columbia, Tennessee. After state highway patrolmen and policemen brutally raid a black neighborhood and arrest over one hundred innocent blacks, Walter White and Thurgood Marshall of the NAACP arrive in town. They set up a joint committee to demand an official investigation into police brutality against black residents and the destruction of property. Eleanor agrees to co-chair the committee.

The United Nations Economic and Social Council (ECOSOC) establishes the "nuclear commission" with the task of developing a permanent UN commission on human rights. Eleanor is later unanimously elected as the head of Human Rights Commission. She leads this group of jurists and scholars in drafting an International Bill of Rights, including a Declaration of Human Rights.

Eleanor debates Soviet delegate head Andrei Vyshinsky over World War II refugee repatriation and gains a reputation as one of the most important defenders of human rights in the United Nations.

Winston Churchill delivers his "iron curtain" speech at Westminster College, Missouri, in which he states that "an iron curtain has descended across the [European] continent," separating areas controlled by the Western powers from states under Soviet influence. Eleanor opposes this assessment, envisioning a world shaped by cooperation and diplomacy rather than fear and hostility.

1947

Eleanor is elected to chair the 18-nation Human Rights Commission, with the task of drafting the Universal Declaration of Human Rights.

W. E. B. Du Bois assembles studies of the mistreatment of African Americans in a petition to the UN. When he and Walter White seek to present these to the Secretariat and the HRC for review, Eleanor refuses to lend her support.

1948

Eleanor gives her speech "The Struggles for the Rights of Man" at the Sorbonne during the United Nations General Assembly meeting in Paris on September 28.

Eleanor opposes President Truman's lack of support for the new Jewish state of Israel and offers her resignation as a UN delegate in protest. President Truman does not accept her resignation.

The Convention on the Prevention and Punishment of the Crime of Genocide is adopted by the United Nations General Assembly on December 9.

Eleanor helps secure the adoption of the Declaration of Human Rights by the United Nations General Assembly on December 10. The Declaration reflects an international collaborative effort and is the first comprehensive agreement among nations on the rights and freedoms of all human beings.

1950–1954

Senator Joseph McCarthy accuses many United States government employees and organizations of being communist and launches Senate investigations into the political loyalties of innocent American citizens. Eleanor opposes McCarthy's accusations and rhetoric, speaking out against the "politics of fear."

1952

Eleanor resigns as a delegate to the UN following the election of President Eisenhower.

1953

Eleanor assumes a central role in the American Association for the United Nations, an organization aimed at educating the American public about the importance of American participation in the UN.

1954

Eleanor applauds the *Brown v. Board of Education* Supreme Court ruling, which outlaws segregation in public schools.

1955

Eleanor supports the Montgomery bus boycott and the struggle for African American civil rights.

1957

Nine African American students, known as the "Little Rock Nine," are the first to enroll in the formerly segregated Central High School in Little Rock, Arkansas. Facing white segregationist resistance, they narrowly escape violence. Eleanor Roosevelt publicly condemns the federal government for its timid approach to desegregation. She later writes an introduction to NAACP leader Daisy Bates's account of the crisis.

1958

Despite receiving death threats from the Ku Klux Klan, Eleanor travels to Tennessee to hold a workshop on civil disobedience and civil rights.

1961

President Kennedy reappoints Eleanor to the United States delegation to the United Nations.

Eleanor serves as the first chairperson of the President's Commission on the Status of Women.

1962

Eleanor dies from complications of tuberculosis at the age of 78 on November 7.

1963

Eleanor's last book, *Tomorrow Is Now*, is published.

INDEX

A

Alexander, C. B. 100, 128
Allied nations 103, 259
American Anthropological Association 154, 157, 190
Anderson, Marian 80, 257
Arthurdale 43, 45, 56, 256
Atlantic Charter, the 132, 180, 258
atomic bomb 18, 19, 107, 118, 247, 259
Axis powers 18, 105

B

balance of power 219
Baruch, Bernard 55
Bass, Leon 95
Bethune, Mary McLeod 48, 75, 253, 255
Black, Allida M. 28, 233
"Black Cabinet" 255
Britain 54, 95, 135, 136, 180, 219, 220, 257, 258
Brown v. Board of Education 234, 261

C

Cassin, René 160, 174, 177, 224, 239, 244, 246
charity 24, 25, 44, 116, 139, 140, 236, 249
China 18, 104, 133, 154
Christianity 174
Churchill, Winston 105, 130, 131, 223, 258, 260
civil rights 19, 28, 47, 49, 51, 52, 74, 75, 77, 95, 98, 123, 140, 161, 162, 164, 166, 167, 191, 192, 194, 205, 206, 233, 232, 234, 235, 247, 255, 261
Cold War, the 179, 185, 222, 226, 244, 247, 259
College Settlement on Rivington Street, the 39
Columbia, Tennessee race riots 163
Committee for the Care of European Children 58, 257
communism 110, 172, 219
Communist Manifesto, the 40
concentration camps 60, 106, 110, 137, 160, 224
Confucianism 155
Conner, Eugene 49
Convention on the Prevention and Punishment of the Crime of Genocide, the 260
Cooke, Blanche Wiesen 35
Cook, Nancy 32, 56, 71, 255
Coughlin, Charles E. 55

D

Daughters of the American Revolution (DAR) 50, 58, 78
Declaration of Independence, the 40, 177, 180, 190, 212

S

T

U

V

W

Z

CREDITS

Grateful acknowledgment is made for permission to reproduce excerpts from the following:

The Eleanor Roosevelt Papers: Volume 1, 1st edition, by Allida M. Black. Copyright © 2007 Gale, a part of Cengage Learning, Inc. Reproduced by permission. http://www.cengage.com

The Promise of Human Rights, by Eleanor Roosevelt. Reprinted by permission of FOREIGN AFFAIRS, Issue 26, April 1948. Copyright 1948 by the Council on Foreign Relations, Inc. http://www.foreignaffairs.com

In Search of Light, by Edward R. Murrow, edited by E. Bliss, Jr., copyright © 1967 by The Estate of Edward R. Murrow. Used by permission of Alfred A. Knopf, a division of Random House, Inc.

The Moral Basis of Democracy, The Seven People Who Shaped My Life, Women Must Learn to Play the Game as Men Do, and *The Minorities Question* all written by Eleanor Roosevelt. Reproduced with permission from Nancy Roosevelt Ireland.

The Autobiography of Eleanor Roosevelt, by Eleanor Roosevelt. Copyright © 1937, 1949, 1958, 1961 by Anna Eleanor Roosevelt. Copyright © 1958 by Curtis Publishing Company. Reprinted by permission of HarperCollins Publishers.

Throng Honors Marian Anderson in Concert at Lincoln Memorial, and *Marian Anderson,* by the New York Times. Articles are copyright © the New York Times. All rights reserved. Used by permission and protected by the Copyright Laws of the United States. The printing, copying, redistribution, or re-transmission of the material without express written permission is prohibited.

Courage in a Dangerous World, by Allida M. Black. Copyright © 1999 by Columbia University Press. Reprinted with permission of the publisher.

CPSIA information can be obtained at www.ICGtesting.com
Printed in the USA
BVOW071021250912

301278BV00007B/38/P

9 780981 954325